ourism and Applied
nthropologists

NKING THEORY AND PRACTICE

m Wallace, EDITOR

T0374811

Contents

Introduction

TOURISM, TOURISTS, AND ANTHROPOLOGISTS AT WORK

TIM WALLACE

North Carolina State University

The anthropology of tourism is a relatively recent topic area within both academic and applied anthropology, having gotten its start in the 1960s and 1970s. Valene Smith's edited work Hosts and Guests: The Anthropology of Tourism *(1977) marks the beginning of the field as a serious academic concern. Since then it has grown rapidly. Anthropologists were (and some continue to be) ambivalent about studying tourists, but initially they were concerned with the impact of tourists and tourism on local communities, especially in rural regions. Much of the initial findings suggested that tourism generally had negative impacts on communities that had become tourist destinations. In this volume, the contributing authors were asked to reflect more on the positive and practical contributions of anthropology to the field of tourism studies and to the tourism industry itself. The authors in their various ways have successfully answered their charge. A brief synopsis of the 13 other papers in the volume is given.* Key Words: anthropology of tourism, development, tourists, ethnography, applied anthropology

INTRODUCTION

As an introduction to the topic of tourism impacts mentioned frequently in the pages to come in this *Bulletin*, let me give the reader a flavor of that tourism from my own experience.

It is only 5:00 a.m., and already it is 72 degrees. I am awakened by rustling, squealing, and an occasional thump from the balcony of my Hotel Costa Verde room, near Manuel Antonio National Park on the Pacific Coast of Costa Rica.

NAPA Bulletin 23, pp. 1–26, ISBN 1-931303-22-3. © 2005 by the American Anthropological Association. All rights reserved. Please direct all requests for permissions to photocopy or reproduce article content through the University of California Press's Rights and Permissions website, www.ucpress.edu/journals/rights.htm.

I push back the curtains to find a troop of the cutest monkeys I have ever seen scampering back and forth along the balcony's railing. They are squirrel monkeys—an endangered species, I later learn—about two and half feet long from nose to non-prehensile tail tips, with small, fuzzy, brown heads, reddish-yellow hair on their backs, and grey legs. They are jumping from palm tree fronds onto the balcony railing on the way across the hotel building to palm fronds on the other side of the building. Two of them are carrying infants on their backs. My wife hears the noise too and unsteadily rises to join me in our discovery. We happen to have a few bananas left over from yesterday and decide to see if they will take some if we leave them on the railing. One of them on the palm frond looks cautiously at us and when we move back away from the balcony he makes his leap, and scoops up one of the pieces and scampers down the railing. Then another one does the same, and another, and some of the ones that had gone ahead come back for more. They seem relatively unafraid of the curious humans watching them. The recent mothers with infants on their backs are much more cautious and are reluctant to jump from the palm tree to the railing. Eventually, both of them take the plunge but don't stop for bananas. One of the males (we think it is a male) watches them protectively in case we humans do something unexpected. We watch them scamper on their way to other treetops, wondering why they made this amazing visit to our hotel room balcony. As we sit on our mountainside veranda watching the sun rise over Manuel Antonio's misty, white sand beaches, we now understand the reason the Hotel Costa Verde uses monkeys in its logo, which is "Still more monkeys than people," and why U.S. tourists have found this destination a magical one.

We later learn from a local biologist that the Hotel Costa Verde was built in the middle of the trail along which squirrel monkeys and the area's other two monkey species (howlers and white-faced capuchins) move. Thus, the hotel was sited smack in the middle of a traditional feeding area, making the balcony visit by our squirrel monkeys something less than an accident, because the building is in an open, treeless space spanning their tree canopy trail. We also learn from a local wildlife conservation biologist that feeding the monkeys is the worst thing to do, since this trains them to become dependent on tourists and hotel owners for food, which changes their diet (reducing the amount of protein, because they don't have to find as many insects to eat, and increasing the likelihood of tooth decay from bananas and other tourist foods) and makes them less afraid of humans and thus easier to capture. By feeding them we have helped to hasten their extinction!

FIGURE 1. Squirrel monkeys being fed bananas.

Later in the day, we walk to the Manuel Antonio National Park itself, originally a United Fruit Company employees' picnic area. Though this is the smallest national park in Costa Rica, with only 683 hectares (1,687 acres), and only about five percent of it is open to the public, it is probably the most popular with tourists. Aside from the postcard-beautiful beaches, it is teeming with exotic wildlife. It seems that the majority of the animals prefer the beach areas, too, where they find plenty of tourists anxious to feed them. To get into the park we have to wade across an inlet (which we later learn is polluted with sewage runoff from local, mostly foreign-owned, hotels, including the Costa Verde, close to the park). At the gated entrance, which is reminiscent of a European grotto, we pay our $6 fee (payable with U.S. cash, Visa, MasterCard, or Costa Rican *colones*) and get our hands stamped, which allows us to come and go all day long.

For about ten minutes and in sight of the pounding surf, we walk along a narrow trail that lines one of the four beautiful beaches of the park, passing other tourists—most in swimwear, carrying picnic gear. We notice large iguanas basking in the morning sun and hermit crabs, scared by our arrival, lurching suddenly back into their shells. Shower stalls and public restrooms are on the left; on the right, we observe trees gnarled by the ocean breezes and hermit

FIGURE 2. Bathers at Beach No. 2 at Manuel Antonio, Costa Rica.

crabs busily scurrying hither and yon. Heavy humidity greets us as we pass in silence. Suddenly, there is some rustling and screeching above us. We look up to find a troop of white-faced capuchin monkeys fighting over some fruit in a tree. Someone in the distance yells in English, "Grab that monkey; it stole my purse!" A guide leads a stunned tour group to find the monkey that stole a bather's handbag while she sunned herself on a beach towel at the famous Playa No. 1 of the park. We watch the monkeys' antics before moving on.

A bit farther down the trail, another nature guide who is leading some tourists through the park has his telescope out and is pointing up in another tree. Excitedly we ask in English what have they found, and the U.S. tourists tell us that the guide has spotted a three-toed sloth. They let us look in the telescope and we spy a hairy, cute-faced miniature Sasquatch ever so slowly moving its arms to reach some flowers on a tree branch. We don't wait for all 25 or so members of the group to look through his imported Swarovksi spotting telescope; we move along, wondering what else we will find here. Suddenly we emerge into a wide cove where placid blue water laps at a white-sand beach shaded by palm trees and flanked by volcanic rocks. It seems like déjà vu— probably because we have just bought a postcard with the same scene on it at the gift shop near the park's bus stop. As we set out our towels among the hundreds of other tourists to relax for a while, we look at each other and smile, silently acknowledging that we sure did make the right decision to spend some quality vacation time together in this wonderful, "natural" setting!

Exotic locales have long been the staple of the received wisdom in anthropological folklore: places where tourists should fear to tread. Costa Rica once might have been such a place. Today, formerly anthropologist-only, exotic, and peripheral four-S (sea, sun, sand, and sex) tourism locales in countries like Indonesia and Costa Rica—the poster child for ecotourism—have become so penetrated by tourism that anthropologists have to study the role of tourism because it is so ubiquitous. I have spent many summers studying the impacts of the four S's on the Costa Rican society and environment. From what I have seen, the speed at which Costa Rica's mass tourism has grown has been stunning. By the 1980s it was already the most deforested country in Central America (Evans 1999:39); every day, more forest and swampland is being removed to make room for hotels and vacation homes.

In many of the well-known cultures and societies in which anthropologists have conducted research over the last century, tourism has become one of the main industries. Indeed, it is often said that tourism is the world's biggest industry, at least in terms of labor and investments.[1] For example, the only export that matters in much of the Caribbean is tourism (Wilkinson 1997:2). In Costa Rica in 2002, there were nearly 1.2 million tourist arrivals—one tourist for every three residents—and the country's tourism sector accounted for 22 percent of exports (UK Trade and Investment 2005:1).

THE GROWTH OF THE ANTHROPOLOGY OF TOURISM

As a field of study, the anthropological study of tourism has grown very rapidly since the 1970s and early 1980s when Valene Smith (1977), Malcolm Crick (1985, 1989), Dennison Nash (1977, 1981), Nelson Graburn (1977, 1983) and Erik Cohen (1974, 1979a, 1979b, 1984), among others, first brought this very important phenomenon to the attention of anthropologists. Earlier anthropologists may have been reluctant to investigate this phenomenon because tourism is too close to what anthropologists do themselves when they are in the field (Crick 1995). There may have appeared to be too little difference between travelers' accounts and anthropological accounts of social and cultural phenomena. Since we anthropologists are professionals by definition, and travelers are not, it was important to distinguish ourselves from mere tourists. Crick (1995:207–208) states that our colleagues are embarrassed to be associated with tourists, for whom tourism is all about a "ludic" state, as contrasted with anthropologists, who are "serious" researchers studying the native perspective with cultural sensitivity, respect, and diligence. Anthropologists denied that there were tourists who might have as much or more knowledge of local cultures than did anthropologists. To admit this would have been threatening, as it might invalidate the entire anthropological belief system. In short, tourism was off limits as a legitimate area of study until Valene Smith's book (1977) was published, institutionalizing the terms "host" and "guest" in the anthropology of tourism. Ten years later, when she published a second edition of the book (Smith 1989), the anthropology of tourism was on its way to becoming a more popular and more seriously regarded area of study among anthropologists and their graduate students. By the publication of a third, completely revised edition (Smith 2001), tourism was a regular topic in the paper sessions of most of the discipline-wide professional anthropology meetings (SfAA, AAA, etc.) and it was widely taught in the United States. In fact, the graduate program in applied anthropology at the University of Maryland now has had a tourism track for at least a decade.

TOURISM AS A NEGATIVE PHENOMENON

Anthropologists already have made a mark in the field of tourism studies. Jafar Jafari, an anthropologist and the editor of *Annals of Tourism Research*, the main journal for this very multidisciplinary field (Jafari 2001:34),[2] advises that anthropologists have submitted as much as 15 percent of the accepted manuscripts for it (Jafari 2004, personal communication). Smith (1989[1977], 2001), Edward Bruner (1995, 1996), Malcolm Crick (1985, 1989) and Dennison Nash (1981, 1996), to name only a few, are well known throughout the field of tourism studies, far beyond the confines of the discipline of anthropology. Increasingly, anthropologists who study tourism have gone beyond the classroom and into a varied range of applied settings, bringing their anthropological expertise to complicated, multisited scenarios, as is shown by the case studies presented in many of the articles printed here. But it has taken a while to get to this point.

In the second half of the last century, anthropologists researching and doing fieldwork in towns and villages distant from urban centers were shocked to see "their" communities become tourist destinations. Consumed with concern about how traditional cultures would fare against the arrival of tourists, unschooled in anthropology, who sought an authentic experience, anthropologists saw this "invasion" as part of an unwanted globalization process. Almost without thought, anthropologists began to study the "impact of tourists and tourism" on local communities. One of the most famous (perhaps notorious) examples of this kind of study was Davydd Greenwood's article (1989[1977], 2004) on the Alarde ritual in Hondarribia, Spain (see the paper by Douglass and Lacy in this volume). His now oft-quoted study itself had great impact on the focus of what anthropologists began to study in tourism. In a recent postscript to his study, Greenwood (2004:166–167) states that he wrote the article out of concern and anger, and that today he finds himself troubled by his judgments—not because they were wrong, but because the way he "researched and delivered this judgment" was "professionally self-serving." Furthermore, he writes,

> In the Alarde I found what I took to be an almost perfect microcosm of the destruction of all that is culturally good and authentic by the "state" and "world capitalism." My response was to denounce this from a position of professional authority—as an [ethnographic] "expert" on a . . . place in a way that has long been conventional for anthropologists. [2004:167]

With regard to tourism studies in anthropology, what followed the publication of Greenwood's article, at least initially, was an investigation of the effects of tourism on native communities, usually under the assumption that tourism had primarily negative effects. In addition, ethnographers felt justified in having no association with tourists and tourism, as it might taint the legitimacy of their own work and diminish their professional academic status. One brief example illustrates. Edward Bruner, a highly respected academic anthropologist who is a frequent contributor to tourism research, wanted to investigate how different populations, genders, and classes travel; and how travel affects them in producing stories, knowledge, and theories about their experiences and observations. To do this, he decided to be an insider, a tour guide to Indonesia for an upscale group of moderately well-educated tourists (see Ingles and Blundell in this volume for other examples of anthropologists as tour guides). Arriving in Bali, he visited a specific temple with which he was familiar and happened upon Hildred Geertz, another well-known ethnographer with long-term research ties to Indonesia. To his chagrin, she was uncomfortable with meeting the tourists he was guiding, and asked to meet him separately after the event. Bruner (1996) concludes from this event and others like it, "To ethnography, tourism is indeed like a poor country, or an illegitimate child that one chooses not to recognize" (Gmelch 2004:226). The disregard for the seriousness of tourism research among anthropology colleagues is also found among colleagues from related fields in the social sciences and humanities. One year I applied for a research grant to study the role of tourism in Hungary's transition to a post-socialist economy. The reviewers were colleagues from nine liberal arts departments. The grant application was turned down. The following year I revised the project slightly and submitted it again, this time without "tourism" in the title. It was funded.

Even though the anthropological study of tourism is gradually achieving some grudging recognition among academic colleagues in anthropology and other related disciplines, tourism itself continues to be regarded suspiciously by most. Even among anthropologists who regularly study tourism there continues to be an uneasy ambivalence about the subject. This ambivalence is well reflected in a new, interesting, interpretive ethnography of tourism by Sally Ann Ness based on her work in Davao City, Philippines:

> The question [of] whether tourism is a nightmare or a godsend or some combination of the two in a given location is not one that currently can be foreseen with any certainty. It depends on an array of circumstances too vast and complex to model in general terms . . . . Regardless of the questions of goodness or evil, however, tourism must be recognized as a subject that brings unique, even vital, insight to the study of contemporary cultural phenomena. [2003:22]

Ness reminds us that tourism is a very complex phenomenon—one that is hard even to describe. Putting a definition on tourism is somewhat akin to the problems evoked by cultural anthropologists trying to define "culture." There is certainly a question of boundary regarding who is a tourist when, where, and how (when engaged in what kinds of activities). For example, a pilgrim visiting the Lourdes shrine seeking a cure is simultaneously a pilgrim and a tourist, as is the Mecca hajj visitor. Both Mecca and Lourdes have developed facilities for those visitors, and though the nature of their destinations is quite different, so have Orlando (Disney World) and Anaheim (Disneyland), two of our most important secular "meccas."[3]

Post-modernist perspectives, too, have been very important in the development of the anthropology of tourism. The works by sociologists Dean MacCannell (1976, 1989), John Urry (1990) and anthropologists Clifford (1997) and Castañeda (1996) are evidence of researchers becoming much more concerned about the "tourist superorganic" (a kind of tourist culture whose specifics are shaped both by the travelers tourists meet and by the cultures tourists have left behind) and the effect of a socially organized, systematized tourist gaze that patterns the relationships among the tourists and the toured (Urry 1990:1).

Regardless of their theoretical perspectives, anthropologists have always had strong concerns with tourists and their effect on small native communities. The famous film *Cannibal Tours* (1987) by Dennis O'Rourke is frequently cited by anthropologists as an example of how tourists have negative effects on native peoples. O'Rourke himself writes:

> I like to think of *Cannibal Tours* not so much as a film about the negative effect of mass tourism on fragile cultures, which should be obvious to everybody; but more as a philosophical meditation set in the milieu of this kind of tourism. The film is much more about the whole notion of the "the primitive" and "the other," the fascination with primitivism in Western culture and the wrong-headed nostalgia for the innocence of Eden. [1999:8]

The underlying assumption is that tourism is bad and that it has negative effects for local communities. A new book by Donald Reid on tourism and development begins with a definitive statement that "Tourism is a dynamic force homogenizing societies and commodifying cultures across the globe" (2003:1) and refers to tourism as a "cancer" (6). Reid also notes that as a form of community development, despite its promise of bringing major economic benefits, tourism in fact brings an uneven development package, with developers and outside entrepreneurs garnering most of the benefits and leaving the local people to bear the cost of development without adequate rewards.

Thus, tourism, seen from the vantage of social scientists like Reid (following Greenwood's 1977 perspective) is doubly cursed. Such scholars believe that tourism does not provide real benefits to local people, that it has a detrimental transformative role in changing local socioeconomic relationships, and that it also destroys local cultural practices and artifacts by converting them into commodities that can be bought and sold.

THE FOCUS OF THIS VOLUME

Academic anthropologists are more attracted to this negative perspective than to one that suggests, as I believe, that tourism is one of many change factors and thus is neither good nor bad but must be recognized for its role as one of the world's largest and most global "industries." In any event, as we have seen above, there are multiple reasons why the negative view of tourism has prevailed among anthropologists. The authors in this issue of the *NAPA Bulletin*, however, reflect a more nuanced view of tourism, one in which tourism is seen as one kind of strategy for change that can have both positive and negative consequences. They also demonstrate ways in which anthropologists can contribute to neutralizing the negative aspects of tourism development projects without losing their wariness over the potential for harm that unrestrained tourism can cause, especially in smaller communities. The authors were specifically asked to find examples from their own work in tourism, illustrating ways in which anthropologists might provide effective and ethically appropriate input into tourism project development. They were also asked to reflect on the impacts their work has had in local communities.

The authors have responded with an extensive examination of issues, ideas, and specific cases from their experience as applied anthropologists working in tourism and with stakeholders (tourism entrepreneurs, travel agency owners, hotel personnel, owners, managers, developers, workers, local community members, etc.). Some of the papers illustrate ways in which the potential for negative impacts can be reduced, while others provide examples of how applied anthropologists working in tourism can assist local communities or help tourists enhance their experience while encouraging sustainable tourism practices. Instead of the usual Sturm und Drang about tourism, what we find in these papers is a different, less impact-focused take on:

1. How anthropology provides context and helps clarify the sometimes different meanings the various stakeholders in tourism assign to the same situation;
2. How the potential roles for applied anthropologists—as researchers, analysts, consultants, advocates, and even as tour guides—vary depending on a context involving multiple actors with differing world views within an ambiguously defined applied setting; and,
3. How universities and academia-based applied anthropologists are often able to leverage huge amounts of resources in the form of human and social capital, sometimes converting this capital into sustained, real-world, tangible resources for the benefit of local communities involved in tourism.

In this *NAPA Bulletin*, we see applied anthropologists putting anthropological concepts and ideas to use in tourism, not only from the perspective of the local community members—as we would expect anthropologists to do—but also from the perspectives of tourists and tour guides, of travel agents and community planners. Tourism, in the view of the contributors, is a very important, common, human phenomenon that needs to be understood in all its complexity. By bringing theory and practice together, a praxis is possible that assists the development of a formal study of tourism and helps tourists—and the people who live and work with tourism—to better understand and control the changes that are connected with the growth of the industry.

TOURISM IN ANTHROPOLOGICAL THEORY AND PRACTICE

This issue of the *NAPA Bulletin* is divided into three sections. The first section concerns the connections between the anthropology of tourism and its practice. The papers here discuss topics of ethics, theory, fieldwork, conservation, ecotourism, archaeology, and the basic elements of "responsible tourism." The second section presents a set of papers dealing with case studies from applied anthropologists who worked in the development of tourism projects. Here we read about anthropologists as consultants, teachers, internship advisors, project researchers, analysts, community development workers, and brokers between NGOs or private enterprises and the community. The issues and themes discussed in the first section—ethical dilemmas, methodological approaches, examining and evaluating project impacts, and the nature of praxis—are exemplified in the work of these authors. The papers in the third section treat the anthropologist as an actor within the tourism sector, primarily as a tour guide or travel agent. The line between anthropologist and tourist begins to blur here, yet it is important to see how anthropology can be applied directly to the tourism industry. In addition, one of the papers provides concrete information about where the jobs in the tourism industry may be found. Now let us turn to the first section and briefly review what lies ahead of the reader.

Tourism as Praxis

This section forces us to take a close look at how anthropological theory and practice (*praxis*) converge in providing important theoretical and practical insights from the study of tourism and applied work in tourism. The first paper gives us many clues about how the knowledge anthropologists have gained about human behavior can be applied to our own tourism experiences. The author of this paper, Erve Chambers (1997, 2000), is a pioneer in the applied anthropology of tourism and is one of the founders of the tourism track in applied anthropology at the University of Maryland. He believes, as do most anthropologists, that tourists often behave irresponsibly. In his paper he lays out a series of tips and suggestions that can make us all better, more responsible tourists. We see from his work that he shares the concerns of Deborah McLaren (1998), whose influential work, *Rethinking Tourism and Ecotravel: The Paving of Paradise and What You Can Do to Stop It*, challenges tourists to rethink the way they travel, where they take vacations, and what they do when they reach their destinations. Both Chambers and McLaren strongly believe that tourists must research their destinations very carefully before taking their vacations, especially when traveling abroad in a different culture. They both worry about unrestrained tourism development in ecologically sensitive areas and in places where tourism is out of the control of local communities. Chambers draws upon anthropological concepts to provide straightforward suggestions about how to guide responsible tourists while on vacation. He asks—and answers— the question "Can anthropology actually teach us anything with regard to becoming better tourists?"

In the second paper, Kathleen Adams is concerned about the ethics of tourism-related studies: a concern arising out of the ethical dilemmas of the research process itself. The anthropologist doing research in tourism might find herself being recruited by her informants; collaborating with local governments, community leaders, business officials, and others to provide a legitimized version of heritage-related events, artifacts, or performances; or even be asked to help promote specific tourist venues in the locality of her research. This presents an ethical dilemma for anthropologists, Adams says, and the refusal to cooperate could produce "unanticipated reverberations."

Adams cites Edward Bruner (1995), who recounts his participant-observation research methodology and experience as a tour guide in Indonesia. In Bruner's article, he is conflicted about his role as interpreter and arbiter of authentic Balinese and Indonesian art and cultural performances. He asks whether he is a closet tourist playing at ethnography or a closet ethnographer working at tourism (Bruner 1995:231). Bruner (1996) is also shocked to find the extent to which anthropological research by earlier researchers—such as Gregory Bateson and Margaret Mead, among others—has influenced the both the art and the practice of art and dance in Bali:

> The gifted group of intellectuals and artists who lived in Bali in the 1930s, including Spies, Covarrubias, Belo, McPhee, Bateson, and Mead, were captivated with the barong [a dance form involving trance] and, in collaboration with the Balinese, commissioned new forms of the barong dance. The famous Bateson-Mead film, *Trance and Dance in Bali*, which is usually regarded as an

early photographic record of a Balinese ritual, was actually a film of a tourist performance for foreigners commissioned and paid for by Bateson and Mead . . . [The barong ritual filmed by Bateson and Mead was not ancient but had fairly recently been created during the period of their fieldwork, and the story performed had been changed from the Calon Arang to the Kunti Sraya, a less dangerous form. The Kunti Sraya barong dance, after various transformations since the 1930s, is still performed for tourists to this day. Further, for the film, Bateson and Mead changed the dance by having women rather than men hold krisses, and they commissioned the dance during the day, when the light was good for photography, rather than having the performance in the evening.] [Gmelch 2004:227–228]

While Bruner notes the unwitting, uncomfortable role of ethnographers in affecting the course of tourism development, archaeologists have sometimes been willful promoters of tourism development and sometimes woeful about what has happened to key archaeological sites overrun by tourists. The tourism dilemma for archaeologists, too, can be great. Archaeologists are key players in interpreting historically significant but fragile archaeological sites and reconstructions while protecting the location's integrity and reducing the impact of the tourist "footprint." In her article on archaeological tourism in Mexico's Yucatan, Cameron Walker describes the importance of tourism both for and in archaeological research, interpretation, and reconstruction. Some of the major funding for archaeological research comes from governments and NGOs that see reconstruction of ancient sites and pyramids such as those in the "Mundo Maya" region of Yucatan and Central America as intimately connected with tourism (cf. Ford 1997; Buettner 2003). Archaeologists face the same kinds of ethical and moral choices as cultural anthropologists in determining when, in what manner, and under what conditions it is appropriate to provide their expertise to projects that may become tourist attractions. While funding for tourism may promote important archaeological research, the commitment to reconstruction of a site for tourist visits may lead to rapid deterioration of key heritage sites by attracting excessive numbers of curious vacationers. Take for example the Late Horizon Inca site of Machu Picchu, Peru's number-one tourist destination. Machu Picchu is one of the most awe-inspiring, ancient destinations in the Western Hemisphere, but overrun by tourists.[4] MSNBC News recently ran a headline entitled, "Tourist glut threatens Machu Picchu: UNESCO calls for drastic reduction in number of visits" (MSNBC News 2003). Each day more than 1,500 people trek the ancient Inca Trail to the ruins, and another 4,000 tourists arrive by train and walk the walls and paths of the site. The daily impact of such numbers is taking a heavy toll. Compare this to the few hundred people who continuously inhabited Machu Picchu in the 16th century. What ethical responsibilities do archaeologists have to protect the site from further deterioration, and how should they respond to governmental pressure to keep it completely accessible to tourists? Walker frames this debate in her paper and shows that archaeological research at the service of the tourism industry is both a responsibility and dilemma for the archaeologist.

Another key area of responsibility and dilemma for anthropologists relates to ensuring that communities participate in the decisions involving tourism and tourists. Applied anthropologists have long held the belief that no applied project can succeed, or should succeed, without some community input. In an article based on her research in the Bay Islands of Honduras (cf. Stonich 2000), Susan Stonich discusses the difficulties of achieving community-appropriate projects in ecotourism, especially since much of the current work in ecotourism is intimately bound up with conservationism. Stonich points out that conservation NGOs often have money to spend but do not want to spend it on humans. Conservationists mainly are interested in biological and ecological issues and often see local people as obstacles to their conservation strategies. American conservationists seem to prefer what Donald Brockington (2001) refers to as the "fortress conservation" model (Igoe 2004:69). By this, Brockington means a model in which the area to be conserved is treated as an exclusion zone—one in which native, non-human life is protected while humans are kept beyond the perimeter of the protected area.

Clearly, anthropologists are among the most outspoken on the side of allowing local residents to have an important role in deciding how their cultural and material resources are to be employed—and whether any of these resources should be used for tourism development. This is especially critical in areas where ecology and nature are the main elements that attract tourists. Ecotourism is seen as a way to protect fragile ecosystems while providing some economic benefit to local communities (Honey 1999), yet the promised benefits have not been as great as expected (McLaren 1998:101; Honey 1999:85). In fact, the term *ecotourism* has been taken over by large tourism companies promoting "alternative tourism," which is merely mass tourism with a different label (Wall 1994, 1996). First World tour operators (including hoteliers and travel agencies) are now mining Third and Fourth World localities for new destinations for the Post-Fordist, alternative tourists from the developed countries of the West. A part of the tour operators' "mining process" is gaining economic and political control over the natural resources of economically poor but environmentally rich communities (cf. Mowforth and Munt 1998). In this way, locations like Ranomafana National Park in Madagascar—set aside largely for the conservation of lemurs—can be reserved for a few well-heeled, elite tourists and endowment-funded scientific primate researchers. Meanwhile, tens of thousands of local people are fenced out of prime forest land they have foraged for generations, jailed when they harvest firewood or crawfish, and denied promised medical benefits. Sometimes they are deemed undeserving of basic governmental services when their traditional farming or hunting systems do not fit within the conservationists' range of acceptable behavior (Harper 2002).

Stonich's article illustrates the disconnect between the public rhetoric of international environmental organizations and their true intent. Stonich forcefully argues for the necessity of an integrated, community-based conservation and development approach rather than the use of exclusion zones, and she provides key suggestions on how such an approach might be realized. Furthermore, she says, anthropologists can play important roles in identifying the stakeholders and facilitating the mediation process in tourism development projects.

Quetzil Castañeda, in his contribution, attempts to dissect the fabric of ethnography in the anthropology of tourism by separating the threads of research from the threads of application, or, as he says, "understanding the entanglement of the anthropologist and the anthropologies at work during ethnographic investigation." In particular, he explores the consequences of a middle path between application and theory, describing an experimental field-work technique he used during his work in Pisté, Mexico, located in the shadow of the famous Post-Classic ruined city of Chichén-Itzá, Yucatan. While studying the toured–tourist relationships among Chichén Itzá-dependent Pisté residents, Castañeda wanted to understand how tourist art is converted into "Art." He thus encouraged the opening of an exhibit of local Pisté artists to see how tourist art production might be converted to developing forms for art collectors. The experimental methodologies he chose had consequences, and he discusses these in his paper. His experimental anthropology falls in the interstices between theory and applied, fitting what Baba (2000:26) defines as *praxis*—a method where theory and application connect.[5] Castañeda wonders about the ethics of his work, and finds himself in situations similar to those discussed by other anthropologists studying tourism, including those who wrote for this *Bulletin*.

Applied Anthropologists as Tourism Consultants, Advisors, and Brokers

The papers in the second section of this volume describe how applied anthropologists have been working in tourism as consultants, researchers, analysts, and mediators. All of them work with local cities and communities in developing tourism projects, some of which are aimed at heritage tourism while others deal with ecotourism that affects indigenous populations. Heritage tourism and ecotourism are both important, major facets of the modern tourism industry and provide opportunities in which the work of applied anthropologists is especially apt.

As independent consultants working in tourism, anthropologists must deal not only with weighty political issues but with significant ethical issues as well. William Douglass, a renowned Basque scholar writing here with Julie Lacy, became both intrigued and suspicious when he was offered work as a consultant in developing a Basque-heritage theme park in the town of Urnieta, Spain. Since any heritage park would be required to seem "authentically Basque," Douglass's involvement would lend authenticity to the project. His enthusiasm for the project was tempered by concern—the angst mentioned in the title of his paper. The mixing of Basque and non-Basque elements might not find favor with traditionalists, especially if the project were to become a Disney-fication of Basque culture.

MacCannell (1989[1976]) was one of the first authors in the field to write specifically about the problem of understanding what *authenticity* means in modern tourism. MacCannell (1989:95) suggests that the search for a travel experience with "the Other" (non-home) is important to many tourists escaping from the pressures of their daily routine. With travel, they can break out of the routine and experience a "real" (but largely imagined) life and let their "inner children" escape from the confines of normal social strictures. Sometimes tourists are satisfied with an almost authentic experience, what MacCannell calls "staged authenticity" (1989:98). This staged authenticity is different from what Boorstin (1961:99) calls "pseudo-events" (MacCannell 1989:103),[6] which are activities or events reflecting the flavor of local culture but in which the natives are quarantined from the tourists, who are thus able to view things in the comfort to which they are accustomed at home.

Douglass and Lacy, like all the anthropologists who write in this issue, are very concerned about the representation of native culture, the tourist gaze, and whether they might inadvertently contribute to the organization of a tourist gaze that would negatively impact the toured. They teach us that much must be considered before undertaking a consulting role in tourism development.

One person who seems to have successfully learned this lesson is Mary LaLone. In her paper, she describes a technique she calls "anthro-planning" that systematically assists Appalachian communities in planning and designing their

FIGURE 3. Civil War heritage re-enactment at Ft. Macon, North Carolina.

own local heritage tourism sites. Several years ago, LaLone organized a group of applied anthropology students at Radford University in western Virginia into a research and planning consulting group. The students were to work with a small Appalachian community that had requested assistance in capturing some of the local tourism, develop plans for showcasing appropriate tourism sites, and suggest ways to exhibit traditional mountain culture. LaLone was so successful that she has been frequently sought out by both communities and regional governmental planning authorities to repeat her successful "anthro-planning approach to local heritage tourism" in new communities. In her article, she provides a simple model that other industrious applied anthropologists could employ with their students, either as a group, class project, or internship. She also gives some wonderful ideas about how to effectively incorporate applied tourism research into our teaching and internships. Her status as a university professor enables her to marshal considerable resources for the communities in her work.

Another participatory "anthro-planning" model for heritage tourism emerges from the work of Amanda Mason, trained in applied anthropology at the University of Maryland, who discusses aspects of her employment by the Western Erie Canal Planning Commission. She emphasizes how difficult but essential it is for anthropologists to convince politicians of the importance of community participatory involvement in developing heritage tourism projects. In fact, the ethnographic research and analysis components of the job appear to be the easiest parts, while the internal and external politics affecting decision-making are what really challenge the skills of the applied anthropologist working in tourism. Mason and her team of ethnographers struggle mightily to provide regional commissioners with the ethnographic data and analysis that will persuade them to become more heavily involved with the local communities in designing tourism projects along the Erie Canal Corridor. Unfortunately, the anthropologists find it very hard to catch the ear of the politicians. Mason shows us how hard it can be to work with local government officials but also how rewarding it can be when the community responds to ethnographic and community-partnership work.

The issue of who decides or leverages the ways in which actual and potential tourism resources are to be used—whether outside researchers, local governments, national and international businesses, or local residents—attracts the attention of many anthropologists working in tourism. The papers in this volume by Amanda Stronza and by Daniela Diamente and myself tackle these issues, albeit with some differences. Both papers deal with issues associated with ecotourism, one of the more controversial types of tourism.

Stronza examines the role of private enterprise in participatory tourism development. Working in Infierno, Madre de Dios, in the southeastern Peruvian Amazon, Stronza studied and played the role of culture broker at an ecotourism destination called Posada Amazonas, a unique partnership between the community of Infierno and the Rainforest Expeditions company. As part of the arrangement, the company would lease Infierno land for 20 years, employ and train local community members, and, at the end of that time, turn the infrastructure over to the community, who would then become the owners.[7] Stronza facilitated the cross-cultural communication between the foreign company and the local community. She was able to alert both sides to the needs and problems presented by the collaboration. Who was to participate in the collaboration, and how, was not clear in the initial contract, but Stronza, in her role as both researcher and broker, was able to assist both sides in grappling with the meaning and practice of *participation*. She also helped to clarify and promote the role of local culture during the evolution of the project. The gradual unfolding of her status as a culture broker, standing as it does at the intersection between applied anthropology and theoretical research, highlights one of anthropologists' common experiences when studying tourism: namely,

FIGURE 4. Mayan woman selling handcrafts on the shore of Lake Atitlán, Guatemala.

that when it comes to good applied anthropology and tourism, the distance between applied anthropology and theoretical anthropology is very small (see also Castañeda, this volume).

Whereas Stronza worked with a private company and a small number of indigenous communities, the case study by Wallace and Diamente concerns a private conservation NGO, The Nature Conservancy, and its "fortress conservation" approach to protecting the biodiversity of the Lake Atitlán, Guatemala, watershed. Our work also illustrates the way applied anthropologists can mobilize an array of human resources to facilitate the interaction between foreign conservationists and local native communities. Furthermore, it provides another example of how to provide training opportunities for students who wish to work in tourism, either as community-development leaders or as research analysts.

The Nature Conservancy wanted to accomplish its mission by restricting community use in areas its in-house biologists and ecologists had decided were primary, while officially espousing the importance of providing local economic benefits through ecotourism development. The Conservancy faced a difficult task in persuading the tens of thousands of Maya living in the area to be "protected." The Maya of the region have a close relationship with the local environment that has evolved over a millennium, and were not easily convinced to change their land-use patterns. Like Stonich, Wallace and Diamente found that the environmental NGO's efforts in ecotourism development were inadequate for the job. Working under the assumption that the Maya could not have been good environmental stewards, The Nature Conservancy prioritized funding for wildlife biologists whose work would document how local Maya cultural and economic practices had had negative impacts on the environment. The biologists' diagnostic studies were to be used to arrive at the next stage of project: establishing biological exclusion zones—euphemistically called municipal parks—to deploy a "site conservation plan." No significant funding was provided for community-building, collaborative conservation and ecotourism partnerships. This paper illustrates the necessity of having social scientists—especially anthropologists—involved in ecotourism development ventures, interfacing with both the project developers and members of the local community to ensure that they participate fully in the planning process. Community participation can ensure that conservationists do not neglect local indigenous preferences and wisdom in their sometimes unwisely conceived projects (Chapin 2004:18).

Anthropologists, Tour Guides, and Travel Agencies

Conservation and ecotourism is also one of the themes in the paper by Palma Ingles. Ingles' paper starts the final section of *NAPA Bulletin 23*, which consists of three papers that focus on anthropologists as tour guides. Like Bruner, who was mentioned above, Ingles has spent several summers working as a tour guide on boat tours of the Peruvian Amazon. In this capacity she was able to see how tourism works from both tourists' and local indigenous communities' perspectives. In this blurring of tourist, tour guide, and anthropologist, Ingles argues that anthropologists should be more frequently involved in guiding tours like the one Bruner led. Ingles has reported elsewhere (2000, 2001) on her research into tourism's largely positive impacts on communities she studied in the Peruvian Amazon. Not only does she support the role of anthropologists as researchers and consultants in tourism research; like Valene Smith (see this volume), she also believes there are many such jobs appropriate for anthropologists who wish to work in tourism. As anthropologists help tour companies and tourists reduce unwanted impacts and better understand local customs, the benefits of their work will accrue for both local residents and fragile environments. Ingles is unconcerned about the blurring of the line between researcher and applied anthropologist because she believes the presence of the anthropologist in tourism has far more positive than negative consequences for tourist and native resident alike.

In contrast to Ingles, who was an employee of a tour company, David Blundell has designed his own tour program. His article describes a very unique case in which he, as an anthropologist, was in the vanguard of designing and conducting tour programs that attempt to break down the stereotypes produced by the tourist gaze. His "traveling seminars" bring together the tourists and the toured and focus on sustainable ecotourism that raises tourists' awareness of their environment and the people who live in it. His work follows McLaren's (1998:131) suggestion to encourage development of and participation in alternative tourist programs that revolve around a cultural exchange between the traveler and the indigenous peoples who are visited. Blundell's program is very interesting for several reasons: (1) it encourages a dialogue between urban tourists and rural indigenous peoples; (2) it emphasizes the role of the tourist in protecting the environment; and (3) it is designed, organized, and led by anthropological concepts. In other words, it puts into practice most of the "tips" that Chambers offers in his paper.

In the final article in this *Bulletin*, Valene Smith—one of the pioneers of anthropology of tourism studies and a longtime travel agency owner—explains why it is important for anthropologists to work in and with the tourism industry. She argues that anthropologists' involvement in tourism would greatly the benefit the United States, which has not done enough to capture the large international tourism market and that, since the events of September 11, 2001, has actually made it harder and less comfortable for foreign tourists to visit. Smith has suggested in another context (personal communication) that more tourism with the United States as a destination would go a long way toward improving our balance of payments. One reason tourism is not as economically potent at home as it could be, she claims, is that the United States has very few trained guides and limited tourist packages for destinations that are off the beaten path—places where foreign tourists might observe "real Americans." Furthermore, the United States devotes relatively little money to promoting itself as a tourist destination. Smith believes that students with baccalaureate and advanced anthropology degrees could fill some of the tour guide positions, work in travel agencies, and design tour programs that would be better suited for foreign tourists and for the communities that receive them. Smith also gives examples of job training and employment opportunities for anthropologists in the tourism field, and describes cases in which anthropologists have worked to develop tour packages for local indigenous communities.

CONCLUSION

Anthropologists can no longer avoid the study of tourism. Tourism is a major factor in bringing change, at home and around the world. Some communities hunger for tourism because they see it as a mechanism by which to formulate, clarify, or validate their cultural identity (through heritage tourism, for example) and bring an economic return to their area. Others, though, experience the darker side of tourism: inflation, crime, drugs, changes in local values and mores, and disruption of the social order, to name a few negative impacts. Tourism also affects tourists themselves. Not only do they "recharge their batteries" but they also learn many things about other communities and other cultures. Sometimes they bring these new ideas and perspectives home and try them out. (Sushi anyone?)

We anthropologists have a better sense of tourism's impacts on local communities, but we have very little theoretical certainty about tourism's effects on tourists themselves and the communities to which they return. In many ways, tourism is like a slate on which many different stories can be written. Tourism is neither inherently good nor inherently bad; rather, it is neutral. The problems with tourism come from how it is employed within specific contexts. Anthropologists can bring a great deal to this field. They know how cultures and systems work; they understand that communities and regions offer multiple interpretations of the "correct" way to represent heritage or to produce a tourist attraction; and they know that ideas and behaviors are broadly diffused as both intended and unintended consequences of contact across communities, societies, and cultures. Furthermore, not only can anthropologists provide culturally appropriate guidelines for ethical and responsible tourists and tourism, but they are well situated to assist local people in the decision-making process so communities can together produce, organize, and control tourist activities.

The applied anthropologists writing in this *NAPA Bulletin* share why it is crucial for anthropologists to be involved in tourism and how their applied work simultaneously contributes to theory and practice. As indicated above, anthropologists—applied or not, knowingly or unwittingly—have influenced the development of tourism and can have positive effects on it. Some would say that anthropologists *are* tourists, though most of us would quickly deny that. We cannot deny, though, that we are affected by our travels. The papers presented here are not only about tourism and what anthropologists contribute to it—theoretically and applied—but also what happens to them in the process of working in it. Not only do anthropologists affect tourism; tourism also affects them. The distance between theory and practice—praxis—is as long as your next vacation or as short as your next research project involving travel.

ACKNOWLEDGMENTS

I would like to thank all of the contributors to this volume for their helpful comments and support over the years and also for their input in bringing this *NAPA Bulletin* to fruition. I would specifically like to thank Chuck de Burlo at the University of Vermont for his very useful comments and suggestions on earlier drafts and Alayne Unterberger, co-editor of the *NAPA Bulletin* series, for giving up so many hours of her limited time to read through and comment on an earlier draft of this issue. Finally I would like to thank all of my students and colleagues in Anthropology and Ecotourism at the Universidad del Valle de Guatemala for their cooperation, support and help during my time in Guatemala.

NOTES

1. In much of the relevant literature, tourism is referred to as an industry, although some would argue that the term should be reserved for the manufacturing sector. In *Webster's New World College Dictionary*, an industry can be "any large-scale business activity."

2. The main researchers in the study of tourism come mainly from the following disciplines: anthropology, economics, geography, history, management science, politics, psychology, regional planning, and sociology.

3. I recently asked one of my anthropology classes how many of them had visited Disneyland or Disney World. Approximately three-quarters of the class had been to either theme park at least once, and one had even worked there!

4. Machu Picchu was rediscovered for Westerners in 1911 by Hiram Bingham, who eventually became a U.S. Senator from Nebraska. Originally thought to be the last city occupied by the Inca resistance to Spanish imperialism, it is now believed to have been a summer residence for the Inca and his court (Thomson 2001:74). I studied in Peru in the mid–1960s and even then Machu Picchu was Peru's major tourist destination.

5. Marietta Baba (2000:26) writes, "Praxis in applied anthropology is a way of knowing that relies on engagement in social reality, on being embedded in the processes of social life. Praxis, is, in part, subjective since the practitioner is not a spectator but an actor. The practitioner is engaged in complex interactions with social reality, as it is lived 'on the ground.'"

6. According to historian Daniel Boorstin (1961:99), "pseudo-events" are "an elaborately contrived indirect experience, an artificial product to be consumed in the very places where the real thing is as free as air. They are ways for the traveler to remain out of contact with foreign peoples in the very act of 'sightseeing' them. They keep the natives in quarantine while the tourist in air-conditioned comfort views them through a picture window. They are cultural mirages now found at tourist oases everywhere" (MacCannell 1989:103).

7. Searching for "Rainforest Expeditions" using Google will reveal a huge number of sites that mention the now-finished Posada Amazonas, the Peru destination that Amanda Stronza writes about. For an interesting contrast with Infierno and Rainforest Expeditions, see the film *Cashing in on Culture: Indigenous Communities and Tourism*, 29 minutes (Harrison 2002). This film examines an ecotourism project in the Ecuadorian Amazon.

REFERENCES CITED

Baba, Marietta L.
  2000 Theories of Practice in Anthropology: A Critical Appraisal. NAPA Bulletin 18:17–44.
Boorstin, Daniel J.
  1961 The Image: A Guide to Pseudo-Events in America. New York: Harper & Row.
Brockington, Donald L.
  2001 Fortress Conservation: The Preservation of the Mkomazi Game Reserve, Tanzania. Oxford: James Currey.
Bruner, Edward M.
  1995 The Ethnographer/Tourist in Indonesia. *In* International Tourism: Identity and Change. M.-F. Lanfant, J. B. Allcock, and E. M. Bruner, eds. Pp. 224–241. London: Sage Publications.
  1996 Tourism in Ghana: The Representation of Slavery and the Return of the Black Diaspora. American Anthropologist 98(2):290–304.
Buettner, Dan
  2003 Groundbreaker: A Plan to Save Guatemala's Mayan Cities with a Park and a Posh Eco-Lodge Has Enviros and Locals Boiling. Outdoor Magazine, August. Electronic document, http://outside.away.com/outside/news/200308/200308_disp_groundbreaker.html, accessed December 23, 2004.
Castañeda, Quetzil E.
  1996 In the Museum of Maya Culture: Touring Chichen Itza. Minneapolis: University of Minnesota Press.
Chambers, Erve, ed.
  1997 Tourism and Culture: An Applied Perspective. Albany: State University of New York Press.
Chambers, Erve
  2000 Native Tours: The Anthropology of Travel and Tourism. Prospect Heights, IL: Waveland Press.
Chapin, Mac
  2004 A Challenge to Conservationists. WorldiWatch, November/December: 17–31.
Clifford, James
  1997 Routes: Travel and Translation in the Late Twentieth Century. Cambridge, MA: Harvard University Press.
Cohen, Erik
  1974 Who is a Tourist? A Conceptual Clarification. Sociological Review 22:527–555.
  1979a The Impact of Tourism on the Hill Tribes of Northern Thailand. Internationales Asienforum 10:373–392.
  1979b A Phenomenology of Tourist Experiences. Sociology 13:179–202.

1984 The Sociology of Tourism: Approaches, Issues and Findings. Annual Review of Sociology 10:373–392.

Crick, Malcolm

1985 Tracing the Anthropological Self: Quizzical Reflections on Fieldwork, Tourism, and the Ludic. Social Analysis 17:71–92.

1989 Representation of the International Tourism in the Social Sciences: Sun, Sex, Sights, Savings, and Servility. Annual Review of Anthropology 18:307–344.

1995 The Anthropologist as Tourist: an Identity in Question. In International Tourism: Identity and Change. M.-F. Lanfant, J. B. Allcock, and E. M. Bruner, eds. Pp. 205–223. London: Sage Publications.

Ford, Anabel

1997 Envisioning the Future of El Pilar: A Model for Conservation and Development of Cultural and Natural Resource in the Maya Forest. The BRASS/El Pilar Program, Mesa Redonda. Electronic document, http://www.marc.ucsb.edu/elpilar/mesaredoda/mesaredonda97/future.html, accessed December 23, 2004.

Gmelch, Sharon Bohn, ed.

2004 Tourists and Tourism: A Reader. Prospect Heights, IL: Waveland Press.

Graburn, Nelson

1977 Tourism: The Sacred Journey. In Hosts and Guests: The Anthropology of Tourism. Valene Smith, ed. Pp. 17–32. Philadelphia: University of Pennsylvania Press.

1983 Anthropology of Tourism. Annals of Tourism Research 10(9):9–34.

Greenwood, Davydd J.

1989 [1977] Culture by the Pound: An Anthropological Perspective on Tourism as Cultural Commoditization. In Hosts and Guests: The Anthropology of Tourism. 2nd edition. Valene Smith, ed. Pp. 171–185. Philadelphia: University of Pennsylvania Press.

2004 Culture by the Pound: An Anthropological Perspective on Tourism as Cultural Commoditization. In Tourists and Tourism: A Reader. S. Gmelch, ed. Pp. 157–169. Prospect Heights, IL: Waveland Press.

Harper, Janice

2002 Endangered Species: Health, Illness and Death among Madagascar's People of the Forest. Durham, NC: Carolina Academic Press.

Harrison, Regina, dir.

2002 Cashing In on Culture: Indigenous Communities and Tourism. 29 minutes. Berkeley: University of California, Extension Center for Media and Independent Learning.

Honey, Martha

1999 Ecotourism and Sustainable Development: Who Owns Paradise? Washington, DC: Island Press.

Igoe, Jim

2004 Conservation and Globalization: A Study of National Parks and Indigenous Communities from East Africa to South Dakota. Belmont, CA: Thomson/Wadsworth.

Jafari, Jafar

2001 The Scientification of Tourism. In Hosts and Guests Revisited: Tourism Issues of the 21st Century. Valene L. Smith and Maryann Brent, eds. New York: Cognizant Communication Corporation: 28–41.

2004 Personal communication. October 24.

MacCannell, Dean

    1989 [1976] The Tourist: A New Theory of the Leisure Class. 2nd edition. London: Macmillan.

McLaren, Deborah

    1998 Rethinking Tourism and Ecotravel: The Paving of Paradise and What You Can Do To Stop It. West Hartford, CT: Kumarian Press.

MSNBC

    2003 Tourist Glut Threatens Machu Picchu: UNESCO Calls for Drastic Reduction in Number of Visits. Reuters. December 5. Electronic document, http://msnbc.msn.com/ Default.aspx?id=3660459&p1=0, accessed September 25, 2004.

Nash, Dennison

    1977 Tourism as a Form of Imperialism. *In* Hosts and Guests: The Anthropology of Tourism. Valene Smith, ed. Pp. 33–47. Philadelphia: University of Pennsylvania Press.

    1981 Tourism as an Anthropological Subject. Current Anthropology 22(5):461–481.

    1996 Anthropology of Tourism. Tarrytown, NY: Pergamon.

Ness, Sally Ann

    2003 Where Asia Smiles: An Ethnography of Philippine Tourism. Philadelphia: University of Pennsylvania Press.

O'Rourke, Dennis

    1987 Cannibal Tours. 70 min. Direct Cinema Ltd. Los Angeles.

    1999 On the Making of "Cannibal Tours." Electronic document, http://www. cameraworklimited.com/download.html?oid=2250047090, accessed November 30, 2004.

Reid, Donald G.

    2003 Tourism, Globalization, and Development: Responsible Tourism Planning. London: Pluto Press.

Smith, Valene L., ed.

    1989 [1977] Hosts and Guests: The Anthropology of Tourism. 2nd edition. Philadelphia: University of Pennsylvania Press.

    2001 Hosts and Guests Revisited: New Horizons in the 21st Century. New York: Cognizant Press.

Stonich, Susan C.

    2000 The Other Side of Paradise: Tourism, Conservation, and Development in the Bay Islands. New York: Cognizant Communications.

Thomson, Hugh

    2001 The White Rock: An Exploration of the Inca Heartland. Woodstock, NY: The Overlook Press.

UK Trade and Investment

    2005 Costa Rica. Electronic document, http://www.trade.uktradeinvest.gov.uk/costa_rica/ opportunities/12_opportunities/introduction.shtml, accessed January 4, 2005.

Urry, John

    1990 The Tourist Gaze: Leisure and Travel in Contemporary Societies. London: Sage.

Wilkinson, Paul F.

    1997 Tourism Policy and Planning: Case Studies from the Commonwealth Caribbean. New York: Cognizant Communications Corporation.

Part 1

CAN THE ANTHROPOLOGY OF TOURISM MAKE US BETTER TRAVELERS?

ERVE CHAMBERS
University of Maryland, College Park

Although the deliberate study of tourism is still relatively new in anthropology, we have over the past couple of decades managed to accumulate an impressive amount of research and experience. This article asks whether our inquiries can provide us with any practical knowledge regarding how tourism is conducted. While it has proven difficult to generalize the impacts of tourism upon particular communities, I argue here that our present knowledge can help us develop guidelines for responsible tourism that are more realistic than those that are usually offered. The danger for well-meaning travelers is that they are often encouraged to assume that their motives alone place them above those mass travelers who are so easily criticized for their lack of cultural interest or sensitivity. The anthropological approach to tourism described here suggests that we might be better off if we recognize that our intrusions into the places of others are not really all that different. This article provides some "alternative travel tips" aimed at creating more aware travelers. Key Words: responsible tourism, tourist behavior, international travel, culture, hospitality

The anthropological study of travel and tourism has progressed considerably over the past couple of decades. We have, for example, moved from a perspective that tended to view tourism as a hugely negative—if not a colonialist—intrusion on largely passive host communities to a more balanced perspective that has begun to acknowledge the complex and pervasive nature of touristic practices, the conventions and agency of hospitality, and the multiple and sometimes conflicting ways in which tourism is mediated by a variety of stakeholder interests. Anthropologists have also begun, as some of the chapters in this

NAPA Bulletin 23, pp. 27–44, ISBN 1-931303-22-3. © 2005 by the American Anthropological Association. All rights reserved. Please direct all requests for permissions to photocopy or reproduce article content through the University of California Press's Rights and Permissions website, www.ucpress.edu/journals/rights.htm.

volume demonstrate, to explore ways in which they can apply their professional skills to the solution of problems and issues related to tourism development.

Over the past several years, my interest in the applied aspects of the anthropology of tourism has focused on preparing graduate students in applied anthropology for employment related to tourism. Through the Resource Management and Cultural Process track of the University of Maryland's applied program, a handful of students are currently pursuing careers in such areas as heritage tourism development, recreation planning, study abroad programs, and tourism marketing. Together, we have at least begun to identify the skills that are likely to lead to rewarding professional opportunities. But skills alone do not prove the efficacy of anthropological training. How can we link our knowledge and our largely implicit theories of tourism to specific tourism practices? Does anthropology itself teach us anything that is generally useful with regards to travel and tourism?

Unfortunately, applied anthropological training, whether applied to tourism development or to some other area of practical concern, does not always address questions that are so disarmingly simple and straightforward. We are too often derailed by an approach that emphasizes training practitioners to conduct original research, and to identify themselves primarily as researchers, rather than encouraging students to explore more innovative ways in which they might draw upon existing anthropological knowledge to entertain careers that are more closely related to such activities as planning, training, advocacy, and directly facilitating change. This latter approach to applied training informs much of the work that we are doing with tourism at the University of Maryland. While some of the graduates of the program might well pursue research careers, many others will not, and their contributions will instead be founded on their ability to derive practical insights and guidance from our discipline in general, and from the anthropology of tourism in particular.

The more popular model of training applied students to be researchers (i.e., evaluation research, impact assessment, appraisal, etc.) emphasizes the acquisition of generic social science research skills. But there is very little pertaining to applied research, including ethnographic methods, that remains distinctly anthropological, and the struggle with this mode of applied training lies in retaining any viable sense of professional identity. On the other hand, the training model that I am suggesting depends upon a close identification with anthropological knowledge. It aims to produce individuals who are able to represent our knowledge in a variety of venues—professional anthropologists whose expertise is rooted in the critical appreciation and practical application of particular domains of anthropological inquiry.

The trick to this second model lies in developing the means by which we might turn knowledge into practices—an endeavor that is all the more challenging because our knowledge is rarely consistent or complete. This suggests the need for a range of skills that we do not usually associate with applied anthropological training, such as the ability to synthesize large amounts of material and to generalize data in a responsible way, as well as the talent for exercising good judgment in drawing conclusions from different and sometimes theoretically incompatible knowledge sources.

TOURISM TIPS AND THE CONTEXTS OF TOURISM

The following discussion is an attempt to demonstrate how the approach to practice that I have described above might be applied to a particular problem. One way to think about tourism is to consider the extent to which it is shaped by the individual decisions of tourists. In this regard, I think it is fair to assume that most tourists are unaware of many of the consequences of their travel decisions, and it is not completely unreasonable to assume that better informed tourists might be less of a burden upon the places they visit. The question is, *can anthropology actually teach us anything in regard to becoming better tourists?*

My thinking on this matter was recently brought to the fore when a colleague shared with me a brief article written by Norman Sundberg (2001). Sundberg is a psychologist who has considerable experience in leading study-abroad programs. His article, entitled "Tips for Tourists," was directed to teachers and students, advising them on ways they might transform their travels—and even brief tours—into more rewarding cultural experiences. To this end, the tips were good suggestions. If the objective of more culturally based travel is to rise above the superficiality of many kinds of tourism encounters and actually learn something about other people and places, then Sundberg's tips were just fine. He recommended ways to get off the beaten track, suggested how to recognize local practices, and explained the value of learning a bit of the language: a variety of suggestions that were meant to turn routine tourism exchanges into something a little more profound.

Still, the article left me dissatisfied, and for a while I was not sure why. What finally occurred to me was that Sundberg's tips served, I suspect quite unintentionally, to mute the act of tourism itself. They provided no insight into the contexts in which tourism occurs. In this respect, his article began to seem more and more abstract, encouraging tourists to focus on travel as an opportunity for cultural enrichment in the same manner as they might be encouraged to read a book or visit a museum, where words and objects are bound or encased and do not have the means to talk back. What is more, Sundberg's discussion seemed to draw a sharp distinction between the art of travel (culturally enriching, of course) and the act of tourism (mundane and superficial). In that respect it joined many other commentaries in which the culturally sensitive traveler, motivated by good intentions and lofty ideals, appears to be relieved of responsibility for the possibly unintended consequences of her or his actions. But despite their intentions, travelers are still tourists. Regardless of the positive values that underlie such justifications of travel, they seem equally compromised by a tendency to deny or at least not to recognize that the environmental and sociocultural consequences of our moving around the world to enrich ourselves in one way or another are not that different from those of other, seemingly less inspired kinds of tourism.

All this thinking, painful as it was, led me to consider whether an alternative set of travel tips might be worthwhile. These could be developed from some of the things that anthropologists have recently had to say about tourism. They would argue, as I do in what follows, that a truly culturally sensitive and potentially enriching travel experience has its foundation in recognizing rather than trying to disassociate ourselves from the tourism consequences associated with our adventures. These tips also would acknowledge that tourism is in its own right one of the most powerful cultural forces of our time, which means that we can acquire greater knowledge of the world by recognizing our relationships as tourists and hosts than we would ever gain by pretending that we are somehow different and exempt from such considerations.

In the tips and suggestions that follow, I have tried to show how this might work, drawing on tourism literature as well as some of my own travel experiences, particularly as they relate to my work in Thailand. I have also, where it seemed appropriate, indicated some ways in which further research might cast even more light upon the consequences of tourism.

Traveler's Tip One: Understand that when you travel you are a consumer of precious goods and places Tourism never occurs in a vacuum. It is introduced to places and environments that have prior uses and standards of consumption, and communities that existed long before they were discovered by tourists have not always benefited from the shift This is especially apparent in places that are relatively confined, such as coastal areas and small islands, and even in some urbanized places, where basic commodities such as food and water can be scarce, and where the provision of electric power, transportation, and waste disposal services for tourism development can place serious economic and environmental constraints on the local population (e.g., Urbanowicz 1989).

In many resort areas, the average tourist consumes many times more water on a daily basis than does an entire local family. Demands for locally produced agricultural products for tourist consumption can result in shortages and higher prices for the local population. You do not have to leave the United States to appreciate this—for example, tourists to Florida are clearly contributing their share to drinking and showering the Everglades out of existence. Land resources and real estate are often dramatically affected by tourism development, resulting in higher local rents and rising land prices that might further diminish a region's ability to remain agriculturally self sufficient, as well as reducing the number of local land holders to the most wealthy alone.

How can this awareness contribute to making us better tourists? Some, although certainly not all, of these problems could be reduced if enough of us were more attentive to our own consumption habits. Do we really need that second shower? What is going to happen to all those plastic water bottles, and what would a customs official have to say if we brought them home with us to have them recycled? Should we make a practice of patronizing hotels and other facilities that at least try to be more environmentally responsible? The larger question, however, lies in the extent to which we might choose to base our travel choices on considerations such as these. Should we, for example, boycott places where our consumption practices are likely to cause to harm? I do not think we have the kind of knowledge that would help us make informed choices in this respect—except, perhaps, in some rather specific, isolated cases.

We have a couple of problems with the existing anthropological literature here, related to both balance and representation. By "balance" I refer to a need for a better way to measure and compare the costs and benefits of tourism, particularly as they apply to the interests of local populations. The problem of "representation" has to do with the observation that the ethnographic focus of much of the anthropology of tourism, valuable as it is, has made it difficult for us to generalize from one case to another and thereby arrive at more comprehensive theories related to such things as the consequences of particular kinds of consumption practices, or the relationships between different kinds of tourism development and the conservation of human and natural resources.

Traveler's Tip Two: Recognize that, in many of the places you travel, your relationship to the local population is primarily economic and is broadly influenced by dramatic differences in wealth We do not like to think in these terms. Many of us are simply not accustomed to thinking of ourselves as wealthy. Besides, travel is adventure. It is learning about other places and people, and it can be the basis for important cross-cultural understandings. These aims are perfectly legitimate, but we should not let them blind us to economic realities. It is far easier for a wealthy tourist to ignore the implications of small economic exchanges than it is for the locals who are involved in such transactions. In this regard, it is worthwhile to be wary of common tourist advice pertaining to how such exchanges should be conducted.

In purchasing goods at local markets, for example, we are often advised that it is important to bargain for a fair price. True enough. Bargain if you will, but be aware that local custom often dictates that you still *should* pay a bit more because of who you are, and that there is a measure of fairness in that expectation. And if you do bargain and reach an agreed-upon price, *never* change your mind and walk away without making the purchase.

Another example has to with how we are often advised to be careful of the ways we express generosity toward the indigenous people we encounter in seemingly remote places. Gifts of money might make such people more dependent on a money economy (don't worry; they almost invariably already are), and gifts of clothing might encourage them to abandon their colorful traditional dress (even though many of them already have adopted modern dress, except for occasions in which they are engaged with tourists).

For yet another example, consider the nearly universal practice of asking strangers for gifts of small change. As tourists, we are often disturbed by the number of "beggars" we encounter in some of our travels, and we tend to regard their presence as deliberately designed to take advantage of our presence and vulnerability. In reality, soliciting alms is an established practice in many countries where social services are lacking and poverty is considerable, and no weakness or naiveté is implied in being generous on such occasions.

Similarly, it is easy to become annoyed at the number of hawkers trying to sell us goods and services in many of the places we visit, and to become equally annoyed at what seems to be an overly tolerant attitude toward such practices on the part of local municipalities and tourist establishments. Once again, we often see such practices as directed specifically against us and as evidence of "inauthentic" tourist encounters. In reality, such informal economic sector practices often predate modern tourism and can be an important part of local culture. Where they are tolerated, it is often because they are recognized as being a vital resource for people in need. The laudable goal of attempting to increase our understanding of local cultures should include consideration of the possibility that many of our common and sometimes annoying economic encounters with the local population have their basis in long-established cultural practices—not to mention colonialist, patron–client relationships.

On the other hand, tourism does seem to give rise to a variety of exploitative practices that are directed toward visitors. In addition to common sense, one way of distinguishing such activities from those discussed above is to be a good ethnographer and make note of how the more privileged members of a place respond to similar encounters.

Traveler's Tip Three: Learn to recognize local customs regarding dress and behavior, but don't overdo it The kinds of "dos and don'ts" that are routinely listed in travel guides are worth considering, but it is equally important to be attentive to the patronizing tone conveyed in many such reports. They sometimes read as though local populations are unable to reflect upon their own conventions or recognize and tolerate differences of custom, when in fact people who routinely play host to large numbers of tourists may well be more flexible in this regard than many of us. In most tourist situations, our hosts do not really expect us to go native or act like they do, and they may be offended if we try (in part because, in trying, we can easily appear so ridiculous as to mock the very practices that we are trying to respect). Effective tourism is very much a process of the negotiation of difference on the parts of both the host *and* the tourist, and those who play host to tourists are usually quite sophisticated in their ability to tolerate the customary behaviors of visitors.

Still, there are occasions in which respecting local practices can be important. I recall, for example, the scandal that arose in Thailand after the local publication of a photograph of a scantily dressed Western tourist standing over a praying Buddhist monk. It is also worthwhile to keep in mind that local customs are sometimes codified into law, and that their violation can have undesirable consequences. In Thailand, again, tourists should not even think about climbing on a figure of Buddha or publicly showing disrespect to the monarchy. (Tourists have been arrested for deliberately crumpling paper money that displays the image of the king.)

Learning how to make a distinction between acquiring respect for local practices and recognizing, on the other hand, the extent to which the "natives" acknowledge and sometimes even count on our being different can in itself be a good way to increase the value of touristic encounters.

Traveler's Tip Four: There are subtleties concerning the uses and conventions of "foreign" language exchanges that you can't find in a phrase book Language is important in several respects. While there are occasions in which trying to adopt local practices might not be advisable, rarely is language use one of these. I have found that most people are appreciative of my attempts to speak their language, if only for the fact that such exchanges can provide opportunity for considerable levity. We cannot, of course, learn the languages of all the places we travel, but an attempt to grasp a few elementary expressions is generally worthwhile. A willingness to expose our limited capacity to communicate in another's language can be a great equalizer, and might actually lead to increased opportunities for sincere communication.

Attempts to practice the local language are sometimes hindered, however, as we encounter people who insist upon speaking with us in our language, perhaps because they consider it a part of their job, or because they realistically prize their language skills higher than ours, or because they seek opportunities to increase their competency in our language. These are legitimate aims that ought to be respected.

As tourists, our expectations regarding language use tend to vary depending upon the situation in which we find ourselves. While we often anticipate having difficulty on the street or in rural regions, we might feel differently when we are dealing with international hotel chains and airlines. Particularly if we are English speakers, we often expect to be able to converse in our language when we visit a Sheraton Hotel or Holiday Inn anywhere in the world. In these cases, our hosts are usually all too ready to accommodate us.

Still, it is not uncommon that language difficulties will arise. Staff might have a language capacity that is completely adequate for ordinary transactions, but that can lead to interesting misadventures in the face of unusual circumstances. It is worth keeping in mind that language is a lot more than vocabulary. English-speaking (particularly American) travelers are infamous for their inability to understand this, in part because our experience of language diversity is among the worst in the world. Our hosts are not only likely to be more adept at language exchange, but also to have greater patience in handling misunderstandings. We can learn a lot from them in this respect.

Traveler's Tip Five: Learn to appreciate the elusive nature of authenticity
Not all forms of tourism require an appreciation of authentic cultural representation. As an activity, tourism frequently encourages frivolity, relaxation, and pleasure-seeking over learning and appreciation, and these are not necessarily unreasonable pursuits (providing, of course, that the impacts upon host communities are taken into consideration). On the other hand, tourism does offer important opportunities for learning about how other people put their lives together. As more tourists come to value such experiences, we note an increase in varieties of "alternative" tourism in such forms as cultural and heritage tourism, ecotourism, adventure tourism, and sustainable or community-based tourism. These approaches to travel are often closely associated with the search for authentic places and environments.

For many tourists, the desire for authenticity is rather simplistically expressed in terms of seeking out that which is not contaminated by outside influences—particularly by the presence of other tourists. There are some important things to keep in mind here. First, nearly all tourism experiences are carefully crafted and staged by someone, specifically for our appreciation and consumption. It is more difficult than most of us realize, and not necessarily desirable, to try to get beyond such experiences and intrude into places where we might not be welcome.

Is it really necessary to get past the touristic staging of culture in order to learn about other cultures? Although much of the scholarship devoted to tourism decries the superficial and "inauthentic" nature of tourism presentations, there is something to say for the idea that practices associated with tourism are as deeply cultural and authentic as any others. The rubber tomahawk offered for tourism consumption in a Native American community that may not have even used "real" tomahawks is an authentic expression of that community's everyday cultural reality. A visit to a McDonald's fast food restaurant in Moscow can teach us a lot about local culture if we are attentive. Culture is not a *thing* produced in isolation. It is a *process* born from the interaction and distinction of peoples, and it is increasingly being produced through tourism.

It is also worthwhile to consider that even attempting to probe into those areas of a community that are not frequented by tourists can have deleterious effects. The most sensitive among us can still be susceptible to the belief that our good intentions and thirst for knowledge are adequate justification for intruding upon the privacy of others, and this is a special danger with respect to tourism, because we are so often encouraged to think of tourism destinations as objects that are created to provide us pleasure and satisfy our curiosity. Our trespasses are even more pronounced because we often do not even realize in cultural terms when we are intruding.

Communities vary considerably in how they distinguish between public and private spaces or between places that can be open to visitors and other places that should be reserved for local use, as well as in the ways in which they mark such distinctions—many of which might be indiscernible to a casual visitor. Communities also vary in their ability to prevent unwanted intrusions. Local conventions pertaining to hospitality might make it difficult for some local hosts to offend their guests in this respect (they rely upon the visitor to understand what the rules are). Other communities might actually be prevented by higher authorities from protecting personal and community spaces from unwanted intrusion by tourists.

In listening to travelers' accounts, including many of our own, we begin to understand how deeply ingrained is the idea of getting beyond the usual tourism experience in order to have a "genuine" cultural encounter. That such an endeavor might also appear to be genuinely rude and intrusive to our hosts is rarely appreciated. In this respect, I do not think the most popular theories of tourism have been of much help, because they tend to replicate the travelers' ethos by privileging certain styles of travel. But it is not the acquisition of remote spaces or the rarity of an experience that makes for authenticity. Perhaps it would be better to measure authenticity in relation to the *sincerity* of an encounter, wherever or however that encounter might occur.

Traveler's Tip Six: Make an effort to understand how tourism operates in the places you visit We can easily get sick of hearing this, but it is both true and significant—tourism represents one of the largest industries in the world, and by some accounts it may be the largest industry of all. It is an important part of the gross national product of many countries and regions, from the most highly developed to less-developed countries. It is the major source of foreign exchange for many developing countries, and, as such, is vital to maintaining financial stability. Although long associated with capitalism, modern forms of tourism are now an important part of the development of many socialist economies.

What all this means is that tourism is developed in a political economic context in which the stakes are great and competition is intense. In such an environment, the needs, interests, and well-being of local communities— particularly of indigenous and ethnic groups and many other "ordinary folk" with relatively little political influence—are not always given the consideration they deserve. One rationale commonly used to justify the social and economic costs associated with tourism is akin to the "trickle-down" notion of economic development (partly expressed in terms such as the "multiplier effect"). In a nutshell, the argument is that the economic effects of tourism will eventually filter down in such a way as to benefit the entire local population.

There are numerous reasons that things do not always work out this way. Calculations might not, for example, take full account of the kinds of economic costs and benefits discussed in the first tip I provided. The promise of local employment generated by new tourism can be negated in cases where the most needy haven't been provided with adequate education or opportunity to compete for even the least skilled jobs, particularly when they are in competition with more highly skilled workers from urban centers or with imported labor. In many countries that are dependent on outside development, the capital and materials (ranging from construction materials to imported food and gasoline) that are required to sustain tourism development can result in considerable "leakage" of tourism profits—estimates for some regions range in excess of 90 percent leakage, with most of the remaining 10 percent or so going to locally based, elite investment "partners" or to government coffers.

It is also important to realize that tourism is valued as a development strategy not only because of its hoped-for economic benefits, but also because it can serve important ideological and political purposes. Whoever controls the imagery of tourism also controls in many respects the ways in which a country is represented, how its symbols are valued, and how its various constituencies and ethnic components are recognized or not recognized. Keep in mind that when the "natives" seem friendly, it is not always because they are happy in our presence, but because they have been instructed to seem so.

The need to provide security for tourists can become overemphasized and serve as a strategy to extend control over local populations and to suppress unpopular ideas. The ways in which the political and economic aims of tourism are expressed are not always predictable with respect to our particular understanding of democratic processes. Tourism-related suppression might take such forms as police surveillance, abridgements of free speech, forced migration and homelessness, and prohibitions against contact between locals and tourists. Places vary considerably in the way they manage their tourism objectives and in the degree to which they value economic and political equity for their citizens.

How can this kind of awareness make us better tourists? Is it reasonable, for example, to expect that travelers of conscience might consider factors such as these as they decide where to invest their tourist dollars? If more of us were better informed about the ways tourism works and made our travel considerations on that basis, might that not encourage governments to support more socially responsible tourism initiatives and thereby help spread the benefits of tourism more equally?

To some extent, this seems reasonable. One example where an international tourism boycott appears to have had some effect is in Myanmar (Burma). Although the intent of that boycott was not directed toward improving tourism in that country, but rather to encourage a relaxation of internal political repression, there does seem to be a relationship between recent political events and Myanmar's interest in attracting tourists. Similarly, increased interest in environmentally sustainable tourism appears to have encouraged some governments to devote more attention to providing such opportunities. On the other hand, a problem with encouraging tourism boycotts is that our knowledge of the political and economic consequences of such acts remains partial and incomplete. While we have gained a fair understanding of the kinds of liabilities mentioned above, we have less of a sense of the kinds of benefits that might accrue even to people who are traditionally repressed.

In Thailand, for example, many of the "hill tribe" people from the north of the country don't enjoy the same political or economic opportunities as do the ethnic Thai, and some of them have clearly been exploited for tourism purposes. Still, international tourist interest in the tribal groups has in other respects increased their value in the eyes of many ethnic Thai, and quite likely improved their relations with national and local authorities. Boycotting tourism to these regions might actually harm the tribal communities, even though there are repressive elements in their current association with tourism. Short of outright boycotts of tourism, travelers might yet have some effect in such situations by selecting experiences that have been designed to respect the rights of local populations and to spread economic benefits more evenly (cf. McLaren 2003).

Traveler's Tip Seven: Consider tourism experiences that are community based Increasing numbers of people around the world understand tourism's potential to contribute to cross-cultural understanding. They are working to provide tourism experiences that offer the opportunity for significant cultural exchange and also provide direct benefits to host communities. These opportunities are not always easy to locate, although the Internet can be a valuable tool that enables alternative tourism advocates to advertise themselves on a more nearly equal footing. Such possibilities include community-based eco-tourism and heritage tourism, various home-stay programs, and a variety of study abroad or volunteer abroad activities.

Certain communities have begun to recognize that tourism can be turned to their economic benefit, and that it also can be used to tell their story to a sympathetic audience. Some of these opportunities are quite well developed, and others seem purely spontaneous and local. I recall hiking into a village in Northern Thailand several years ago and encountering a sign outside a building that said "tourists welcome to visit." The building turned out to be the local school house, and the teacher there proved to be a gracious and informative host. He described how tourists had visited from around the world, and how many of them had later donated school materials from their home countries. One Norwegian tourist even returned to spend an entire summer helping rebuild the school.

Intensive community-based tourism experiences might not be for everyone, but they certainly do have a lot to offer. They generally require the adoption of a different frame of mind and the ability to adjust one's expectations to local conditions and talents. On the other hand, there are many less strenuous possibilities. For example, there are numerous places in the world where different approaches to rural and agricultural tourism have been developed to assist small farmers in diversifying their incomes and to help them preserve their holdings and way of life.

Much of the growth related to opportunities for community-based tourism has occurred within the past decade. It is an area that is deserving of greater attention on the part of anthropologists, who could help us better understand both the potentials and pitfalls of such efforts.

Traveler's Tip Eight: Still, be wary of overly simplified distinctions between "mass" tourism and the "new" tourism Sophisticated travelers, and not a few scholars of tourism research, tend to cringe at the idea of mass tourism, associating it with superficial encounters and hardships foisted upon local communities. There are places in the world where, at least during particular seasons, tourists can outnumber locals by ten to one. Group tourism *can* be quite superficial, and the social and environmental carrying capacities of popular tourist destinations are easily exceeded. Still, many of our attitudes related to mass tourism have more to do with our own expectations and prejudices than they do with impacts upon local populations.

I have a colleague who has studied tourism in Australia. She once visited an Aboriginal village that was on a popular tourist route, where she asked the Aborigines what they thought about the different kinds of tourists they encountered. Their preference was for the mass tourists who arrived by the busload. These people piled out of their buses, bought a lot of stuff, then got back on their buses and disappeared. Less desirable were the tourists who arrived in smaller numbers and wanted to hang around for a while to become acquainted with the Aboriginal way of life. These folk interfered with daily routines, sometimes introduced undesirable practices, and were in general a real bother.

Something else to consider is that many of the increasingly popular forms of "new" tourism discussed above (e.g., ecotourism, heritage and cultural tourism, adventure travel) that have been put forth as alternatives to mass tourism are rapidly becoming routinized, co-opted, and "massified" by the tourism industry. Ecotourism, conceptually justified as a means to encourage local populations to place new value on the preservation of their environmental resources (Wearing 1996), has in some places become the greatest threat to those same resources. In other places, adequate controls have served both to protect the environment and to provide the local population with added sources of income (Honey 1999). Possible resources that can aid us in making informed travel choices in these respects include the United Kingdom-based organization Travel Concern and the United States-based International Ecotourism Society. There are also a growing number of local or indigenous organizations, such as the Alliance for Tribal Tourism Advocates, which represents American Indian communities, and the Caribbean Alliance for Sustainable Tourism.

Traveler's Tip Nine: Be aware of the "child" that travels with you No, I do not mean your actual children, who often prove to be important assets in bridging cultural gaps. I refer to the child in each of us. The sociolinguist Graham Dann (1996) has discussed the extent to which the tourist industry caters to a kind of "parent–child" relationship in its promise to satisfy some of our most basic needs related to nurture, comfort, and security. Again, there is nothing particularly wrong with this. Tourism is often associated with leisure activity, a measure of indulgence, and relief from everyday responsibilities. But there is another aspect of this "parent–child" relationship that merits scrutiny.

If, as tourists, we prove eager to accept a greater degree of coddling and nurturing than we would expect in our everyday lives, what happens when our expectations are not met? Too often we respond in a way that is well out of proportion to the source of our disappointment. A perceived slight in service at an expensive restaurant or a persistent hawker on the street can result in an angry outburst. Stand for a while (it usually doesn't take long) at the front desk of any hotel and you will almost invariably find otherwise reasonable travelers throwing childish tantrums at the slightest provocation.

Tourism, especially international travel, puts us in vulnerable and often dependent relationships. We are faced with satisfying our needs and looking after our safety in uncertain and sometimes threatening environments. It can be helpful to recognize our vulnerability and try to gain insight into how each of us as individuals tend to express our dependency, especially since many of the possible responses, such as fearfulness and anger, can lead us far from the kinds of positive cultural experiences we seek.

Traveler's Tip Ten: Strive to be a good host Tourism and hospitality are opposite sides of the same coin, and people often judge their tourism experiences in relation to their own acquired traditions of hospitality, most of which they may only vaguely recognize. In many respects, the kinds of tourists we will be, and the things we are likely to gain from our travels, have been shaped by the kinds of hosts we have learned to be. Flipping the coin the other way, we should consider that our hosts are generally accomplished tourists in their own right, although the means of their travels might be different from ours.

Tourism is not an "us" versus "them" kind of relationship, although it is often expressed as such in much of the literature. By thinking of myself as both a host and a tourist, I think I have begun to better appreciate the reciprocities that are necessary to keep the kinds of exchanges associated with travel from becoming reduced solely to commercial ventures. By considering the extent to which my attitudes and expectations regarding hospitality have a cultural base, I feel that I have become better able to appreciate differences in the hospitality traditions in places where I travel.

What we learn of the world is never simply a result of how often or how far we travel. It is just as intimately related to how sincerely we receive strangers amongst us. Here I refer not only to our interactions as hosts with wealthy tourists, students, and associates from other places, but also to our relationships with others who are perhaps less fortunate although equally insightful visitors— those coincidental tourists, such as guest workers, recent immigrants, and refugees.

To my mind, there is no greater gap in the anthropological study of tourism than the one that exists in our reluctance to study hospitality as an important and dynamic partner to travel. We have allowed ourselves to imagine that the commercialization of much of the tourism industry has replaced culturally based conventions of hospitality, and that's simply not true. A better appreciation of the vital role played by hospitality would not only help mature our theories of tourism, but would, I believe, make us all better travelers.

So there we have it. Upon reflection, I am convinced that the anthropological study of tourism does provide us with information that can help us become better tourists, and that there is the potential for even greater guidance as the field develops and as we continue to expand upon our interests. If there is one major lesson to be had, I feel it must be that we (as travelers, and perhaps as anthropologists) cannot afford to let our good intentions and lofty objectives stand in the way of recognizing that we're indeed tourists, and that we have responsibility for the consequences that accompany our travels. Without this recognition, I believe our excursions are as superficial as any others because, like the forms of travel that we so enjoy disparaging, they separate us from the very acts in which we are engaged.

SOME COMMENTS AND CONSIDERATIONS

The "traveler's tips" suggested above are meant to be representative of a particular approach to applying anthropological knowledge in the service of improved tourism practices. In this sense the tips are simply exemplary—the same model might be applied, for example, to developing criteria associated with planning new tourism facilities, evaluating existing tourism destinations and events, rethinking the roles and training of various kinds of hospitality professionals, as well as attending to the sustainability of tourist-receiving communities. The tips are also clearly based on my own experience of the tourism literature as well as my own travel activities; they are, in other words, subject to interpretation and revision. My major purpose in developing these tips has been to try to imagine a practical, applied way of summarizing the kinds of knowledge that have been produced from our interests in tourism.

For me, this exercise has served to emphasize how important it is to recognize the contexts of tourism in relation to all kinds of travel experience. There is much in the tourism industry itself and in our own desires as travelers that encourages us to ignore these contexts and, in effect, to associate the act of tourism with superficiality and a lack of authenticity. I believe this has led us to a kind of *tourism of denial*, out of which we try to imagine ways of traveling that seem to disassociate us from tourism's unseemly posterior. The industry itself is all too eager to try to accommodate our wishes to think of ourselves as "real" and "genuine" participants in the world of travel, recognizing that some of the most marketable new forms of tourism are those that promise some measure of relief from the banality of common tourist experiences.

Ironically, I believe it is this desire for escape and these acts of denial—our attempts, in effect, to be better than mere tourists rather than to be better tourists—which helps reproduce the very banality and irresponsibility that we claim to abhor. Our tourisms persist despite us, and thrive as they always have in our ignorance of the consequences of our journeys.

This is why I have come to believe that a responsible approach to tourism is one in which the act of tourism is clearly recognized. In this respect, tourism and hospitality might together be thought of as a very particular kind of acting in the world, as real and important in its own right as any other pursuit. There are any number of ways in which we might represent this view in practical terms. The modest collection of travel tips offered above is one example, in which travelers might be encouraged to view the act of being a tourist as a part of their *authentic* travel experience. It would be interesting to imagine how this perspective might be applied to other practical concerns, such as the marketing of tourism, the design and planning of tourism experiences, and the evaluation of tourism endeavors.

My remarks in this article have assumed travel experiences in which Western, primarily North American, tourists are visiting their own or other places. It is clearly just as important to consider other kinds of tourism relationships. For example, the anthropology of tourism has paid little attention to the consequences of dramatic rises in domestic tourism in developing countries (Ghimire 2001). While many of the tips I have offered might also apply in such cases, especially where there are significant class or ethnic differences between tourists and receiving communities, it is likely that our view of the contexts of tourism exchanges would have to be modified to recognize regional, national, and class differences in styles of tourism.

There are quite obviously different views even within anthropology as to the consequences of tourism, and it is clearly a field from which it is difficult to draw many firm generalizations (Chambers 2000). To put forth a viable applied approach to the anthropology of tourism, we have at a minimum to be convinced that the human consequences of tourism are not so terribly negative as to defy solution (cf. McLauren 1998). We then have to recognize ways in which anthropology might specifically serve to improve some aspect of tourism practice.

In this article I have maintained that one such contribution can be to advocate for a critical awareness of the social and cultural contexts of tourism. This critical awareness would stand in opposition to current trends that lead to a tourism of denial, in which often well-intentioned travelers and the tourism industry conspire to imagine ever more ways to conceal the acts of tourism. Rather, such an awareness would encourage us to think of ways in which the tourism enterprise might be appreciated for what it has become. It is one of the major social and cultural forces of our time, and as such it is among the most genuine and authentic of all modern human experiences.

REFERENCES CITED

Chambers, Erve
    2000 Native Tours: The Anthropology of Travel and Tourism. Prospect Heights, NJ: Waveland Press.
Dann, Graham
    1996 The Language of Tourism: A Sociolinguistic Perspective. Oxon, England: Cab International.
Ghimire, Krishna B., ed.
    2001 The Native Tourist: Mass Tourism within Developing Countries. Sterling, VA: Earthscan.
Honey, Martha
    1999 Ecotourism and Sustainable Development: Who Owns Paradise? Washington, DC: Island Press.
McLaren, Deborah
    2003 Rethinking Tourism and Ecotravel: The Paving of Paradise and What You Can Do To Stop It. 2nd edition. West Hartford, CT: Kuamarian Press.
Sundberg, Norman
    2001 Tips for Tourists. International Psychology Reporter 18:4–5.
Urbanowicz, Charles F.
    1989 Tourism in Tonga Revisited: Continued Troubled Times? In Hosts and Guests: The Anthropology of Tourism. V. Smith, ed. Pp. 105–117. Philadelphia: University of Pennsylvania Press.
Wearing, Stephen
    1996 Assessing and Managing the Sociocultural Impacts of Ecotourism: Revisiting the Santa Elena Rainforest Project. The Environmentalist 16:117–133.

GENERATING THEORY, TOURISM, AND "WORLD HERITAGE" IN INDONESIA: ETHICAL QUANDARIES FOR ANTHROPOLOGISTS IN AN ERA OF TOURIST MANIA

KATHLEEN M. ADAMS
Loyola University, Chicago

This article is broadly concerned with the unique ethical quandaries anthropologists face when conducting research in touristic milieus, as well as the ethical dilemmas that ensue once we have left the field and are engaged in constructing theoretically informed portraits of the communities we researched. Specifically, drawing on experiences in two contrasting Indonesian field settings (Tana Toraja and Alor), I explore the ways in which contemporary anthropological theories about culture, identity, and identity politics can collide with local perceptions and local tourism-generating aspirations, placing researchers in potentially problematic ethical terrain.
Key words: ethics, tourism, Indonesia, identity politics, Toraja, Alor

INTRODUCTION

My initiation into the personal and professional negotiations embedded in field research in a touristic setting began on a June morning in 1984 in the much-toured Toraja village of Ke'te' Ke'su. I had arrived on the Indonesian Island of Sulawesi two months earlier with a plan to conduct dissertation research on Toraja art and identity politics in the context of tourism development. Newly settled into the comfortable household of my host family bordering a "traditional carving village," I was in the midst of interviewing one of the family's sons when my host burst into the room. Waving her arms excitedly, she called out to me "Katlin! Do you hear? There is a big tourist bus coming! Quick, come down to the *tongkonan* [ancestral house] to work." Assuming I'd been granted

NAPA Bulletin 23, pp. 45–59, ISBN 1-931303-22-3. © 2005 by the American Anthropological Association. All rights reserved. Please direct all requests for permissions to photocopy or reproduce article content through the University of California Press's Rights and Permissions website, www.ucpress.edu/journals/rights.htm.

tacit permission to begin interviewing tourists while they toured the village, I grabbed my notebook, and together we scurried down the path to the cluster of traditional houses where other villagers were already setting up their wares.

As my host hurriedly unloaded carved wall plaques, trays, key chains, and textiles onto the front porch of the *tongkonan* (which doubled as a souvenir stall), she recited selling prices to me, urging me to repeat her. I began recording these prices in my notebook but was quickly interrupted by my host. Gesturing towards the European tourists leisurely ambling down the village path, she instructed me, "You can write in your book later—your foreign tourist friends are almost here. Quick, call them over, or they'll end up buying things next door!" Not knowing what else to do, I complied, and soon we were encircled by a large group of tourists and their guide, all of whom seemed quite intrigued to discover an anthropologist in the midst of this "traditional village."

As my savvy host had anticipated, with me there to serve as translator and object of touristic curiosity, the trinkets flew off her shelves. While her competitors' sales were sluggish that morning, hers were better than ever. As the tourists clambered back onto their bus, she chuckled and declared that she would enjoy having me work with her each day, though her neighbors might not be too pleased. Nodding awkwardly, my heart sank, as I realized that I was headed into an ethically murky zone and that my research project could ill afford such an overt economic allegiance. Although I was ultimately able to navigate my way out of this particular situation, other potentially more troubling situations followed, all of which were outgrowths of my role as a foreign anthropologist researching a touristic setting.

This article is broadly concerned with the unique ethical quandaries anthropologists face when conducting research in touristic milieus. It is also concerned with the ethical dilemmas that ensue once we have left the field and are at home constructing theoretically informed anthropological portraits of the toured communities we studied. Whether we anticipate it or not, those of us involved in academic research in touristic settings often find ourselves inadvertently drawn into more applied endeavors in the tourist sector. In some cases, government officials to whom we are indebted for research permits request our assistance in assessing potential and existing tourist sites. In other instances, hoteliers, guides, and travel agency owners who have generously shared insights and indulged our incessant requests for interviews subsequently solicit us to promote their enterprises abroad. And in still other cases, we are asked to "market" particular locales, or to promote particular versions of local history, or more simply to hawk touristic merchandise for particular hosts (as in the vignette above). Finally, once we become established in the academic or practicing world, those of us working in tourist destinations are often invited to lecture on tourist cruises and to serve as anthropologist guides (cf. Bruner 1995; Kaspin 1997). As paid authorities, it is expected that we will present captivating, entertaining, and tantalizing accounts of the cultures being toured. In short, our own identities as "cultural authorities" and "representatives" of tourism-generating countries can prompt unanticipated reverberations that deserve our consideration.

Not only do these situations suggest a pressing need for more careful and systematic ethical reflection, but they also bear relevance for the theories we develop in the field, particularly those concerning tourism, agency, and identity politics. In her insightful article exploring the risks and rewards of involvement in heritage tourism, Benita Howell (1994:150) refers to the intellectual and ethical challenges of work in this arena as a potential "Bermuda Triangle," concluding nevertheless that we should not simply observe from a distance and steer clear of direct involvement. I would add that most of us conducting research in tourist sites do not have the luxury of choice: our research projects are superimposed on a stage on which there is already an ongoing local drama. Our voices and subsequent writings have implications for this drama and invariably become drawn upon by local, national, and international actors with very different sets of interests and orientations. Ironically, the biases and weaknesses of our earlier theories concerning tourism left us a legacy of blind spots in this area. Earlier theories assumed that tourism struck local communities from the outside like a billiard ball, to quote Robert Wood's now-famous analogy (Wood 1980:585, 1998:223),[1] jostling and transforming these passive local communities. As tourism denied local people agency, it was assumed that a researcher could stand by the sidelines and chronicle this process of touristic transformation. However, as more recent research has shown (Adams 1995; Silverman 2001), local communities are hardly passive, and touristic phenomena are actively manipulated by local community members for their own objectives. Likewise, anthropologists working in toured settings are drawn upon in these local and often politicized dramas. It is therefore imperative that we reflect more carefully on the ethical (and entwining theoretical) dimensions of our enterprise.

In the pages that follow, I draw on my experiences in two contrasting Indonesian field settings to elaborate on the ways in which contemporary anthropological theories about culture, identity, and identity politics can collide with local perceptions and local tourism-generating aspirations, placing researchers in potentially ethically problematic zones. These two field settings represent opposite ends of the continuum in terms of tourism development. The dilemmas in the first portion of this chapter are drawn from my research in the heavily toured Toraja highlands, in Upland Sulawesi, Indonesia. Higher-volume tourism in this area was established over twenty years ago, and local villagers—as well as regional, national, and international businesspeople and politicians—have established interests in this area. The second portion of this chapter concerns cases drawn from my research on the remote Eastern Indonesian island of Alor, where tourism is, at present, more a fantasy than a reality. However, it is a vibrant fantasy that animates local actors and fuels relationships with outside researchers. In both of these locales, as I will illustrate, my role as researcher and my theoretical interests and perspective posed challenges requiring careful ethical reflection.

ETHICAL TIGHTROPES IN TANA TORAJA, SULAWESI

Tourism to the Tana Toraja highlands of Sulawesi, Indonesia, began to flourish in the 1970s, when Toraja entrepreneurs who had visited Bali began to recognize the potential for tourism in their homeland. Noting the trickle of adventure tourists lured to their homeland by rumors of spectacular scenery, pageantry-filled funeral rituals, scenic traditional villages, and carved cliff-side tombs, these Toraja entrepreneurs began to produce articles and guidebooks touting their homeland. Soon the national Indonesian government took note and, in 1974, added Tana Toraja Regency to their second Five Year Plan as a site for tourism development. By 1984, when I first arrived in Tana Toraja, the region was receiving thousands of domestic and foreign tourists annually and local Toraja leaders were eager to add new villages to the list of official "tourist sites," hoping to extend tourist stays and spread revenues to other areas of the region.

Within several months of my settling into one of the most-toured "traditional" villages, my host (an elite, locally respected elder) and I were invited to serve on the newly-formed Toraja Jelita Tourism Planning Team.[2] Specifically, we were asked to participate in a community-based team to assess and nominate potential new tourist sites. I was told that my invitation stemmed from my identity as a Westerner who spoke Indonesian, and not from my status as an anthropologist studying tourism. That is, the team leader envisioned me as someone who could represent and communicate "Western tourists' tastes." I felt indebted to the individuals on the team, who were local politicians and respected elders with various tourism involvements. One of them had helped me get situated, and others had granted me interviews or had provided essential data. Moreover, I recognized this as a potentially rich research opportunity. However, I had great trepidations about agreeing to assume an active role in tourism planning, given my objectives as a researcher. Clearly, "mapping" sites for future tourism development would have tremendous economic implications for competing local villages; should I allow myself to become involved in such politically charged activities? Given my research debts, could I refuse?

The fact that the "community-based team" was largely composed of like-thinking elites from the Northern areas of Tana Toraja Regency also gave me pause. Chambers' (1983) work had impressed upon me that development planning projects needed to recognize indigenous pluralism and the range of ideological positions within local communities. However, as a young female graduate student in my first months of fieldwork, I did not feel comfortable questioning the planning strategies of my benefactors (particularly as the "traditional" model of fieldwork I embraced at the time dictated that my task was simply to observe and, where possible, to reciprocate local community members for their favors and time). Nothing in my training had prepared me for the dilemma I faced. My research debts rendered me morally obliged to participate in the planning team's activities, yet I also felt that actively participating risked compromising my impartiality by publicly aligning me with Northern Toraja elites inclined to nominate tourism development sites in their own area.

As discussed earlier, some of my ambivalence about joining the team stemmed from the problematic theory of culture to which I subscribed at the time: I simplistically assumed that active involvement in tourism planning would locate me on the extreme "participant" end of the spectrum, hence removing me from my desired position as "observer–participant" and sideline chronicler of changes. I did not yet appreciate that this neatly drawn participant–observer dichotomy was predicated on a static vision of culture.[3] It was only after a number of months in the field that I began to perceive that my very presence as a researcher meant that a personal engagement in the unfolding local drama of tourism was inevitable.

Ultimately, I decided to join the small team of four on a rollicking three-day survey of local sites. I resolved to remain in the background and weigh in with my "tourist taste" perspective only after the Toraja team had made its decisions about which villages were worthy of inclusion on the new expanded list of *obyek turis* (literally, "tourist objects," or sites). In subsequent discussions with the members of the team, I gently encouraged them to seek input from the lower-ranking residents of the villages they had selected (most Toraja villages are comprised of nobles, commoners, and descendants of slaves),[4] as well as from Toraja people residing in the southern portion of the Regency. However, I suspect my suggestions had little impact on the biases inherent in my friends' approach to tourism management in their community.

My Toraja friends were hardly alone in their approach. As Natcher and Hickey (2002) recently observed, while many community-based resource management programs have met with success in including local voices in the planning process, these local voices are often drawn from a small, non-representative pool, as there is still a tendency to approach local communities as "homogenous sites of social consensus." In similar situations today, a tactful solution might entail providing such planning teams with a translation of Natcher and Hickey's article, as well as other writings illustrating the long-term advantages of a more broad-based approach to representing the "community" in tourism resource planning. Unfortunately, this diplomatic option was not available to me at the time.

Despite my ethical dilemmas and misgivings, for a variety of reasons I do not regret my decision to participate in the Toraja Jelita Planning Team. As Fischer (2003) recently noted, ethnography is uniquely situated to amass and articulate observations essential to the creation of new social institutions. Certainly, practicing anthropologists are well aware of the value of ethnographic skills for calculating potential impacts of development projects. Although my participation on the planning team was not predicated on my anthropological background, it turned out that my ethnographic training and my fieldwork among tourists visiting the Toraja area enabled me to discern and convey the potentially disruptive ramifications of several dimensions of the planning team's visions for village-based tourism development. Several projects which would likely have resulted in sites spurned by tourists were dropped, sparing great expenditures and subsequent local disappointment.

In some cases, unexpected ethical quandaries may arrive long after we have left the field and are back at our home institutions writing up our ethnographies. My second example illustrates some of the entwined theoretical and ethical issues that emerged for me years later, in writing about Tana Toraja for scholarly audiences. While in Tana Toraja Regency, various community members cautioned me that much of what was written about Toraja was "inflated," elevating certain groups at the expense of others.[5] One Toraja acquaintance repeatedly urged me to write about "the true Toraja," "the Toraja without makeup." Another Toraja friend urged me to put an end to rivalries between local elites whose natal villages had become tourist sites "by determining once and for all which village had the oldest and most authentic *tongkonan* [ancestral house]." He presumed this might have ramifications for the flow of tourists and revenue through his own village, but claimed he was interested in "truth." Many of my Toraja friends who reflected on tourism were deeply interested in issues of authenticity and in sorting out "true" culture from "false" culture. They envisioned culture as a bundle of traditions passed down from the primordial past. For these local intellectuals, one of the challenges posed by tourism development was to separate out the "true" elements from the more recent "false" accretions of culture and present only the "true" elements to tourists. For them, culture was not something that gets invented, reconfigured, constructed, and rearticulated while still remaining "authentic."

However, over the past two decades anthropological and historical theorists have embraced a more constructivist approach to culture (cf. Handler 1984; Hanson 1989; Hobsbawm and Ranger 1983; Linnekin 1983, 1990, 1991; Handler and Linnekin 1984; Keesing 1989). As these writers have conveyed, "tradition" and "authenticity" are problematic concepts, as cultures are fluid and people routinely invent culture as they go along. With regard to tourism theory, Crick (1989:336) summed up the heart of the issue when he raised the question, "What in a culture is not staged? What does cultural authenticity consist of?" and cited Greenwood's (1982:27) observation that "all cultures are in the process of 'making themselves up' all the time. In a general sense, all culture is 'staged authenticity'." Such anthropological approaches to culture have the potential to come in direct conflict with local cultural perspectives, as Hanson, Linnekin, and others have discovered (cf. Linnekin 1991). Moreover, in settings where cultural heritage tourism is being developed, the stakes become even higher. As Howell observed, this theoretical shift in anthropology

> forces us to ask: what is the tradition that heritage tourism planners and other cultural conservationists supposedly conserve? Perhaps cultural conservation is a cruel illusion. We ineluctably conserve only what we ourselves construct, guided implicitly or explicitly by our own or clients' political agendas. . . . In practical terms, popular interest in cultural conservation encourages countless groups and localities to discover, create, or rehabilitate "traditions" that serve their social, political, or economic ends, and these are our clients. [1994:152–153]

Although Howell is primarily concerned with applied work in cultural heritage management, even those of us not actively consulting on such projects can find ourselves drawn into ethical dilemmas due to the theoretical disjuncture between our constructivist perspective and differing conceptions of tradition and heritage, be they local or be they embraced by external heritage agencies.

I became personally conscious of the problematic ethical ramifications of this theoretical disjuncture when I was invited to participate in a scholarly conference on the politics of UNESCO's World Heritage Sites, which also included UNESCO leaders.[6] In spring 2001, the village in which I had based my field research was nominated for possible inclusion on UNESCO's lists of World Heritage Sites. I shared in the excitement of my friends in the village, who had long lobbied for this recognition, but also experienced anxiety knowing that UNESCO's conceptions of heritage are different from anthropologists' conceptions of heritage, which differ yet again from local Toraja conceptions of heritage.

My documentation of the village's history illustrated that the village was very much a product of local interactions and adaptations to a series of global forces, including Dutch colonization,[7] independence, and tourism development. From a constructivist theoretical perspective, these factors did not challenge the village's authenticity and merit as a World Heritage Site. Yet UNESCO officials appeared to embrace a more static concept of heritage,[8] and I feared that misinterpretation of my discussion of the village at the conference could potentially jeopardize the village's hard-earned status as a potential World Heritage Site. Anthropological ethics rightly dictate that our first obligation is to protect our informants and ensure that no harm befalls them as a result of our work. However, it also did not seem ethical to reinvent the village's history to mesh with UNESCO's more static conception of heritage. Ultimately, after much reflection, I opted to use my talk to argue that most culturally oriented UNESCO World Heritage Sites were actually products of histories of interactions with the global world and that the village in which I worked was typical of many World Heritage Sites. In short, I reframed my talk as an opportunity to stimulate UNESCO officials to reconsider their more static notions concerning heritage.[9]

The case discussed above reveals some of the collisions between contemporary anthropological theories and those embraced by others (be they locals or external groups such as UNESCO) and illustrates some of the emergent ethical dilemmas such collisions prompt for anthropologists working in heavily toured settings. I turn now to address tourism-related ethical dilemmas that emerged in the more remote setting of Alor, Indonesia, where tourism is in its infancy.

In contrast to Tana Toraja Regency, tourism on Alor is embryonic at best. The island of Alor has never figured prominently in Indonesian tourism promotion. Although a few English-language adventure tour books give the island passing references as the site of celebrated anthropologist Cora Du Bois's field research and as the island of bronze drums and tradition, most give it no mention whatsoever. More significantly, Alor is not mentioned in the government's *A Tourism Master Development Plan for Nusa Tenggara Timor*. In 1994, prior to the political and religious turmoil which have decimated tourism in Indonesia, just 220 foreigners stayed overnight on the island and only three small cruise ships docked for half-day visits on the island (several dozen small diving groups also toured offshore reefs, never actually landing on the island).

The rarity of tourists, however, does not render Alor insignificant for our understanding of tourism-related issues and ethics. As I have argued elsewhere (Adams, in press), even in such remote Indonesian locales, where tourism is barely existent, ideas and fantasies about tourism can color local politics, flavoring discussions of identity and channeling local actions. Moreover, such fantasies about tourism can have reverberations for interactions with and expectations from visiting anthropologists. Hence, looking at tourism-related research ethics in a locale where tourism is embryonic can be instructive.

Despite Alor's lack of touristic celebrity, as I visited potential field sites on the island in the 1990s,[10] it became clear to me that the expectation of tourism animated local activities and fantasies. Since the late 1980s, the discourse on tourism has become increasingly ubiquitous in Indonesia. In the 1990s, the Indonesian government developed an active and extensive Tourism Consciousness Campaign. In preparation for Visit Indonesia Year (1991) and Visit ASEAN Year (1992), the Indonesian government launched a national Tourism Consciousness Campaign (*Kampanye Nasional Sadar Wisata*). As part of this campaign, the Minister of Tourism, Post, and Telecommunications proclaimed the Seven Charms (*Sapta Pesona*) to which all Indonesian groups should aspire. These tourist-pleasing charms include security, orderliness, friendliness, beauty, comfort, cleanliness, and memories. The Tourism Consciousness Campaign was widely discussed in the Indonesian media, and the Seven Charms were posted on plaques in villages. The campaign helped prompt even villages off the beaten track in Outer Indonesia to consider their own touristic charms and attraction powers, as I discovered on my research visits to Alor.

When I arrived on Alor in 1996 for longer-term research, I registered at the local Office of Education and Culture, as is legally required in Indonesia. As one of the first foreign anthropologists interested in conducting research on the island since the days of Du Bois (the 1930s), I was embraced by officials at the Alor Office of Education and Culture, who urged me to assist them in their project of "inventorying" local culture while I searched for a field site. For several weeks, my hosts took me to a series of scenic villages to photo-document traditional houses, megalithic remains, and various village-rebuilding rituals. It soon became apparent that the villages selected for me to help "inventory" were hardly random: many of the sites were the natal villages of my official sponsors. Moreover, our inventory clearly sparked an array of powerful fantasies about tourism development and the riches it would bring. Residents in each locale enthusiastically declared that the "seven touristic charms" were present in their villages and speculated that their own dances, architecture, and scenic landscapes would be of interest not only to other anthropologists, but to tourists.

In many sites, residents lobbied for me to write a book about their local cultural area, just as Du Bois had done for Atimelang (which was one of the few sites for sporadic touristic pilgrimage on the island, largely by anthropology fans). The mythic power of Du Bois's classic 1944 ethnography to generate trickles of tourists and revenues for the village in which she worked was palpable to my Alorese acquaintances. Although only a few copies of her book existed on the island, many village leaders were well aware of the celebrity-creating results of Du Bois's 1930s research in Altimelang. As anthropologists writing texts for largely academic audiences, we tend to overlook the unanticipated ramifications our publications may have for the communities in which we work. Clearly, Du Bois's writings had prompted a certain local perception—and an appreciation often lost on us—of the powers of anthropological publications. In short, our footprints may be larger and last longer than we tend to assume.

The villagers I met on Alor were not shy in conveying their expectations about the publicity and funds they hoped I would generate via my anthropological publications. At several stops, villagers described the hardships of seasonal droughts and the difficulties of getting by, and urged me to help rescue them from poverty by publicizing their village's touristic charms.

As rumors of my plans to conduct research on the island spread, people from an assortment of Alorese ethnic groups appeared daily at my temporary lodgings, each lobbying me to write a book like Du Bois's but on their group, so that they, too, could stand out. As a number of these lobbyists told me, their own cultures were even more interesting than Atimelang's and deserved to be made famous by the book they imagined I would write. As many claimed, Atimelang was no longer traditional. Even Du Bois's house, I was told, had decayed, like the Atimelang traditions. But in their distant villages, tradition was still alive. Although I attempted to convey to my Alorese acquaintances that my writings were destined for obscure journals and would never be able to generate the tourist flocks they imagined, their disbelief was obvious. For them, anthropologists were amplifiers of identity, with the potential to transform impoverished, off-the-beaten-track villages into prosperous international celebrities.

Grasping the enormous expectations tagged to associating myself with a particular village, I wrestled with the ethics of the situation. To avail myself of the hospitality of villagers who had clearly conveyed their expectations for the longer-term results of their generosity was clearly a breach of ethics. Ultimately, I decided to remain based in my temporary lodgings in the main town.

The problematic role researchers in touristic and proto-touristic settings may play as "amplifiers of identity" presented itself to me in a new form when, two years later, I was invited to lecture on a luxury cruise ship slated to stop on Alor for an afternoon. Given my research interests in internal and external constructions of Alorese identity, the cruise ship position offered an irresistible opportunity to interview some of the normally difficult to access, fleeting visitors. The cruise passengers were largely composed of members of the American Academy for the Advancement of Science and several upscale American travel groups. These tourists were unusually intellectual in their approach to travel. A number of them had read as many Indonesian ethnographies as they could in preparation for the trip, including Du Bois's (1944) classic work on Alor. Accordingly, the tour organizers had devoted careful attention to selecting an array of experts to offer the serious educational experience expected by the passengers.

However, just as Kaspin (1997) observed when she lectured on a Yale trip to Kenya, our "expert" constructions of Indonesia were mediated by the largely Balinese and Javanese cruise ship tourism personnel and infrastructure. For many of the shipboard Javanese and Balinese travel industry employees, Eastern Indonesia (where we were voyaging) was a land of "primitives." As I struggled to convey a sense of the complexity of Alor and the issues faced by contemporary Alorese and the other groups we were to visit, the shipboard Balinese tourism director put forth a very different "iconography of primitivism"[11] when he offered his daily itineraries and commentaries. Politeness and professional ethics prohibited me from directly contradicting my shipboard superior, yet we were both acutely aware that I offered a less exotic and, to his eyes, less marketable narrative. As Kapin observed in the Kenyan setting, the local tourism industry "actively marketed an iconography of primitivism that found anthropological expertise useful [primarily] when it operated according to the parameters of that iconography" (1997:53).

In my role as shipboard anthropological teacher, I was determined to out-amplify the Balinese tourism director's sensationalized imagery of the Alorese. Also, given some passengers' familiarity with Du Bois's work, an additional challenge was to address and contemporize Du Bois's pioneering yet dated research, which had been conducted in the 1930s and was no longer an up-to-date portrayal of life on Alor. Sensitively engaging with, yet adjusting, these competing images of Alor seemed to offer the most ethically responsible path. However, I was unprepared for the scene which greeted us on Alor as we debarked. Assembled in the bustling port was a troupe of bare-chested, spear-clutching male dancers, as well as female dancers, barefoot and clad in hand-woven ikat sarongs. The troupe proceeded to perform a series of dances billed as "welcome dances," "hunting dances," and "headhunting dances." The "Alorese = savage" iconography I had worked to dispel was apparently being embraced by our local greeters.

As I later learned, these Alorese dancers came from an array of different Alorese ethnic groups and had been schooled by a local tourism official who believed that the imagery of primitivism was a surefire way to captivate tourists. He may well have been right. As the tourists looked to me in my role as anthropological teacher to authenticate or question the welcoming performance, my own sensibilities concerning my ethical responsibilities to the Alorese to deconstruct certain problematic popular images suddenly became more complicated. As anthropologists working in tourism, it pays for us to be acutely aware of our own identities as amplifiers and authenticators of local identities. Our consciousness of this is crucial, as the ethical quandaries of trafficking in representations are multiple and murky.

CONCLUSION

Whether we anticipate it or not, those of us conducting academic research in touristic settings frequently find ourselves inadvertently drawn into more applied tourism activities. As I have illustrated, our contemporary anthropological theories and perspectives can collide with local perceptions and local tourism-generating activities, landing researchers in ethically murky zones. However, I would not advocate withdrawal as a solution. Rather, we should devote more energy to careful and systematic anticipatory ethical reflection as we embark on these projects.

Moreover, for practicing anthropologists, active involvement is more the norm. As tourism projects mushroom around the globe, anthropologists have the potential to play key roles in understanding and ameliorating some of the more troubling dynamics of tourism. As some have noted, our critical perspective and awareness of power issues (cf. Errington and Gewertz 1989) enable us to serve as useful voices in tourism-related development projects in our field communities, as does our community-oriented, diversity-attentive approach. As authoritative outsiders, we are also aptly positioned to address externally imposed stereotypes of the peoples with whom we work, as long as we are reflective and responsible about ethical issues and our roles as identity amplifiers.

NOTES

1. Also see Picard 1990:74.
2. Toraja Jelita roughly translates as "Charming Toraja."
3. It seems to me that this theme is also at the heart of the class dichotomy between anthropology and development. For a relevant discussion of these issues, see Gow 2002.
4. Slavery is illegal in Indonesia, although in the 1980s some older rural Toraja elites still had difficulty adjusting to the more egalitarian dictates of the nation.
5. They were largely referring to the tourist literature. For a fuller discussion of the politics underlying such concerns, see Adams 1995.
6. For a summary and sample proceedings of the conference, see David Harrison and Michael Hitchcock (2004).
7. Soon after the arrival of Dutch colonialists, for example, the primary ancestral houses comprising the village were moved from various mountaintops to the current site, so that the elites could be closer to the new Dutch sources of power.
8. This assertion is based on UNESCO reports concerning criteria for World Heritage Sites.
9. See Adams 2003.
10. I conducted field research on the island of Alor in 1989, 1993, and 1996, with a brief return in 1998.
11. Kaspin's term (1997:53).

REFERENCES CITED

Adams, Kathleen
    1995 Making-up the Toraja: The Appropriation of Tourism, Anthropology and Museums for Politics in Upland Sulawesi. Ethnology 34:143–154.

2003 The Politics of Heritage in Southeast Asia: Interplaying the Local and the Global. Indonesia and the Malay World 31(89):91–107.

In press The Genesis of Touristic Images: Politics and Poetics in the Creation of a Remote Indonesian Island Destination. Tourism Studies.

Bruner, Edward

1995 The Ethnographer/Tourist in Indonesia. *In* International Tourism: Identity and Change. Lanfant, M.-F., John Allcock, and Edward Bruner, eds. Pp. 224–241. London: Sage.

Chambers, Robert

1983 Rural Development: Putting the Last First. Harlow, England: Longman.

Crick, Malcolm

1989 Representations of International Tourism in the Social Sciences: Sun, Sex, Sights, Savings and Servility. Annual Review of Anthropology 18:307–344.

Du Bois, Cora

1944 The People of Alor: A Social-Psychological Study of an East Indian Island. Cambridge, MA: Harvard University Press.

Errington, Fredderick, and Deborah Gewertz

1989 Tourism and Anthropology in a Postmodern World. Oceania 60:37–54.

Greenwood, Davydd

1982 Cultural "Authenticity." Cultural Survival Quarterly 6(3):27–28.

Gow, David D.

2002 Anthropology and Development: Evil Twin or Moral Narrative? Human Organization 61(4):299–313.

Fischer, Michael J.

2003 Emergent Forms of Life and the Anthropological Voice. Durham, NC: Duke University Press.

Handler, Richard

1984 On Sociocultural Discontinuity: Nationalism and Cultural Objectification in Quebec. Current Anthropology 25: 55–71.

Handler, Richard, and Jocelyn Linnekin

1984 Tradition: Genuine or Spurious. Journal of American Folklore 97: 273–290.

Hanson, Alan

1989 The Making of the Maori: Cultural Invention and Its Logic. American Anthropologist 91:890–902.

Harrison, David, and Michael Hitchcock, guest eds.

2004 The Politics of World Heritage: Negotiating Tourism and Conservation. Special double issue, Current Issues in Tourism 7(4–5).

Hobsbawm, Eric, and Terrance Ranger, eds.

1983 The Invention of Tradition. Cambridge: Cambridge University Press.

Howell, Benita J.

1994 Weighing the Risks and Rewards of Involvement in Cultural Conservation and Heritage Tourism. Human Organization 52(2):150–159.

Kaspin, Deborah

1997 On Ethnographic Authority and the Tourist Trade: Anthropology and the House of Mirrors. Anthropological Quarterly 70(2):53–57.

Keesing, Roger

    1989 Creating the Past: Custom and Identity in the Pacific. The Contemporary Pacific
    1:19–42.

Linnekin, Jocelyn

    1983 Defining Tradition: Variations on the Hawaiian Identity. American Ethnologist
    10:241–252.

    1990 The Politics of Culture in the Pacific. *In* Cultural Identity and Ethnicity in the Pacific.
    Jocelyn Linnekin and Lin Poyer, eds. Pp.149–173. Honolulu: University of Hawaii Press.

    1991 Cultural Invention and the Dilemma of Authenticity. American Anthropologist
    93:446–448.

Natcher, David C., and Clifford G. Hickey

    2002 Putting the Community Back into Community-Based Resource Management: A Cri-
    teria and Indicators Approach to Sustainability. Human Organization 61(4): 350–363.

Picard, Michel

    1990 "Cultural Tourism" in Bali: Cultural Performances as Tourist Attraction. Indonesia
    49:37–74.

Silverman, Eric

    2001 Tourism in the Sepik River of Papua New Guinea: Favoring the Local Over the Global.
    Pacific Tourism Review 4:105–119.

Wood, Robert

    1980 International Tourism and Cultural Change in Southeast Asia. Economic Development
    and Cultural Change 28(3):561–581.

    1998 Touristic Ethnicity: A Brief Itinerary. Ethnic and Racial Studies 21(2):218–241.

ARCHAEOLOGICAL TOURISM: LOOKING FOR
ANSWERS ALONG MEXICO'S MAYA RIVIERA

CAMERON WALKER
University of California, Riverside

Located on the Caribbean coast of Mexico's Yucatán Peninsula, the village of Cancún was radically transformed when mass tourism development began there in the early 1970s. Cancún and the surrounding "Maya Riviera" quickly became a wildly popular tourism destination offering a variety of cultural experiences, including visits to ancient Maya archaeological sites. Now, some of those archaeological sites are in danger of being "loved to death," while others are only just beginning to appear on the tourist radar. There is increasing pressure to balance tourist accessibility with conservation of the ancient buildings and to find a balance that incorporates architectural and ecological conservation, management of the tourist procession through the site, and effective interpretation of the site to enhance the visitor experience. Sites need to be presented within historical, temporal, and geographical contexts, and tourists must be educated about the host region and local indigenous cultures to enhance the tourism experience and encourage tourist behaviors that promote sustainability at the site. Key Words: Mexico, tourism, archaeological sites, public interpretation, sustainability

Heritage tourism has been called "travel designed to experience the places and activities that authentically represent the stories and people of the past" (Hoffman et al. 2002:30; National Trust for Historic Preservation 2001). This definition incorporates travel to archaeological sites, parks, museums, and places of traditional or ethnic significance, as well as to foreign countries for the opportunity to experience "exotic" cultures.

Archaeological ruins are compelling to tourists for at least three reasons. Visitors are often genuinely interested in archaeology or history and want to view the archaeological remains firsthand. Others may have enough curiosity

NAPA Bulletin 23, pp. 60–76, ISBN 1-931303-22-3. © 2005 by the American Anthropological Association. All rights reserved. Please direct all requests for permissions to photocopy or reproduce article content through the University of California Press's Rights and Permissions website, www.ucpress.edu/journals/rights.htm.

about the ruins that they will make time to visit an archaeological park when on vacation, while still others will sign up for organized excursions or accompany companions for the opportunity to experience something new and different. For example, as the construction of Cancún as a tourist destination got underway, it became apparent that tourists were indeed enthusiastic about venturing into the countryside to take day trips to such famous Maya archaeological sites as Chichén Itzá and Tulum. As Henry Cleere succinctly puts it:

'Cultural tourism,' visiting primarily monuments and art galleries, represents only a minor proportion of the visitors to such monuments: for every 'cultural' tour group visiting Ephesus or the Pyramids at Teotihuacan and spending several hours studying them in detail there are 20 groups arriving by bus *en route* between one visit and the next, spending half an hour in a hurried and unprepared tour before buying their souvenirs and boarding their buses for their next destination. The value of such tours is debatable; for the individuals concerned it is probably minimal, since they will have little time to absorb even the basic facts about these important and complex sites. Nevertheless, there is an intangible benefit in that many of them will be almost subconsciously influenced by a feeling of respect for the past and for the human achievement that such monuments represent— though few are likely to be able to articulate these feelings in such terms—and as a result they may well be instinctively sympathetic to 'archaeology' when they are confronted with it in their home environments, whether in a television programme or an excavation in their home town. [Cleere 1989:9]

Archaeological tourism has become a particularly important economic asset for developing countries, where archaeological sites are often situated in remote settings, on dramatic promontories or within lush forests, and thus also offer opportunities for other non-archaeological or even ecotourism interests as well. For example, the relatively protected archaeological parks often serve as havens to many species of birds, providing excellent bird-watching opportunities. Archaeological sites also provide access to exotic and indigenous plants, while hiking enthusiasts may seek out archaeological sites to explore the trails and surrounding landscape. Local people interact with heritage sites too. There is a visible interdependence between the community and nearby archaeological ruins that contributes a sense of vitality to the site's atmosphere that is especially conducive to tourism (Nuryanti 1996:256).

Archaeologists and public officials who are concerned with managing archaeological sites as tourism venues face many problems in trying to balance the goals of education, sustainability, and conservation. Even as funding opportunities are declining, more archaeologists are turning to the public to support their scholarship. However, to gain public recognition and much-needed financial and political support, archaeologists are challenged to demonstrate that there is value in the past and to publicize the importance of archaeology in ways that will convince the public they should care about it in the present. Lessons learned from this type of interdisciplinary research are useful for breaking down intellectual and political barriers by promoting cultural understanding and, ultimately, contributing to the larger field of anthropology (Beltrán and Rojas 1996).

Because archaeological sites are popular with tourists, they also provide an important perspective for understanding the delicate balance between sustainable tourism and sustainable development. In a discussion on sustainable tourism at World Heritage Sites, Anne Drost (1996:479) makes the point that these sites not only generate revenue and attract public interest, but tourism can provide a potential means for their preservation. If revenue from archaeological tourism could be applied to meeting a site's maintenance and educational needs, it might actually be contributing to the sustainability of the site, including its ecological, social, cultural, political, economical, and educational concerns.

Many archaeologists, concerned about the public consequences of their research and restoration, especially at major sites such as Chichén Itzá, Copán, Tikal, Angkor Wat, and Cuzco, are making important efforts to provide archaeologically and environmentally responsible, sustainable, and educationally sound contributions to local communities and national governments. However, the solutions are as complicated as the problems. In this paper, I discuss the major issues confronting archaeologists and archaeology in relating to the touring public and suggest ways they have tried to assist in both simultaneously protecting and making accessible the architectural achievements of earlier human cultures. My own experience has brought me into frequent contact with Mesoamerican archaeology, so I will illustrate these contributions through the discussion of tourism to Mexican sites.

TRADITION IN MEXICAN ARCHAEOLOGY

Mexican archaeology has a very old tradition going back to at least 1776 with the establishment of an *Instrucción* of the Royal Cabinet of Natural History (León 1994:70). The purpose was to build up royal collections by excavating antiquities in Spanish territories, with soldiers and bureaucrats performing the first excavations of Maya ruins at around this time (León 1994:69–72).

By the turn of the 20th century, Mexican officials already understood that archaeological tourism showed great promise for making use of the country's natural and cultural resources. Captain Leopoldo Bartres began work on the magnificent ancient city of Teotihuacan under the appointment of then-President Porfirio Diaz as part of a program to celebrate the centenary of Mexican independence and stress the importance of archaeology to the Mexican heritage (León 1994:70–71; Muriel 2001:57).

Marketing archaeological tourism was such an obvious course of action that Teotihuacan, just 50 kilometers northeast of Mexico City, became the first archaeological site to be specifically promoted for tourism purposes (Muriel 2001:57). Eventually, the Mexican government also began to promote several other sites because they demonstrated certain features: they were famous enough to attract public interest, they were fairly easy to get to, and they were located in spectacular landscapes. As this strategy proved successful for tourism, especially tourism from North America, the Mexican government began to consider strategies conducive to attracting the newly emerging mass-tourism market. Mass tourism offered affordable vacations in locations with cultural attractions and beautiful landscapes, and became an important component of modern life in North America, Europe, and Asia. This kind of tourism concentrated on bargain destinations in developing countries such as Mexico.

Over time, Mexico has developed five integrated tourism centers that are associated with mass tourism: Los Cabos, Ixtapa, Loreto, Huatulco, and the most wildly successful of them all, Cancún. Within these beach resorts designed for international mass tourism, various state and federal agencies took on a series of roles that ranged from buying and selling land to planning and provisioning the essential infrastructure to making loans to private investors and overseeing local governance of the development (Clancy 1999:10).

ARCHAEOLOGY AND TOURISM ALONG THE MAYA RIVIERA

Located on the eastern coast of the Yucatán Peninsula in the state of Quintana Roo, the small village of Cancún was radically transformed when mass tourism development began there in the early 1970s. For the Mexican government and major investors, Cancún tourism development has clearly been an economic success—so much so that plans for development are ongoing and the Cancún model has been replicated elsewhere (Bosselman et al. 1999:127–128).

Although the Cancún model began with an overall plan to integrate development with responsible environmental considerations, the enormous success of tourism marketing, combined with pro-tourism growth and loose oversight in the enforcement of regulations, has earned the Cancún model a mixed reputation at best among various concerned groups. Now, some environmental groups, residents, tourists, and even a few politicians regard the rampant development as a less desirable alternative for the long-term health of the region.

Prior to the early 1970s, Cancún was a small village with about 400 inhabitants, used primarily as a base for hunters and *chicleros*. Over the last 30 years, an average annual growth rate of more than 20 percent has resulted in a permanent population of more than 400,000 residents, with millions of tourists rotating through as temporary "residents" (Daltabuit and Leatherman 1998:320).

Although the vast majority of Mexican tourism is of the sun-and-sea variety, an estimated 10 to 15 percent is specifically related to ethnic and cultural tourism, making it a profitable niche for the industry (van den Berghe 1999:568–599). The presence of ancient Maya archaeological sites became an important selling point to distinguish this part of the Caribbean from other, more established destination resorts in the Bahamas and Virgin Islands. Cancún became a tourism destination that offered a variety of cultural experiences, with visits to ancient Maya cities as one of many exotic enticements. As expressed by Miguel Borge Martin, head of the Cancún Convention and Visitors Bureau, "Modern Cancún, with all the quality and variety that it offers, is also the gateway to a thousand years of Mexico's archaeological history—and to a natural history that is even older" (Sidron 2000:1).

Quintana Roo's eastern Caribbean coastline offers plenty of the requisite attractions for mass tourism: sun, sea, sand, and sex ("the four S's"), but there are also what tourism anthropologist Valene Smith (1996:287–300) has called the "four H's" of cultural or indigenous tourism: habitat, history, handicrafts, and heritage. Habitat refers to the geographic setting and underlying platform for the visit, whereas the term history implies post-contact relations between Westerners and aboriginal groups. Handicrafts, often manufactured by indigenous groups, commemorate a tourist's visit and reflect the market demands of tourism. Lastly, heritage is used to describe the body of knowledge and skills associated with human survival in terms of individual values and beliefs. The tourism interaction sphere around Cancún offered all of these attractions and more, thereby earning the designation of the "Maya Riviera," referring to the expansion of tourism development along the coastline of Quintana Roo:

> The Maya Riviera is a tourist-industry designation for the coastal strip of land and beaches that begins at Cancún and extends about 160 km south to the modern town of Tulum. Much of this area has been, or is being, developed with hotels, resorts, and so-called "ecoparks." The development of Cancún and the Maya Riviera has resulted in striking contrasts and conflicts between modern development and the "traditional" Maya way of life. [Fedick 2003:158 n. 3]

In many respects, Quintana Roo has now become an economic extension of the United States and Europe (FONATUR 1993:12; Pi-Sunyer, Thomas, and Daltabuit 2001:129). Private owners—often expatriates from the United States, Canada, or Europe—control many of the beachfront resort enclaves south of Cancún, and at least some of these resorts have inadequate waste disposal and use up huge quantities of water, to the detriment of surrounding communities. However, this is unfortunately a generic problem in the enclave tourism of the Caribbean and not specific to archaeological heritage sites alone.

HERITAGE INTERPRETATION AND ARCHAEOLOGY

Archaeological tourism is often considered to be a variation of heritage tourism, and is associated with the term "inheritance," suggesting the transfer of cultural traditions from one generation to another. The ramifications of transferring cultural traditions between generations can easily be seen in the modern world of Cancún, where the debate between tradition and modernity has become especially reverberant. However, budgetary problems within the Mexican government and the need to reduce the fiscal deficit have led to reducing federal support for archaeological programs in the Cancún area and elsewhere in the nation and have necessitated finding new funding sources.

In a study (Beltran and Rojas 1996) on public visits to three important Mexican archaeological parks, Templo Mayor in Mexico City, Cacaxtla, and Cholula were all chosen for their historical significance and for the disparity in their accessibility to the public. The study by Beltrán and Rojas (1996:463–478) concluded that visitors were not currently able to appropriately enjoy Mexico's enormous archaeological heritage, but if services were improved, visitors would get higher levels of utility and satisfaction from their visits. Therefore, these authors advocate the establishment of self-financing mechanisms at each site, reasoning that if the public learns to value archaeological zones, they will be more likely to contribute support for their preservation. Most importantly, the research by Beltrán and Rojas (1996) confirmed that Mexicans do assign a significant overall value to the preservation of their archaeological heritage and will support conservation techniques if they are adequately informed about them.

Tourism is an activity that requires some degree of interpretation and representation, which people then re-interpret through the filter of their own experiences. It is often the case that interpreted messages reflect different, competing interests and that a popular place for tourists to visit may change over time, making tourism both a cause and consequence of globalization (Mowforth and Munt 1998:7–8). Archaeological interpretation is important for discovering the story of a place, although this does not seem to be acknowledged by many archaeologists today (Slick 2002:221). Few of the archaeology courses offered in U.S. universities relate to appropriately interpreting ancient artifacts and sites for the public. Moreover, even though there is some thought in the United States about trying to rectify this situation, little is being done here at home, and far less is being done abroad.

The U.S. National Park Service, the U.S. government's leading preservation agency, has developed a number of strategies for public interpretation in national parks. From the 1930s to the present, standards in U.S. policy have evolved and are outlined in the Guidelines for Cultural Resource Management; these guidelines also closely parallel the laws and guidelines for managing the nation's natural resources (Jameson and Hunt 1999:35; National Park Service 1994).

Schwimmer states, "Tourism is now the primary mode of reciprocity between countries, ethnic groups, regions, and classes" (1979:232). Although international tourism has long been touted as a valuable educational experience, a study by two educational anthropologists, J. M. and Gaetane Thurot (Crick 1989:328; Thurot and Thurot 1983) raised serious doubts about the validity of this conclusion. Their study suggested that tourists actually tend to be rather poor culture-bearers because they have temporarily left behind their usual cultural roles and the symbols that would make them more understandable to others. Additionally, tourists are often more intent upon hedonism and conspicuous consumption than in education and cultural understanding (Crick 1989:328-331). As the study states, "Tourism is very much about *our* culture, not about *their* culture or about our desire to learn about it" (Crick 1989:328; Thurot and Thurot 1983:187).

Some would go so far as to argue that tourism perpetuates and reinforces stereotypes rather than breaking them down (Crick 1989:329). Tourism has often been accused of contributing to commodifying cultures, especially in situations where visitors and their hosts regard each other as exploitable resources rather than as human beings, and it is not uncommon for host communities to consider tourists as a nuisance (Castañeda 1996; Crick 1989:329; Pi-Sunyer 1978:155). On the other hand, indigenous people are not always satisfied with the way their country's image has been presented to tourists by the dominant commercial interests (Crick 1989:317; Pi-Sunyer and Thomas 1997:201).

In Mexico, the long period of colonialism disrupted the organization of indigenous traditions, and as with other colonized nations, this disruption was eventually counterbalanced by political interests determined to build a national character (Mexico Profundo) and to demonstrate a continuous cultural identity in which colonialism was just one of many episodes. Over the intervening years, Mexican politicians employed the archaeological heritage to symbolize the strong sense of a shared cultural identity before, during, and after the Mexican Revolution, particularly with the social movements of "mestizaje" (a blend of indigenous and imported traditions into a new synthesis) and "indigenismo" (the idealization of indigenous cultures)(Gutiérrez 1999:19; van den Berghe 1995:569–570).

Around the wildly successful tourism destination of Cancún, a growing number of lesser-known archaeological sites are currently undergoing tourism development. Effectively interpreting an archaeological site plays a critical role in guaranteeing a successful visitor experience, and includes putting the site within historical, temporal, and geographical contexts. Effectively educating tourists about the host region and local indigenous cultures not only enhances the tourism experience but also encourages tourists to engage in behaviors that promote sustainability at the site (Drost 1996:481; Moscardo 1996:377). Proper interpretive techniques can distribute visitors to different locations throughout a site by incorporating self-guided walks, for example, to relieve traffic pressure on any one particular monument or location.

DISCUSSION

According to Henry Cleere (1989:1), academic archaeology and archaeological heritage management are twins that developed at different rates. Numerous articles feature archaeology in periodicals and television documentaries and testify to a keen public interest in archaeological sites and ancient civilizations. The thrill of discovery is inherent in the pursuit of archaeology and offers a fundamental link between the past and the present that is meaningful to most everyone. However, funding by the National Science Foundation and the National Endowment for the Humanities in support of archaeological research has been steadily declining over the last several years.

On the other hand, public interest in archaeology continues to thrive and has been successfully exploited by numerous pseudoscientific books and television programs that spew out dubious information about archaeology (McManamon 2000:20). These popularizers have even been known to accuse archaeologists of participating in conspiracies to withhold information about exciting discoveries from the public for reasons that remain unclear. Even though these popularizers rarely have archaeological training, they continue to successfully communicate their own uncontested conspiracy theories in books and documentaries, detailing fabulous tales such as the Sphinx being built by a pre-Egyptian civilization over 10,000 years ago (Fagan 2003:47–50; McManamon 2000:20). They have proposed that Teotihuacan was built by extraterrestrial visitors and can be linked to the Nazca Lines in South America and to the temples of Angkor Wat in Cambodia. In the last several years, Chichén Itzá and Tulum in the Yucatán have become meccas for New Age devotees who are captivated by legends of virgin sacrifices and promises of spiritual healing. In many respects, professional archaeologists have allowed their own field to be usurped by these archaeology popularizers, who essentially disregard scientific theory and methodology along the way to selling their stories.

It is important for the public to learn about archaeological work from professional archaeologists themselves. Archaeologists, in turn, need the financial and political support of the public to ensure that their research, conservation, and education efforts will continue. Therefore, archaeologists should try to balance the excavation and subsequent conservation of a site with the appropriate educational and aesthetic expectations of a visiting public (Kwas 2000; McManamon 2000).

In a discussion on effective interpretation and education approaches, Gianna Moscardo (1996:381–392) adapted E. J. Langer's work (1989) on "mind-ful" and "mind-less" behaviors to identify two sets of factors for determining whether visitors to heritage sites will have a mindful (meaningful), or a mindless (non-meaning) experience. Langer considered that "Setting Factors" include maps, signs, brochures, and guided tours, while "Visitor Factors" are concerned with a visitor's companions, familiarity with a place, and motivation for the visit. Interpretive techniques that produce a more mindful visitor experience are much more likely to be associated with a satisfying and enjoyable visit. Equally important, mindful visitors generally report a deeper appreciation after a visit to a heritage site and come away with a heightened awareness of the consequences of their own behaviors.

Oftentimes, the marketing of heritage tourism has missed the mark by emphasizing Maya archaeological ruins as somehow separate from the forest rather than resulting from a long-term and complex cultural interaction with the environment. Extensive removal of vegetation from around archaeological buildings gives the impression that the Maya don't belong in the forest and may even set up a subconscious oppositional perspective of people versus forest (Fedick 2003:134–136). To the contrary, there is growing evidence that removing the protective forest not only exposes the ancient buildings to even more rapid decay, but also that the forest may actually have protected the buildings for thousands of years (Ford 2001:2–3). Archaeological, architectural, and botanical data support the premise that the Maya supported large populations over a long period of time by utilizing highly efficient forest-management techniques (Gomez-Pompa and Bainbridge 1995; Gomez-Pompa and Kaus 1999).

Maya archaeological sites such as Muyil in the Yucatan and Lamanai in northern Belize provide examples of sites that combine excavated, consolidated buildings with unexcavated mounds while still preserving a strong sense of the forest around them. Muyil and Lamanai stand in contrast to stripped cities like Chichén Itzá or parts of Mayapan, which now have the vegetation almost entirely cleared away from their ceremonial centers.

A primary objective of interpretive archaeology is to instill in the public a sense of stewardship toward the archaeological record and to make clear the connection between people and their heritage. The underlying idea is that if citizens are able to understand the tangible evidence of ancient monuments and artifacts, they may come to value and be more likely to support conservation issues and trade laws that are designed to protect them. A successful approach to archaeological interpretation for the visiting public can be facilitated by using unobtrusive and simple informational signs, providing brochures or other explanatory literature, employing the use of personal guides whenever possible, and combining several different informational techniques whenever feasible. Emphasizing the value of interpretation not only offers a more satisfying tourism experience, but also garners support for the often tenuous political and economic realities of the site.

As archaeological sites are opened for tourism, more reconstruction and consolidation of the structures may be seen as necessary. This quickly becomes controversial because there is always a component of subjectivity, not only in the technical methodology used in the reconstruction, but also in the extent to which the reconstruction is to be accomplished. In Quintana Roo, as in all of Mexico, decisions on the philosophical merits of the reconstruction or consolidation of monuments are made by the National Institute of Anthropology and History (INAH). INAH has a pattern of working with some combination of three approaches: consolidate and reconstruct certain of the more imposing or prominent buildings, display others as they were left after excavation, and leave other mounds in an unexcavated state. Alejandro Muriel's (2001) experience with INAH suggests that a visit to a site is most successful when there is an appreciation of architectural variety, urban design, and different periods of occupation, which must be supported by appropriate signage and a printed guidebook. It has also become important to show visitors something of the ordinary life through exposure to different types of houses and food-production activities, for example.

In the Yucatán Peninsula, the pattern has been to heavily promote the mega-sites of Chichén Itzá and Tulum, with the interpretation mainly provided by tour guides and guidebooks. A number of other lesser-known sites—Ek Balam and Mayapan, for instance—have been opened for tourism but receive far fewer visitors, probably due to a lack of promotional marketing, a minimal effort toward interpretation, and the fact that they are not yet on the beaten path of mass tourism. There is an advantage to this in that lesser-known sites will be better preserved for the future, though the extensive visitations by tourists endanger the conservation of the mega-sites. In the light of this case and others like it, tourism to archaeological sites has a very mixed record. On the one hand, archaeological tourism promotes the development of local cultural and social identities and provides income to the national (and often the local) coffers, but, on the other hand, tourism itself makes it harder to preserve the site for future generations.

ARCHAEOLOGY AND NATURE TOURISM

Xcaret Ecoarchaeological Park, located a short distance south of Cancún in the Maya Riviera, is a highly controversial natural history theme park literally built around the ruins of an important ancient Maya settlement. These ancient archaeological buildings—not replicas—are treated as opportunities for amusement and unfettered exploration in the model of Disneyland theme parks. Xcaret, whose name refers to "inlet" in Yucatec Mayan, attracts crowds of tourists who are bused in from Cancún and resorts along the Maya Riviera. Once there, tourists are entertained by glamorized presentations of the Maya culture, including reenactments of ancient Maya ceremonies and the famous ball game. By paying an entrance fee of about $39 per person, visitors are able to view exotic animals such as jaguars, sea turtles, spider monkeys, and dolphins housed around the archaeological ruins. The initial building and subsequent expansions of Xcaret Park have been highly controversial among archaeologists and environmentalists, who became particularly alarmed by the massive amount of dynamiting and bulldozing done to produce the two underground rivers now used for swimming and snorkeling.

Occasionally, tour agencies attempt to market a visit to a Maya community in conjunction with a tour to an archaeological site, implicitly linking the ancient and modern Maya. In most situations, however, tourists to the Maya Riviera are left with the overall impression that the Maya are now extinct, despite the presence of more than a million Maya living there today. Enlisting the cooperation of local communities as stakeholders for archaeological tourism may help to reduce conflicts now and in the future—especially conflicts that arise from continuing conditions of poverty, loss of cultural identity, and destruction of the environment.

Currently, there are many threats to the biodiversity of the Maya Forest, to the archaeological sites, and to the cultural heritage of the contemporary Maya people. Problems associated with the cutting down and burning of vast sections of the forest for development have been extensively documented (Nations, Primack, and Bray 1998:xvi–xvii; Pi-Sunyer and Thomas 1997:198), making preservation of the remaining forest more than a noble goal; it is an economic necessity for the socioeconomic future of the entire region (Galleti 1998:33–46; Primack et al. 1998). In addition, many of Mexico's archaeological sites are in danger of literally "being loved to death," as there is little effort to mitigate against the destructiveness associated with mass tourism. In writing about protecting archaeological sites from being damaged by tourism, Mexican archaeologist Nelly Robles Garcia has this to say:

It is equally important to point out that in spite of the noteworthy growth in tourism, and that its promotion has become an important part of government policy vis-à-vis INAH and the Secretary of Tourism, with few exceptions there is little long-range planning for conservation. A few sites such as Cacaxtla or the Templo Mayor have received some of the infrastructure needed to reduce degradation caused by constant use, e.g., walkways and railings, but these are the exceptions. The result is that while more visitors generate more income they also generate greater deterioration through increased use of the original architectural elements such as floors, stairs, walls, or tombs, yet there is little recognition of this in the allocation of funds and human resources. [Robles Garcia 2002:3]

Ultimately, in order to lessen the harmful effects for both present and future scenarios, sustainable tourism planning must combine education and regulation strategies in a sort of "carrot and stick" approach (Drost 1996:481–482). Educating the visiting public about archaeological, cultural, and environmental issues—such as heritage preservation, the development of cultural identities, sustainability, etc.—has the potential to raise the level of awareness in visitors, particularly when it is reinforced by a clear code of behavior when visiting archaeological sites.

CONCLUSION

Sustainable tourism and sustainable development are linked together ethically, and require a compromise between balancing the needs of the past and the present with the needs of the future. However, sustainability is as difficult to define as it is to measure, assess, and monitor at each and every location.

It should be a priority to understand which aspects of low-impact, sustainable tourism can be adapted to archaeological sites in the Cancún area, as well as other regions undergoing tourism development. It may also be possible to remedy some of the more negative repercussions at sites previously developed for archaeological tourism. When a major archaeological park such as Chichén Itzá has been excavated, reconstructed, and successfully promoted as a major tourism destination, it is usually marketed as a commodity, which externalizes the site. As such, it may come to be seen as lacking in authenticity, even though the buildings are authentic in the archaeological sense. In any event, as Quetzil Castañeda (1996:105) points out, because archaeological investigation is inherently a destructive process, uncontested authenticity is an unrealistic concept under any circumstances.

The state of Quintana Roo is currently trying to diversify its travel market, which in November 2001 was reported to have dropped by about 30 percent after the tragedy of September 11. Although Americans still represent 60 percent of the total visitors to the region, Cancún has been trying to appeal to European, Asian, and Latin American travel markets to maintain the usual high numbers, as well as to diversify the market base. An especially successful but problematic niche has been established by appealing to "spring breakers," the college students who visit on cheap package plans during spring vacation. Additionally, several more golf courses are planned, along with a new $600 million tourism and residential project. Probably the most controversial plan involves the building of a $35 million cruise ship terminal called Puerta Cancún-Xcaret, already under construction in the Puerto Morelos area. This homeport, the first in all of Mexico, will have the capacity to berth four mega-ships with a capacity of 2,500 passengers each, and will be able to process customs and immigration services for up to 10,000 passengers at a time (Arellano 2001:1–2).

Thus, the juggernaut of tourism development continues at breakneck speed along the Maya Riviera, providing a wealth of research opportunities for archaeologists and other anthropologists. It is crucial that we are prepared to meet the challenges that lie ahead. It is also essential that the local Maya be included in seeking solutions to those challenges. The Yucatec Maya have been living here for hundreds if not thousands of years. The Yucatán was already a large, urban, developed community prior to the arrival of the Spanish, and Yucatecans fought long and hard against them. They did not succumb until the mid–20th century, and Maya resistance continued even while Cancún was being considered for development. Tourism, and archaeological tourism in particular, can help either to destroy or to revitalize the value and the beauty of Yucatec Maya history and tradition.

REFERENCES CITED

Arellano, Luisa E.
    2001 New Strategies: Quintana Roo, Mexico. Travel Agent, November 12. Electronic document, http://www.highbeam.com/library/doco.asp?DOCID=1G1:80164025&num=17, accessed March 7, 2002.
Beltrán, Ernesto, and Mariano Rojas
    1996 Diversified Funding Methods in Mexican Archaeology. Annals of Tourism Research 23(2):463–478.
Bosselman, Fred P., Craig A. Peterson, and Claire McCarthy
    1999 Managing Tourism Growth: Issues and Applications. Washington, DC: Island Press.
Castañeda, Quetzil E.
    1996 In the Museum of Maya Culture: Touring Chichén Itzá. Minneapolis: University of Minnesota Press.
Clancy, Michael J.
    1999 Tourism and Development: Evidence from Mexico. Annals of Tourism Research 26(1):1–20.

Cleere, Henry

1989 Introduction: the Rationale of Archaeological Heritage Management. *In* Archaeological Heritage Management in the Modern World. H. Cleere, ed. Pp. 1–19. London: Unwin Hyman.

Crick, Malcolm

1989 Representations of International Tourism in the Social Sciences: Sun, Sex, Sights, Savings, and Servility. Annual Review of Anthropology 18:307–344.

Daltabuit, Magali, and Thomas Leatherman

1998 The Biocultural Impact of Tourism on Mayan Communities. *In* Building a New Biocultural Synthesis: Political-Economic Perspectives on Human Biology. Alan H. Goodman and Thomas Leatherman, eds. Pp. 317–337. Ann Arbor: University of Michigan Press.

Drost, Anne

1996 Developing Sustainable Tourism for World Heritage Sites. Annals of Tourism Research 23(2):479–492.

Fagan, Garrett G.

2003 Far-Out Television. Archaeology Magazine, May-June.

Fedick, Scott L.

2003 In Search of the Maya Forest. *In* In Search of the Rain Forest.Candace Slater, ed. Pp. 133–164. Durham, NC: Duke University Press.

Fondo Nacional de Fomento al Turismo (FONATUR)

1993 Panel Aeropuerto: Estudio Continuo de Visitantes pro via Aerea. Cancún, Mexico: FONATUR, Subdirection General de Comercializacion.

Ford, Anabel

2001 El Pilar Landscape: Gateway Between Two Nations. Rolex Application. ISBER/MesoAmerican Research Center, University of California-Santa Barbara.

Galletti, Hugo

1998 The Maya Forest of Quintana Roo, Mexico. *In* Timber, Tourists and Temples. R. Primack, David Bray, Hugo Galletti, and Ismael Ponciano, eds. Pp. 33–46. Washington, DC: Island Press.

Gomez-Pompa, Arturo, and David A. Bainbridge, eds.

1995 Tropical Forestry As If People Mattered. New York: Springer Verlag.

Gomez-Pompa, Arturo, and Andrea Kaus

1999 From Prehispanic to Future Conservation Alternatives: Lessons from Mexico. Proceedings of the National Academy of Sciences 96:5982–5986.

Gutiérrez, Natividad

1999 Nationalist Myths and Ethnic Identities. Lincoln: University of Nebraska Press.

Hoffman, Teresa L., Mary L. Kwas, and Helaine Silverman

2002 Heritage Tourism and Public Archaeology. The SAA Archaeological Record 2:30–32.

Jameson, John H. Jr., and William J. Hunt, Jr.

1999 Reconstruction Versus Preservation-in-Place in the U.S. National Park Service. *In* The Constructed Past: Experimental Archaeology, Education and the Public. Peter G. Stone and Philippe G. Planel, eds. Pp. 35–62. London: Routledge.

Kwas, Mary L.

   2000 On Site and Open to the Public: Education at Archaeological Parks. *In* The Archaeology Education Handbook. Karolyn Smardz, ed. Pp. 340–351. Walnut Creek, CA: Altamira Press.

Langer, E. J.

   1989 Minding Matters: The Consequences of Mindlessness-Mindfulness. Advances in Experimental Social Psychology 22:43–50.

León, Luis V.

   1994 Mexico: The Institutionalization of Archaeology, 1885–1942. *In* History of Latin American Archaeology. A. Oyuela-Caycedo, ed. Pp. 69–89. Aldershot, UK: Avebury.

McManamon, Francis B.

   2000 Public Education: A Part of Archaeological Professionalism. *In* The Archaeology Education Handbook. Karolyn Smardz, ed. Pp. 17–24. Walnut Creek, CA: Altamira Press.

Moscardo, Gianna

   1996 Mindful Visitors: Heritage and Tourism. Annals of Tourism Research 23(3):376–397.

Mowforth, Martin, and Ian Munt

   1998 Tourism and Sustainability: New Tourism in the Third World. London: Routledge.

Muriel, Alejandro M.

   2001 Archaeological Research in Mexico's Monumental Sites. *In* Archaeological Research and Heritage Preservation in the Americas. R. D. Drennan and Santiago Mora, eds. Pp. 56–62. Washington, DC: The Society for American Archaeology.

Nations, James D., Richard B. Primack, and David Bray

   1998 Introduction: The Maya Forest. *In* Timber, Tourists and Temples. R. Primack, David Bray, Hugo Galletti, and Ismael Ponciano, eds. Pp. xiii–xx. Washington, DC: Island Press.

National Trust for Historic Preservation

   2001 Heritage Tourism Program. National Trust for Historic Preservation. Electronic document, http://www.nthp.org/heritagetourism/index.html.

Nuryanti, Wiendu

   1996 Heritage and Postmodern Tourism. Annals of Tourism Research 23(2):249–260.

Pi-Sunyer, Oriol

   1978 Through Native Eyes: Tourists and Tourism in a Catalan Maritime Community. *In* Hosts and Guests: The Anthropology of Tourism. Valene Smith, ed. Pp. 149–155. Oxford, UK: Blackwell.

Pi-Sunyer, Oriol, and R. Brooke Thomas.

   1997 Tourism, Environmentalism, and Cultural Survival in Quintana Roo. Life and Death Matters. B. Johnston, ed. Pp. 187–212. Walnut Creek, CA: Altamira Press.

Pi-Sunyer, Oriol, R. Brooke Thomas, and Magali Daltabuit

   2001 Tourism on the Maya Periphery. *In* Hosts and Guests Revisited: Tourism Issues of the 21st Century. Valene Smith and Maryann Brent, eds. Pp. 122–140. New York: Cognizant Communication Corporation.

Primack, Richard B., David Bray, Hugo Galletti, and Ismael Ponciano, eds.

   1998 Timber, Tourists, and Temples. Washington, DC: Island Press.

Robles Garcia, Nelly M.

    2002 The Management of Archaeological Resources in Mexico: Oaxaca as a Case Study. Jack Corbett, trans. Society for American Archaeology. Electronic document, http://www.saa.org/publications/oaxaca/cover.html, accessed January 4, 2005.

Schwimmer, E. G.

    1979 Feasting and Tourism: A Comparison. *In* Semiotics of Culture: Approaches to Semiotics, 53. I. P. Winner and Jean Umiker-Sebeok, eds. Pp. 221–236. The Hague: Mouton.

Sidron, Jorge

    2000 Cancún Offers Natural Preserves Unknown to Many Visitors. Travel Weekly, April 14.

Slick, Katherine

    2002 Archaeology and the Tourism Train. *In* Public Benefits of Archaeology. B. J. Little, ed. Pp. 219–227. Gainesville: University Press of Florida.

Smith, Valene L.

    1996 Indigenous Tourism: the Four H's. *In* Tourism and Indigenous Peoples. Richard Butler and Thomas Hinch, eds. London: International Thomson Business Press.

Thurot, J. M., and Gaetane Thurot

    1983 The Ideology of Class and Tourism: Confining the Discourse of Advertising. Annals of Tourism Research 10:177–189.

Van den Berghe, Pierre L.

    1995 Marketing Mayas: Ethnic Tourism Promotion in Mexico. Annals of Tourism Research 22(3):568–599.

ENHANCING COMMUNITY-BASED TOURISM DEVELOPMENT AND CONSERVATION IN THE WESTERN CARIBBEAN

SUSAN C. STONICH

University of California, Santa Barbara

The principal goal of this article is to make specific suggestions regarding how to enhance community-based tourism development and conservation in tourist destinations with heterogeneous social and cultural contexts and fragile environments. The article uses the example of the Bay Islands, Honduras, to demonstrate the obstacles and opportunities for integrated community-based tourism and conservation. These recommendations stem directly from almost twenty years of research efforts in the region and are among the major conclusions of my recent book, The Other Side of Paradise: Tourism, Conservation, and Development in the Bay Islands (Stonich 2000). Key Words: tourism and social impacts; tourism and environmental impacts; community-based tourism; conservation; Bay Islands, Honduras

INTRODUCTION

The economic development aspect of this project [*Paseo Pantera*] is baloney. We're a conservation organization: We want to save turtles. If that other stuff comes along, that's fine, but we only put that in the proposal for the funders [primarily USAID]. [U.S. conservationist referring to the *Paseo Pantera* project, quoted in Royte 1992]

I tend to agree of having to confront political and economic realities in the Bay Islands. And it may take a more direct approach from the international community, including ourselves. [Senior IDB staff member discussing implementation of the IDB environmental management project for the Bay Islands, Honduras; personal communication, 1997]

NAPA Bulletin 23, pp. 77–86, ISBN 1-931303-22-3. © 2005 by the American Anthropological Association. All rights reserved. Please direct all requests for permissions to photocopy or reproduce article content through the University of California Press's Rights and Permissions website, www.ucpress.edu/journals/rights.htm.

NABIPLA agrees with the world's environmental movement, but we need to fight the battle from the root. NABIPLA believes that our children are the #1 endangered species. [Native Bay Islanders Professional and Labourers Association (NABIPLA) 1995:3]

The three remarks provided above—by the U.S. conservation specialist, the official from the Inter-American Development Bank (IDB), and the grassroots organization Native Bay Islanders Professional and Labourers Association (NABIPLA)—divulge contending perspectives and major obstacles to achieving integrated community-based conservation and equitable tourism development in the Bay Islands and in the Western Caribbean more broadly. The unguarded comment by the environmentalist associated with the *Paseo Pantera* project (the precursor of the Meso American Biological Corridor) discloses the underlying values and motives of the international environmental organizations that designed and managed the project—the preservation of turtles. In addition to revealing that environmental goals are paramount, the remark also exposes the insincerity of these organizations in terms of their commitment to achieving the economic development aspects of the project. In contrast, the statement by the IDB official was made in order to explain the lag in implementing the local management aspect of the IDB project in the Bay Islands, Honduras, which had community-based conservation and development as a major goal. It attributes delays in implementation in part to the failure to directly confront the social, economic, and political realities on the islands.

These two comments represent extremely different but equally critical factors that impede integrated, community-based conservation and development initiatives in the Bay Islands: the first based on underlying ideology, values, and goals, and the second on disregarding the structure of island society, especially relations of power. The quote published in the NABIPLA newsletter reveals a very different perspective on ethnically and culturally based values and on associated perspectives regarding the relationship between conservation and development. The primary goal of this paper is to make specific suggestions as to how to enhance community-based tourism development and conservation in the Western Caribbean and elsewhere in the many other tourist destinations with heterogeneous social and cultural contexts and fragile environments. These recommendations stem directly from almost twenty years of my own research efforts in the region and are among the major conclusions of my recent book, *The Other Side of Paradise: Tourism, Conservation, and Development in the Bay Islands* (Stonich 2000).

Although so-called "integrated community-based development and conservation" have become buzzwords in national and international environmental and conservation circles over the last two decades, the great disparity between the rhetoric and the reality of such efforts has caused many people to begin to give up on such efforts entirely. In many places, including the Bay Islands, where I have worked for almost twenty years, efforts to enhance community-based conservation and development have significantly exacerbated existing local conflicts and created new ones. Despite the gap between the concept and implementation of community-based conservation and development efforts, it is my cautious hope that efforts to enhance community-based development and conservation continue—albeit with eyes wide open.

INTEGRATED COMMUNITY BASED CONSERVATION AND DEVELOPMENT

The U.N. Conference on the Environment and Development (also known as UNCED or the Rio Summit) that took place in Rio de Janeiro in 1992 catalyzed a global agenda around the connections between development and the environment. In fact, the development–conservation nexus was recognized by the international community as early as the 1970s. The Rio Summit marked the 20th anniversary of the U.N. Conference on the Human Environment, which convened in Stockholm in 1972 to consider how human activities alter the global environment. The recommendations of subsequent international councils, such as the United Nations World Commission on Environment and Development that published the influential *Bruntland Report* in 1987, and the numerous environmental initiatives that followed, testify to the expanding global awareness that complex interconnections exist between development processes and the state of the environment. While a great deal of the discussion at these international meetings emphasized global and national policies, the environmental initiatives that ensued also included limited efforts to integrate environmental conservation (especially biological diversity) with the maintenance of people's livelihoods at the local level. Many if not most of these efforts were connected with the establishment of protected areas—and tied to growth in the international tourist sector. For example, the *World Conservation Strategy* in 1980 stressed the importance of linking protected area management with the economic activities of local communities (United Nations Environment Programme, International Union for Conservation of Nature and Natural

Resources, World Wildlife Fund, Food and Agriculture Organization of the United Nations, and Unesco 1980). Two years later, the World Congress on National Parks in Bali, Indonesia, called for greater support for communities located adjacent to parks through such measures as education, revenue sharing, participation in decisions, appropriate development schemes such as ecotourism, and access to crucial resources (McNeely and Miller 1984). Shortly thereafter, in 1985, the World Wildlife Fund (WWF) confronted the messy and problematic challenge of integrating conservation and development by initiating the Wildlands and Human Needs Program. Originally encompassing about twenty integrated conservation and development projects (ICDPs), the program attempted "to improve the quality of life of rural people through practical field projects that integrated the management of natural resources with grassroots economic development" (Larson et al. 1997:5). According to a 1997 review of their decadelong experience implementing ICDPs, WWF concluded:

> All international conservation organizations now seek in varying degrees to address local needs while conserving biodiversity and ecological processes.... In the mid-1980s, ICDPs were a radical divergence from the norm. Today, such projects constitute over half of WWF's funding. [Larson et al. 1997: 5–6]

Based on their experience, the WWF divided ICDPs into two generations. The first generation, designed in the early 1980s, attempted to reduce conflicts between people and protected areas by compensating local residents for the loss of natural resources, sometimes with cash but more frequently with health clinics, schools, and other social services. Unfortunately, many of the early ICDPs became large, multifaceted, and inevitably unmanageable. Similar to the large, integrated rural development projects of the 1970s, large ICDPs became impossible to manage effectively due to their unrealistic goals and timetables and excessive dependence on outside funding and expertise (Larson et al. 1997:7). Despite their name, first-generation ICDPs were not very integrated at all. Instead, conservation organizations and their partners implemented alternative income-generating activities in communities adjoining protected areas on the assumption that the new sources of livelihood would replace those judged to be harmful to the environment. People in local communities rarely had an opportunity to express their needs and remained alienated from the management of protected resources as well as many of the development interventions (Larson et al. 1997:7).

Based on lessons learned from these initial efforts, conservation organizations significantly refined and modified the second generation ICDPs that were developed in the early 1990s. One significant change is that recent projects focus more on land outside of protected areas—where much of the world's biodiversity exists. In addition, whereas first-generation ICDPs tended to see local people as the source of environmental and conservation problems, second generation ICDPs perceived local people as having the rights to and the responsibilities for resource management. Commonly referred to as community-based conservation projects, second-generation ICDPs tend to be more community driven, focused on improving community skills in resource planning and management, and aimed at achieving collaborative management arrangements between communities and governments. Supporters contend that these kinds of projects are more likely to succeed, because they are designed and implemented with more community involvement and more directly link conservation and development activities (Larson et al. 1997:7).

Several issues regarding the present generation of ICDPs have been raised in connection with efforts in the Western Caribbean and elsewhere. Among the most important are those primarily centered around conceptualizations of community, participation, representation, and accountability. Various additional problems have been raised about ICDPs, including the need to provide adequate funding over longer time frames, to ensure more explicit linkages between conservation and development initiatives, to incorporate monitoring and evaluation programs throughout the lifetime of projects, to build on local knowledge, and to promote active participation of community stakeholders (Brown and Wyckoff-Baird 1992; Wells et al. 1992). Several recent reviews of ICDPs have raised other serious questions about the approach. Larson et. al (1997:9) caution that ICDPs, increasingly funded by development agencies like USAID, have become too focused on rural development and tend to be located in areas that are either biologically unimportant or too fragile or small to support resource extraction by local communities. In part to address such criticisms, current efforts by the WWF and others, such as the Atlantic Reef Conservation Project, tend to focus on the ecoregion or landscape level rather than on smaller spatial areas such as communities. These diverse criticisms disclose the ongoing conflicts about the relative primacy of the human and environmental goals of ICDPs.

It is difficult but feasible to place development and conservation efforts in the Western Caribbean within the framework outlined above. First, in contrast to the predominant rhetoric of ICDPs, the vast majority of tourism development in the region has either ignored or attempted to circumvent environmental laws and regulations and conservation initiatives rather than to integrate conservation goals into tourism development schemes. Second, the conservation efforts either already implemented or in process frequently virtually overlook development objectives for less powerful residents of the islands. Meager attempts to train local people to be park guards, dive masters, or craft producers often are inadequate in terms of compensating local residents for diminished access to natural resources and are at the root of growing enmity toward such efforts. In some respects, conservation efforts throughout the region frequently correspond most closely to first-generation ICDPs. They tend to see local people as the problem and attempt, albeit feebly, to compensate them for losses to livelihoods. In contrast to the strategies of ICDPs, the best-known local level conservation effort on the Bay Islands where I have worked, the Sandy Bay–West End Marine Reserve (SBWEMR), is dominated by an overwhelming emphasis on regulations and enforcement. As regards the Bay Islands, three major "lessons learned" by the WWF are most relevant:

- In densely settled areas, strict enforcement of protected area regulations cannot by itself prevent the illegal use of resources . . . strict enforcement is costly both in financial and political terms;
- Compensation does not necessarily change peoples' attitudes and behaviors;
- Changing peoples' resource use patterns is a complex undertaking and requires a sophisticated understanding of the political, economic, and social context of their lives (Larson et al. 1997:6).

MOVING TOWARD EFFECTIVE COMMUNITY-BASED TOURISM AND CONSERVATION

My work on the Bay Islands suggests several recommendations to enhance the success of community-based tourism development and conservation initiatives. These recommendations are based on the argument that effective community participation essentially is based on an understanding of extant social relations.

1. Define and operationalize "participation." There are two main dimensions of participation: participation as a goal in itself that allows communities to have greater control over their lives and resources, and

participation as a means of achieving improved social, economic, or environmental objectives. These two objectives are not mutually exclusive. In many cases the second dimension may prove impossible unless the first objective is achieved.

2. Realistically address the major weaknesses in many community-based initiatives. Some of the most important of these are:
   (a) An unrealistic understanding of local social and cultural dynamics;
   (b) Lack of understanding of competing interest groups both within and outside the local community; and
   (c) Ignorance of the larger political and economic structures that generate local competition and conflict.

3. Conduct a thorough, informed assessment of the meaning of the "local," paying close attention to local–extra-local linkages.

4. Use sociocultural analysis to attain a realistic understanding of the "community" in terms of heterogeneity of nationality, ethnicity, class, and gender.

5. Identify relevant stakeholders at all levels—from the local through the global—including their ideologies, values, interests, and behaviors. The development and conservation literature is full of examples of unsuccessful efforts due to failure to collaborate with important interest groups or segments of the population. This involves:
   (a) Identifying major interest groups and their motives, strategies, and behaviors; and
   (b) Identifying conflicts among and between stakeholders over such things as jobs and resources.

6. Stipulate the structure of power and extant power relations among stakeholders.

7. Identify the benefits and costs or risks (the winners and losers) from current trends in development and conservation.

8. Collaboratively (i.e., with all stakeholders) identify feasible stages (from problem formation and design through implementation, monitoring, and evaluation), facilitating conditions (sharing, dispersing, or redistributing power among stakeholders), and actions or steps to ensure that power is distributed among stakeholders.

9. Collaboration among local, community, and extra-local stakeholders may involve establishing new institutions or enhancing existing ones.

10. Establish means by which to resolve conflicts.

11. Engage in direct and vigorous attempts to channel greater power and authority to less powerful local groups during processes of coalition building.

12. Establish networks among communities.

13. Ensure that local representatives of communities are truly representative and accountable.

14. Ensure that local people (especially the poor and women) benefit economically and in other ways from the development and conservation projects. Cases in which local communities in poor regions manage their resource base with the prime objective of conservation are virtually nonexistent.

15. Integrate cultural survival into community-based tourism development and conservation.

Strengthening Anthropologists' Contributions to ICDPs

These recommendations point to the enhanced role of anthropologists in participating in successful and effective efforts at community-based conservation and development. These recommendations suggest the following expanded roles for anthropologists and other social scientists:

Applied Political Ecological Analyses Political ecology provides the means to conceptually and methodologically integrate the human and environmental consequences of tourism development and conservation strategies into a single analytical framework and to disaggregate these impacts by relevant social actors or stakeholders within the existing structure and relations of power (Stonich 2000). Political ecological analysis also illuminates the factors that are essential to effective local community participation by (1) identifying the major interest groups or stakeholders, (2) examining the motives and behaviors that affect the use of resources by diverse interest groups, (3) exposing and confronting actual and potential conflicts among stakeholders, and (4) identifying potential winners and losers as a result of current or planned development and conservation initiatives.

Thorough Sociocultural and Stakeholder Analyses The cost of slighting sociocultural studies can be high. A comprehensive analysis of ex post evaluation findings and World Bank and USAID analyses indicated that "the average economic rate of return for rural development projects which have incorporated sociocultural analysis was more than double that for projects which had been poorly appraised from a sociocultural viewpoint" (Cernea 1992). Sociocultural analyses are complex, always site specific, and take time (although financial costs are relatively low or moderate). Without sociocultural analyses, stakeholder analysis is apt to be shallow and pro forma.

Moreover, subsequent "community participation" in development and conservation projects is likely to be mere rhetoric, and without community participation, projects are apt to be inefficient, inequitable, not cost-beneficial, and
short-lived.

Interdisciplinary Projects The recommendations strongly suggest the necessity that interdisciplinary projects address the complex set of social, cultural, economic, political, environmental, and other factors implied. It seems
to me that anthropologists are in a good position to lead such projects.
Recent work by Sara Alexander and Jane Gibson (2001) and by anthropologists in this volume (e.g., Wallace and Diamente) are wonderful examples of how a few anthropologists have taken up this challenge—not
only to advance scholarship and practice but also to train a new generation of interdisciplinary scholars and practitioners—but we could do much
more.

Big Science The above suggestions imply "big" projects—far removed from
the relatively small projects in which anthropologists typically have been involved. There is a great need I think to move beyond such small-scale efforts
toward *big science* projects—traditionally not the domain of anthropologists.
This, in turn, implies fundamental changes in the way we educate and train
most of our anthropology graduate students—but that's a big problem to take
on another day.

REFERENCES CITED

Alexander, Sara, and Jane Gibson
    2001 Tourism Impact Assessment. Paper presented at the Annual Meeting of the Society for
        Applied Anthropology, March 28–April 1, Merida, Mexico.
Brown, Michael, and Barbara Wyckoff-Baird
    1992 Designing Integrated Conservation and Development Projects. Washington, DC:
        Biodiversity Support Program of the World Wildlife Fund, The Nature Conservancy,
        and the World Resources Institute.
Cernea, Michael
    1992 The Building Blocks of Participation. Washington, DC: World Bank.
Larson, Patty, Mark Freudenberger, and Barbara Wyckoff-Baird
    1997 Lessons from the Field: A Review of World Wildlife Fund's Experience with Integrated
        Conservation and Development Projects 1985–1996. Washington, DC: World Wildlife
        Fund.

McNeely, Jeffrey A., and Kenton R. Miller
    1984 National Parks, Conservation, and Development: The Role of Protected Areas in Sustaining Society. Proceedings of the World Congress on National Parks, Bali, Indonesia, October 11–22. Washington, DC: Smithsonian Institution Press.
NABIPLA (Native Bay Islanders Profession and Labourers Association)
    1995 Bay Islanders Echo. The Way We See Things 1(1):1–20.
Royte, Elizabeth
    1992 Imagining *Paseo Pantera*. Audubon 94(6):76–89.
Stonich, Susan C.
    2000 The Other Side of Paradise: Tourism, Conservation, and Development in the Bay Islands. New York: Cognizant Communications.
Wells, Michael, Katrina Brandon, and Lee Hannah
    1992 People and Parks: Linking Protected Area Management with Local Communities. Washington, DC: The World Bank, World Wildlife Fund, U.S. Agency for International Development.

BETWEEN PURE AND APPLIED RESEARCH: EXPERIMENTAL ETHNOGRAPHY IN A TRANSCULTURAL TOURIST ART WORLD

QUETZIL E. CASTAÑEDA
Open School of Ethnography and Anthropology

This article reports on an ethnographic project designed and conducted as an experimental fieldwork practice. The research was a study of the modern Maya artwork of Pisté, Yucatán, that developed in the context of archaeological heritage tourism at the Maya site of Chichén Itzá, México. The article discusses how the research was designed to explore experimental fieldwork as an alternative path between pure and applied research paradigms. The use of art exhibition and installation was developed as a method of studying tourism phenomena in ways that positively contributed to community life. The research included exhibitions of art conducted as fieldwork encounters. Further, the experimental methodologies allowed the research to be designed and conducted so that the historical and ongoing involvement of anthropology in the art tradition was also studied and formulated as part of the object of study. Concepts of research positioning and transculturation are used to elaborate these principles of research design and practice. Key Words: transculturation, experimental fieldwork, research positioning, heritage tourism, art exhibition, methodologies

THE PROBLEM: ENTANGLING RESEARCH

This essay explores the methodological problem of studying transcultural relationships in which the anthropologist and anthropologies form an intrinsic part of the sociocultural phenomena under ethnographic investigation. This issue is explored in relation to an ethnographic study of the modern Maya art and artisans of the community of Pisté, Yucatán, México, and the archaeo-tourist site of neighboring Chichén Itzá that contextualizes and frames the setting of this

NAPA Bulletin 23, pp. 87–118, ISBN 1-931303-22-3. © 2005 by the American Anthropological Association. All rights reserved. Please direct all requests for permissions to photocopy or reproduce article content through the University of California Press's Rights and Permissions website, www.ucpress.edu/journals/rights.htm.

transcultural art world. From 1997 to 1999, an experimental practice of ethnographic fieldwork was developed to study this modern Maya tourist art with this issue in mind. The historical entanglement of diverse forms of anthropology—in art worlds generally and in the world of the Maya specifically—points to certain inadequacies in both "pure research" and "applied research" models: both models tend to obscure certain kinds of transcultural dynamics and processes that inhabit in objects of study such as tourism. The goal of this essay is to discuss the experimental and transcultural ethnography that was developed in order to comment upon this methodological problem.

Context and Questions: The Pisté Maya Art World, 1970s to 1999

In the 1930s, Morris Steggerda conducted ethnographic research in the town of Pisté. He was a member of the multidisciplinary research project studying the Maya at Chichén Itzá, Yucatan, Mexico, that was sponsored by the Carnegie Institution of Washington. In Steggerda's 1941 monograph, he described the history and culture of the town, noting that there was no production of handicrafts (Steggerda 1941:25; cf. Castañeda 1995, 2001, 2003). Forty years later, in the mid–1970s, the unique Pisté tradition of stone and wood carving was invented by a man, Vicente Chablé, who worked at Chichén Itzá as an employee of the federal anthropology agency (i.e., the INAH or Instituto Nacional de Antropología y Historia). Inspired by the images of gods and personages depicted in Maya hieroglyphic books and by statuary from archeological sites with which he was either personally familiar or knowledgeable about through archeology books, Chablé began to carve idols in the soft wood of the acacia tree (chaká) and in soapstone (see Figure 1).[1]

In the early 1980s, there were only some twenty carvers, but by 1983 the number of artisans in the Chichén tourist market had escalated to two or three hundred, including "part-timers," due to the boom in the tourist economy of Cancun. Compelled to invade the archeological zone of Chichén illegally to sell their wares, artisans were politically marginalized and devalued by governmental institutions of art and anthropology (see Figure 2). During the 1980s, the first and second generations of wood carvers primarily produced a cheap and "rudimentary" style of tourist souvenir art that was only sanded after being carved (Figure 3). In the early 1990s, a third generation of artisans emerged who transformed the handicraft into a distinct and established tradition through the addition of forms, figures, modes of paint finishes, and media (Figures 4, 5, and 6). Bolstered by tourists' seemingly insatiable consumption of the product,

FIGURE 1. These two examples of the work of Vicente Chablé were brought to the 1999 *concurso* of Pisté Maya Art by Chablé's surviving sons and wife. The basic *ídolo* form can be carved into two distinct and standardized figures as shown here. On the left is the Corn God, who holds a corn cob between hands and knees, and the right is the Ixchel, or Goddess of Life and Death, who has a child emerging from between the legs. The simple headdress of the Corn God is changed, in the Ixchel figure, into two serpent heads that frame a skull. The figures are carved only in the front, as three-quarter and fully in-the-round carving of idols were only developed in the early 1990s and late 1990s, respectively. These figures are rare as they are carved in stone. In the 1980s actual stone was substituted by a concrete and limestone mix that is sold as stone to tourists (see Notes).

artisans achieved a certain legitimacy and began to participate in regional tourist fairs in México City and in state sponsored handicraft competitions in Mérida. One Pisté artist, Gilberto Yam, was even awarded first place in one of these competitions in 1995.

Starting in 1997, I initiated a three-year research and field school program that included ethnography with artisans as part of an anthropological study of the artwork. Central to this ethnographic research, which focused on production and marketing, was the development of exhibitions in the town of Pisté for local audiences in the summers of 1997, 1998, and 1999. In December 1999, a major grant from the Fideicomiso México-USA (a bi-national granting agency

FIGURE 2. This is a typical "invasion" scene from 1995, showing artisans selling their products and two vendors of Popsicles. While food vendors were mobile, most of the handicraft vendors set up their wares alongside paths. During the initial invasion from 1983–1987, all vendors were quite aggressive and were known for frequently intimidating tourists. The vendors and artisans were criticized for their unruly and illegal presence and for disrupting tourists' "good image" of Chichén, Yucatán, and México. In January 2005, at the time of the publication of this essay, the venders had re-invaded the archaeological zone due to a conflict with the owners of the Hotel Hacienda Chichén, the Barbachano family, who assert claims of private ownership of parts of the federal zone of cultural patrimony.

comprised of the Mexican National Fund for Culture and the Arts, Bancomer Cultural Foundation, and the Rockefeller Foundation) allowed us to extend this series of exhibitions to include a showing at a gallery on the campus of a small liberal arts college in the United States. A group of five Pisté Maya artists participated in this exhibition of their artwork (Figures 6 and 7).[2] In short, in some 25 years, the artwork had developed based on a improvised opportunity that led from an "invented tradition" (Hobsbawm and Ranger 1985) of rudimentary tourist souvenirs to a sophisticated art tradition that includes diverse styles, aesthetics, media, and figures.

There are many different issues raised by this artwork and its history of development. Thus, there are many different ways to formulate ethnographic research on this art, its artisans, and the art world.[3] The research that is discussed in this essay was developed from my prior research. One set of questions concerns the politics and political history of the artisans, artists, and related

FIGURE 3. This typical, makeshift display was set up on the side of the road at the entrance to Chichén in 1989. The figures, all unpainted and untreated, include three different mascaron forms leaning against the table. The *ídolos* on the table include Feathered Serpents (left corner), two Corn Gods (left front row), a God of Medicine, the Young Corn God (bust based on a Palenque statue), another Corn God, and another God of Medicine (leaning against a very large Young Corn God). This artwork is a development of the second generation of artisans from the 1980s and demonstrates the beginning of a dramatic expansion of forms and figures that was to occur in the early 1990s with the development of different varnishes and painting styles.

vendors of handicrafts (cf. Castañeda 1998; Himpele and Castañeda 1997; Peraza López, Rejón Patrón, and Piña Loeza 1987). A second set of questions concerns the aesthetic classification, economic markets, cultural-symbolic identity, and mode of production of the art (Castañeda n.d.; Castañeda, Fumero, and Breglia 1999; Armstrong Fumero 2000). A third set of issues centers on how this art tradition emerged within, articulates with, and affects the tourist economy of Yucatán at the levels of micro-region, the regional state society, and the peninsular region of the Cancun-Mérida-Tulum tourist network, as well as the broader history of the community (Morales Valderama et al. 1992; Peraza López and Rejón Patrón 1989; Castañeda 1996:203–231, 2001, 2003).

Within this context, the continued or renewed ethnographic study of the modern Pisté Maya artwork—or *arte pisteño*—and art world would necessarily need to address the methodological problem already mentioned. The art raises this problem in three ways. First, many studies in the anthropology of art have

FIGURE 4. In this photo from 1997, the daughters of Victor Tun are shown painting gold trim on *idolos* in a traditional Maya hut that is used for storage of corn. In this household, the males spend the morning until about 11 a.m. carving pieces while the women finalize the pieces. Later, the pieces are divided up among the extended family, who then go to sell the artwork at their favorite spots in front of different restaurants and hotels in Pisté. The painting or *acabado* (a "finishing" consisting of a either a type of varnishing or painting and varnishing) of the wood originates from conversations I had with Hilberto Yam in the summer of 1992, suggesting the possibility of "antiquing" the carvings so as to provide greater allure to tourists. Inspired by my confidence that this would increase the commercial value and attraction for foreign consumers of the pieces, Hilberto experimented with different materials such as gasoline, tar, shoe polish, and paint based in oil, water, and other materials. Until the development of this *acabado*, the carving of wood was completely a man's job; finishing introduced new steps in the production process that could be assumed by women, specifically sanding, painting, and polishing.

demonstrated the mutual complicity between institutions and practices of art and anthropology in the creation and maintenance of art worlds based on non-Western artworks and objects (e.g., Clifford 1988, 1997; Errington 1998; Mullin 1995; Steiner 1994; Marcus and Myers 1995; Garcia Canclini 1993, 1995).

Second, the historical interdependence between anthropology and tourism is a well-documented complexity that continues to shape and inform the creation of tourist attractions and anthropological practices (e.g., Castañeda 1996; Hervik 1999; Price and Price 1992; Garcia Canclini 1995; Clifford 1997). A statement made by Alfred V. Kidder, the archaeologist in charge of the Carnegie

FIGURE 5. On the same day as the photograph above, students from the Field School conducted participant-observation on the processes of art production at Victor Tun's house. Here one student, Fernando Armstrong, is learning to carve with Victor Tun, while Carlos engages in conservation with Victor's son-in-law in the shade of the hut. Meanwhile, Ana Wandless (standing center) and Catherine Deane (far right) are doing photographic and video documentation (respectively) of the work. The hut in Figure 4 above is located five meters behind the photographer of this image.

Institution of Washington (CIW) program of Maya research headquartered at Chichén Itzá (1923–1941), clearly demonstrates this point. Kidder locates the development of tourism not only as the consequence and positive responsibility of archaeology, but as necessary for the continued development of archaeology itself:

> If Chichén Itzá can be kept both interesting and beautiful [through archaeological excavation and restoration], it will without question become a Mecca of Travel and incidentally, a most valuable asset for archeology which, like every other science, needs its "show-windows" because public interest must be aroused and eventual public understanding must be achieved if archeology is to go forward. [Kidder 1930:99]

Third, given the above, we might begin to recognize that the emergence of a local artisanry tradition in the face of a burgeoning tourist economy at the local, regional, and national levels is not to be explained as simply a function of locals responding to tourism. Pisté Maya artwork is created within particular contexts that are deeply shaped, structured, and infused by a complex history of anthropological intervention and interaction with anthropologists

FIGURE 6. This true bas-relief, titled "Sacrifice to Life," is carved into a 2-inch-thick cedar board that measures 1 × 1.3 meters. The *chapopote* finishing accentuates the natural color variation of the wood. This piece, which was awarded first place in the 1999 *Concurso* in Pisté under the "tabla" category and showed in the December 1999 exhibition at Lake Forest College, manifests an aesthetic style that resonates with the bas-relief styles found on benches and altars at Chichén, especially in the building complexes archaeologists call Mil Columnas and Mercado, and with styles of the archeological site Tajin, which features extensive use of feathered serpents in its iconography. The content of the piece, although clearly inspired by and borrowing from "ancient Maya" iconography, is, however, original and not a replica of any existing pre-Columbian artwork.

and government officials, as well as a 100-plus-year development of a tourist economy based on archeological ruins and beach–sun–sex attractions. Thus, in terms of the historico-empirical realities of anthropology, art, tourism, and the transcultural art world of Pisté Maya art, scientifically distanced positions of objectivity, neutrality, and value-free approaches are not available from which to analyze, or even to describe, the object of study.

ENTANGLEMENTS: METHODOLOGIES AND OBJECTS OF STUDY

Anthropological discussion of the mutual entanglement of subject and object is not recent. It is, however, an issue that has been primarily debated

FIGURE 7. In 1998 and 1999, the ethnographic research included a workshop with the artisans that was run as a focus group to study transcultural elements of the artwork. On one hand, the workshop was a forum for artisans to learn more about the symbols, iconography, and art history of the ancient Maya art traditions so as to incorporate this knowledge as they saw fit in their own practices. On the other hand, the workshop was a site of ethnographic fieldwork and research on both artisan aesthetics and the lived transcultural dynamics between art worlds and anthropology. The workshop was student directed by Fernando Armstrong Fumero (2000) and is written up as a master's thesis. Shown left to right are Sara Saso (student researcher) and the artists Alvaro Balam and Wilberth Serrano Mex.

by proponents of contrastive paradigms in terms of epistemology and politics. Many have given up on the argument and debate between positivist and humanist philosophies; many have sought to move beyond it in order to constructively devise new modes of analysis that build from the assumption that subject and object are mutually implicated in one another. In the realm of the anthropology of art, for example, Marcus and Myers (1995) suggest the need to develop research methodologies (which would be a kind of "critical ethnography") that are conceptualized from the fact of the historical and reciprocal complicity of the institutions and practices of art and anthropology.

It should be noted, however, that much of the discussion about this complicity, as in Marcus and Myers, presupposes a "pure research" mode or form of ethnography. Anthropological practices of social and cultural critique can

FIGURE 8. Before and after the opening of the exhibit at Lake Forest College in 1999, the Maya artists led "tours" for different groups of students from art and anthropology classes, as well as for a private high school from the greater Chicago area. Here, Hilberto Yam explains symbolic and production aspects of an *idolo* (the God of Medicina, a figure he invented) to an anthropology student during a tour prior to the opening.

be identified as falling under the "pure research" model when they are strongly conditioned by—and aim toward—the scholarly criteria of university or academic knowledge production rather than commercial, communitarian, or governmental agendas of directly effecting social change. On the other side of

FIGURE 9. During the exhibit at Lake Forest College, students from the author's course on ethnography sit in the gallery space while listening to an artist (not shown) discussing his artwork in the days after the opening.

science, work that operates within the model or sphere of applied research has often sidestepped or ignored this entangled complicity of subjects and objects of study. This seems to be the case historically; in the present, this approach is just as often a side effect of the constraints established by funding agencies and sponsoring clients. The tendency is for such sponsoring or funding agencies—if not for the anthropologists as well—to consider this question as a theoretical or scholastic issue that has little real-world relevance in terms of the bottom line (see Pels 1999 on ethnographic ethics as caught in a tension between obligations to patrons and responsibility to subjects of research).

Given these tendencies, there is a significant need to interrogate the complicated entanglements of subjects and objects with the explicit aim of reconceiving and reconfiguring the always problematic distinction between pure, basic, theoretical research and applied, practical, policy science. The ethnographic study of Pisté Maya art and artisans provides a welcome occasion for such an exploration.

In 1997, I organized and led the Field School in Experimental Ethnography. In it we initiated a program of research in three areas of study that was conducted over the course of three summer seasons (1997–1999) and one period of fieldwork in the fall of 1999 (Castañeda and Breglia 1997–1998; Logan 1997).[4] Two overarching principles governed the program's conceptual design and organization. First, the field school program combined intensive and long-term field research with a pedagogical agenda of training students in ethnographic fieldwork. In three summer seasons of research, the program trained more than 30 undergraduates and five graduate students and worked in three areas of investigation—one of which, the Ah Dzib Project in Maya Art and Anthropology, is the focus of this essay. Second, the field school program sought both to theorize and to put into practice a mode of ethnography that is called experimental ethnography.

Experimental ethnography in the present context does not refer to the commonly held meaning of the "writerly" attempt to experiment with the conventions of ethnographic writing and representation. Instead, the term refers to a process of fieldwork and, more specifically, to a theory and practice of fieldwork that emerges from and works within the dynamic tensions between the articulation of basic and applied research and subject–object dichotomies. The experimentality, or experimental nature, of this ethnography can be defined as an exploration of the methods and practices of fieldwork. Methodologically this experimentation has three aspects. First, there is the detailed re-evaluation of the existing toolkit of ethnographic procedures and reconceptualization of their uses and connections to theoretical concerns shared among sectors of anthropologists. Second, there is the incorporation into ethnographic fieldwork of methods and concepts borrowed from diverse fields of art, such as performance studies, installation art, museology and curation, scenography, street theater, performance art, and theater anthropology. Third, there is the development of innovative combinations of such interdisciplinary techniques to create "new" kinds of dynamics and processes of fieldwork. It must be strongly reiterated that the agenda is not to create "new" methods of fieldwork, but alternative uses and conceptualizations of existing practices so as to create new analyses. This experimental ethnography does not pretend to create new dynamics of fieldwork so much as to create new understandings, perspectives, and uses of the dynamics of fieldwork that have always existed, but have sometimes been obscured within fieldwork.

Conceptually, this experimentation is a different notion than that offered by scientific paradigms. In the present framework it does not refer, as in the positivist and neo-positivist philosophies of science, to a strictly defined methodology or set of procedures and prescriptions aimed at the production, testing, and verification of facts. Following the etymology of the word, the idea here is that of "putting into peril." In other words, experimentality is an exposing or putting out into the open for questioning, inspection, and exploration the utility of methodological tools; this is a "playing with the possibilities at hand" in such a way that there is a "testing" of methods without the surety of an answer such that there is a risk of "failure"—that is, inadequacy, shortcoming, or limitation in terms of the expectations of the research design. The status of "failure" needs to be discussed more,[5] but for the moment note that this notion of experimentality is precisely what is put into practice with, in, and through fieldwork as this last concept is conceptualized within the humanist paradigm of social science. The distinction here, however, is that whereas the various phenomenological–hermeneutic approaches aim toward understanding and comprehension of the cultural life-worlds of others as pre-given and autonomous, this experimental ethnography assumes that *cultural worlds are created and based on transcultural processes.* Thus, this framing transforms the subject–object binary in a radical way that is not too often theorized in even dialogical-based anthropologies. The notion of experimentality here is different from both (1) the scientific model of experiment that is governed by the teleological objective of the production of new knowledges regarding an object of study and (2) the phenomenological model of experience that is also governed by the goal of producing knowledge in the register of existential, experiential, axiological, and culturo-logical understandings. The reason for this is that experimental ethnography, in this third framework, aims not to produce knowledge per se, but to differently deploy the already given understandings and knowledges in ways that have an explicit, direct, and immediate relevancy or significance for the communities in which the fieldwork is conducted.

To clarify: the production of knowledge does occur but does not constitute the ultimate objective or teleology as in the scientific paradigm of accumulating knowledge for its own sake. This point might suggest that this experimental ethnography therefore fits into the paradigm of applied or practical science. However, other differences intervene: for example, the use and valorization of the experiential and the theoretical in the conceptualization of research designs, which make experimentality a different mode of social science than the "applied" paradigm as well. Although there is affinity to "action research," experimental ethnography is also different from this methodology. Neither the basic research objective of the accumulation of knowledge (in either mode of neo-positivist or phenomenological science) nor the applied objectives of creating public policy, giving local aid or assistance to communities, or effecting social change and improvement are governing principles.

There is, as noted, a double bricolage of experimentality in this alternative conception of fieldwork: both (1) methodological practices are reconfigured and (2) existing knowledges, understandings, and experiences are recirculated in new modalities that are in turn mediated by the experimentation with fieldwork practices. This double articulation of an experimental bricolage of knowledges through an experimentation with fieldwork methods makes this mode of research both like and unlike existing visions of scientific, humanist, and applied science. It has affinities to all, but crucial counterpoints to each. It would, however, be a mistake to understand these contrastive similarities as a "blurring" of boundaries, as well as an error to think of it as a blurring of the very entities or paradigms whose boundaries are nonetheless porous and malleable. Rather, experimental ethnography is an alternative modality of ethnography that is still emergent and in process of definition. The Field School in Experimental Ethnography was conceived as an ongoing project in furthering the development of this possible mode of ethnography.

THE AH DZIB P'IZTÉ' PROJECT IN MAYA ART AND ANTHROPOLOGY

The Ah Dzib P'izté' was developed on the basis of 12 years of ethnographic research conducted from 1985 to 1997 in Pisté (pop. 5,000) and Chichén Itzá.[6] Interestingly, this period of ethnographic experience in Pisté roughly coincides with the coming of age of the art tradition among second and third generations of local, Pisté artisans. During this time, however, my prior investigations had objectives that did not take into account the artwork either as an aesthetic–meaningful system of commodities or as a tourist industry. While my previous research had treated the political history of the Pisté artisans and handicraft venders of Chichén Itzá (see Castañeda 1996, 1998; Himpele and Castañeda 1997), the research initiated in 1997 shifted objectives to the cultural politics of the artwork. Specifically, the project sought to intervene in the political economy of aesthetics with research that emphasized both the cultural dimensions of the art production and the aesthetic elements of the artwork as they articulated actual and possible markets. However, before describing in detail the research agenda and methods, it may help the reader to first have a synthetic summary of the ethnographic context and situation that was studied.

The Tourist Market of the Pisté Art World

The concept of art worlds as developed by Howard Becker (1982; cf. Danto 1964) refers to a configuration of diverse agents, institutions, social relations, and technological forms that contribute necessarily in the making, marketing, distribution, and consumption of works of art. As Marcus and Myers (1995:28, 39 n.) point out, Danto (1964) "originated [the concept of artworld] in his argument that the meaning and value of works are produced in . . . an institutional matrix" (39 n.). Although Becker and Danto offer similar concepts, one nuance is that whereas Danto argues for an "artworld" in the singular, Becker conceptualizes "art worlds" in the plural. This difference is further differentiated typographically by the use of one word and two words by Danto and Becker, respectively.[7] The fuzziness and fluidity of the concept is not a handicap but an advantage, as it helps both to identity the art world of Pisté Maya art and to design research that can trace its different aspects.

The Pisté art world is marked by a complicitous entanglement of business interests, state institutions, tourism agencies, handicraft production, marketing, and anthropological authorities. Without giving further details of this complexity that is described elsewhere (e.g. Castañeda 1996, 2003, 2004), we can synthetically characterize the tourist market (both generally and in this specific case) in terms of how it not only positively enables the art or artisanry production but constrains, delimits, and informs aspects of production, value, and aesthetics. Ten aspects of the Pisté Maya art world can be identified as the baseline for analysis of the conditions in which the project in experimental ethnography was designed to intervene. Although each of the following merits greater elaboration, the focus of this essay only allows a summary listing:

1. State intervention by governmental anthropologies, which both propagates (or "reconverts") folk or popular handicrafts[8] and asserts legal claim as the only juridically and aesthetically legitimate authority to replicate or copy pre-Columbian art, works to delegitimize any grounds for assertions of Pisté artists as cultural inheritors, renovators,

and protagonists of an "ancient tradition" based on an organic continuity.

2. Tourist demand for handicrafts tends to be for lower-priced and lower-quality artwork and to eschew items that are high in price compared to the products available in the market.

3. A tourist preference for kinds of artwork, as well as the sale volume of different figures or styles, are subjectively tracked by artisans and generate a creative conservatism among artisans that is fed by an economic competitiveness.

4. This conservatism leads to specific forms of copying and reproduction that both constitute the basis of the tradition (and its "continuity") and raise a set of interesting analytical or theoretical issues centered on the problem of mimesis in art.

5. Countering the conservatism is a creative or innovative spirit among some producers, especially the third generation of artisans, which is fed by an artistic competitiveness or competition in technical and aesthetic mastery of the art of carving.

6. This artistic spirit not only brings some "artisans" within or in proximity to the domain of the ideological category of "artist," but is a motivational structure that results in some particularly creative, challenging, innovative, and intricate artwork.

7. The production of highly elaborate, high-priced pieces is "punished" by the structure of the market and artists must necessarily find an economic balance between the production of high-priced, unique figures and high-volume-sale "stock figures" that require less investment in terms of time, skill, materials, and technical know-how.

8. This market punishment of the artistic or creative element is, in part, a function of the lack of a system of art writing[9]—or specialist commentary or knowledge—about the art tradition, which would give tourists knowledge through which to make informed aesthetic distinctions.

9. The exhibitionary structure of market display, based on a "flat" front stage of diverse handicrafts,[10] is a second determining factor that effects a market punishment of the pricing of intricate, elaborate pieces and constrains the aesthetic categorization or meaning of Pisté artwork to "artisanry" rather than "art."

10. The market is structured on a three-tiered system of sale by producers, vendors, and handicraft stores that does not include a brokerage of the artwork by metropolitan curators, critics, collectors, dealers, and other agents—the existence of which

would allow alternatives to the market punishment of high-end artwork.

In summary, the Pisté Maya art world emerged from, and has remained within, the handicraft markets of Chichén and nearby tourist attractions such as Mérida and the Cancún region. In this market it sells as local "folk" or "indigenous" art to tourists, whether Mexican or foreign, since it is embedded within the context of the diverse national, regional, indigenous, folk, and popular arts of México. Its authenticity resides therefore in its physical or visual market relation to other contemporary crafts, even if it is dynamically inspired by and draws from pre-Columbian traditions. These conditions combine to create a structure of meaning in which the Pisté Maya artwork can only have significance as a contemporary art form defined within the domains of handicrafts and tourism markets. The value of the artwork is therefore constituted—that is, both enabled and contained—as tourism handicrafts.

The absence of one factor is crucial in effecting this closure on the possibilities of value: there is, as of yet, neither a production of knowledge about it in the forms of art criticism, ethnographic representation, or museum/gallery exhibition of the art, on the one hand, nor the development of a patronage and "discovery" of the art by wealthy patrons, collectors, galleries, or other agents of metropolitan capitalism. These two elements are mutually interdependent, since these agents write the commentaries about and critiques of the artwork and circulate it in new exhibitionary networks of museums, galleries, and markets within Western art worlds but do so primarily on the basis of a prior history of insertion of the art into the circuits of critique, commentary, and exhibition. Thus, from the perspective of an "applied anthropology," the task is clearly one of creating, from a blank slate, a system of art writing that would trigger or initiate this opening into new circuits of exhibition and commentary. How can ethnographic research conceived as applied anthropology work to stimulate the "discovery" of an art tradition by transnational art critics, patrons, and collectors? Note here that the concept of art writing includes within it not only the idea of verbal and published commentary and critique by art critics, anthropologists, dealers, collectors, et cetera, but the art's curation in diverse settings of exhibition. Indeed, the curation of the artwork in gallery and museum space is a fundamental mode of commentary that is both the result and the production of perception, reception, and valorization of art.

The Research Agenda and Methodology of the Ah Dzib P'izté' Experimental Ethnography Project

The foregoing analysis or "pre-understanding" of the political economy of aesthetics provided the foundation for an experimental ethnography. This understanding of the transcultural art world of Pisté and its tourist markets suggested a strategy of fieldwork based in the methodological principle of installation. This strategy would allow us to center the investigation on problems of aesthetics and value as articulated through display, staging, and exhibition. With the goal of contributing to the opening up of the conditions of production and marketing in which Pisté Maya art and artisan exists, the Ah Dzib P'izté' Project in Maya Art and Anthropology had five objectives. The agenda below was formulated through a consideration of the intersection of (1) the issues of the empirical and conceptual entanglements of subjects and objects of study (as well as of anthropology and tourism, anthropology and art), (2) the objective of developing a theory and practice of experimental fieldwork, and (3) the transcultural reality of the life worlds and art worlds of Pisté and Chichén Itzá.

1. Explore—that is, conceive and operationalize—experimental practices of ethnographic fieldwork that are linked to quotidian processes of cultural invention, intercultural exchange, and transcultural interaction.
2. Create and organize exhibitions of the contemporary Maya art of Pisté in the community of Pisté for audiences that are formed by the local community, regional society, and international tourism, as well as international exhibitions for broader transnational publics.
3. Realize different publication projects that include academic and popular books, scientific journal articles, and ethnographic art catalogues that target tourist and popular readerships.
4. Contribute to the opening of the conditions of production and commercialization of the aesthetic work of producing Pisté Maya art and artisanry through the diverse processes of experimental ethnography, which include fieldwork, exhibition, installations, and print and video publications.
5. Theorize and further develop in actual practice new uses of ethnographic fieldwork in the creation and fomentation of communicative links and networks between anthropology and the cultural communities in which it operates.

Notable in this research agenda is the recognition of open-ended processes and specific, particular strategies by which to address and intervene in them. In turn, the actualization of fieldwork, aiming toward these objectives, was designed out of "standard" ethnographic techniques and procedures, such as interviewing, observation, participation, and documentation, in conjunction with procedures and methods that were borrowed from diverse fields of art, such as installation art, performance art, museology, and curation, as well as theater anthropology. Specifically, the Ah Dzib P'izté' Project was based in fieldwork that used interviewing; participant-observation, both "alone" and with multimedia documentation; modified focus group workshops; the staging of sites of fieldwork (or fieldwork interaction–exchange); the exhibition and curation of art as sites of fieldwork; expanded documentation of the collaborative fieldwork processes; and research workshops to collectively design and operationalize agendas. The remainder of this ethnographic report of fieldwork focuses on processes of installation and exhibition.

The ideas of installation and exhibition are quite closely related. In the context of the development of experimental ethnography, the concept of "installation" was developed as a methodological principle and strategy in a way different than that of "exhibition." Whereas "exhibition" is used in the common-sense meaning of "display," the notion of ethnographic installation refers to other processes. Specifically, "installation" was used as a strategy of proactively intervening in space to create or stage an environment in which to conduct ethnographic fieldwork. Staging in fieldwork can range from something as invisible as the rearrangement of social relations necessary to conduct an interview or a conversation with an "informant" to something as spectacular as an art exhibition. The diagnostic element of ethnographic installations is that they are strategically constructed and staged spaces in which to realize fieldwork activities.

The Art of Staging Fieldwork: Installation In the fourth week of an eight-week season in 1997, a core team of three student researchers, the two field school directors, and the graduate student assistant instructor[11] was assembled and established an agenda: to organize and install an exhibition of Pisté Maya art in the town center. The first step, after getting approval from community authorities, was to make an invitational call and campaign to all artisans asking for their participation. Having established logistical issues regarding the exhibit, students began to conduct participant-observation of the art world (production and sale) as they went to various locations to invite artisans to participate. Student researchers were directed to spend days "hanging out" with different groups of artisans and to move from group to group, making acquaintances if not friends and explaining the project agenda as well as the logistics of the exhibition. Artisans were obliged to register on a day set well in advance of the exhibition date. For registration, the research team prepared a structured questionnaire which was administered in an area of the town hall by the team. Questions concerned (1) the social aspects of production, (2) the typical kinds of artwork produced by the artisan, (3) the artisan's sources and mode of learning the art, and (4) the projected piece or pieces the artisan would produce for the exhibition. Artisans came in groups and asked questions, often with a substantial amount of hesitancy and perhaps even unspoken doubt. Although almost forty artisans initially registered, many artisans approached students to register late. However, in the final count, only 19 participated.

The attempt to organize an exhibition was an experimental process in several ways. On the one hand, Pisté Maya art had been an "invented tradition," in that the community of Pisté itself recognized that the artwork had no authentic continuity or connection to the ancient traditions that inspired it and that it imitated, regional "folk" or Maya traditions of carving wood, or to the history of the community. Further, the artisans themselves were of questionable character, not only for their history of illegal invasions of the archeological zone to sell handicrafts but for their general tendency—as males from the lowest socioeconomic sectors of society—to publicly consume their substantial profits in beer and liquor. The intensely political history of the artisans included several episodes of violence—not only between their groups but as a whole with police, military, anthropological authorities, state agencies, private capitalists, and tour guides. In short, there had never been any kind of organized effort oriented toward the "collective good" that was not in fact simply an elaborate, self-interested scheme (on the part of one or more vendors or artisans) or an attempt to liquidate the artisans as a commercial force (on the part of authorities or handicraft store owners).

An overwhelming culture of conspiracy theory, skepticism, self-interest, double crossing, deceit, and rejection of communal action has prevailed throughout México in the last decades of the Partido Revolucionario Institucional (PRI) and had entrenched itself in Pisté. In this context, not only was the project of an art exhibit exceedingly suspect, but my motivations and objectives as project director were open to extremely jaded interpretations for a variety of reasons (see Castañeda 1996:259–297, 1998; Himpele and Castañeda 1997).[12]

On a more practical level, the structure of the exhibition itself was logistically antagonistic to the modus operandi of all artists. In order to effectively design and construct an exhibition space, one needs to have collected the pieces sufficiently in advance. The tourist demand for this artwork is so high, however, that artisans usually sell what they produce within a few days. There is no stockpiling or warehousing of pieces by producers, only by buyers or vendors. Further, the domestic economy of many of the artisans is such that what is produced today must be sold today in order to have any income whatsoever. It is true that everyone uses this ideological line as a way to protest one's poverty and humility, not simply as a bargaining chip with tourists or dissimulation for ethnographers, but as a way of safeguarding against neighbors who might get *envidia* (i.e., a case of vengeful, harm-causing jealousy). Thus, the decision to hold an exhibit—an activity that had never before been attempted, much less accomplished—was perilous for the simple fact that it could have been totally and completely rejected by all those concerned. Thus, the fact that nearly fifty artisans registered (out of some two hundred) and that nearly twenty actually participated is a successful achievement in and of itself for an event that had never previously been attempted.

It was mostly achieved, however, through the promise that virtually all the pieces would be purchased by the field school or by individual researchers. Further, it was made known that "good" prices would be paid as part of a stimulus to improve quality and open up pricing. While such an objective was only viable as part of a long-term process, the most immediate and tangible success of the exhibition was a function of its actualization. Although the exhibition itself was rudimentary, makeshift, and handicapped by the mid–August rains prior to hurricane season, it was a successful, well-attended cultural event that received rare newspaper publicity. Despite inadequacies in several registers, for the broader Pisté community it opened up an awareness of the artwork as aesthetic objects as well as an understanding of the artisans as truly skilled craftsmen and legitimate artisans, if not exactly artists.

One example of this shift in local perception and reception of the artwork and artisans is an interaction that occurred on the last night of the exhibition in 1997. Ruben, a tour guide at Chichén since the early 1980s, during the period of exacerbated antagonism toward the artisans (Castañeda 1998), had entered the exhibit space, and I gave him a tour so he could inspect the artwork. Standing within hearing distance of a group of three artists who were evaluating the artwork in front of them, he marveled at a particular piece and commented in surprise about the exceptional talents of its creator. Ruben had never seen work of this aesthetic and technical quality, and his loud, surprised response told me and others that the *chavo* (roughly "dude") who had made this piece should be *orgulloso* (proud); that indeed this was not just artisanry but art, high art. Furthermore, Ruben said that he, too, was *orgulloso* to be of Pisté because this artwork, which had been created in Pisté, had finally developed into something so beautiful and complex. He was surprised and proud of Pisté, its artists, and its tradition of Maya art. The artist who had carved the piece and two of his friends, who were standing nearby, pretended to not hear, but the comment reverberated in the room.

If the 1997 exhibit indeed contributed to a shift in the popular understanding of and attitudes toward the aesthetic merits of the local art tradition, it did not amount to a revolution in pricing and valorization. This was just an initial impulse that had the added benefit of establishing a precedent for the 1998 field season and exhibition. A focus group workshop on Maya iconography, hieroglyphs, and art styles was created as one forum in which artists could create a piece specifically for the art exhibition. However, due to real-life constraints, skepticism, and other reasons, only nine artists responded to the invitation to participate in this weekly forum led by one of the student researchers. Staged as a space or site of fieldwork, the workshop featured a leader (a student researcher) who exchanged knowledge about ancient traditions as a means through which to investigate questions of the artisans' aesthetics, sources, techniques, and culture of work, all within a problematic of transcultural exchange. Although participation in the workshop was explicitly not a condition of participation in the exhibition, the workshop dynamic was apparently a factor that may have precluded other artisans from registering for and participating in the exhibit. Another reason for the low turnout, at least according to everyday talk as reported by student researchers, was our dissemination of the fact that the field school could not guarantee the purchase of the participating artwork.

In addressing low turnout, it was determined that the researchers would scope out artwork at Chichén and other venues to request "loans" for the exhibition. Interestingly enough, this circumstance may have been helpful in counteracting a rumor that had spread to the effect that the exhibition was simply a means by which to procure artwork that would be sold in the United States for exponentially increased prices and, of course, private gain. It had the added benefit of allowing for pieces to be collected sufficiently in advance to be able to design the exhibition and display of objects. While the conceptualization and design of this exhibit, which sought to put into play a style of curation borrowed from conceptualism or conceptual art (c.f. Kosuth et al. 1991; Foster 1995), are important elements to discuss, the space of this essay permits only two further points. First, the exhibition again served an important pedagogical function in training students in fieldwork and in the anthropology of art; it also allowed the research team to explore concepts of experimental ethnography. Second, the 1998 exhibition, although based on limited artisan participation, continued to stimulate community engagement and, for all appearances and based on local gossip, positively shifted attitudes towards the field school agenda as well as the artisans of Pisté.

The Fieldwork of Staging Art: Exhibition In this context, it was critical for the 1999 season to build on the successes of the previous years but also to develop a more successful strategy for artisan participation. Two additional factors enabled this to happen: First, major funding from the U.S.-México Grant provided the necessary resources for a more ambitious exhibition, and, second, a number of community groups—primarily the town authorities and representatives of the Chichén employees of the INAH—sought to collaborate actively in the organization of the ethnographic installations. It was decided that the exhibition would be structured as a *concurso* or competition, with prize monies solicited from local businesses. The *concurso* proved to be an excellent decision, not only because this format of exhibition was culturally familiar and intelligible to artisans and the broader community alike—unlike the exhibition of artwork for its own sake—but also because it was sociologically congruent to local marketing practices. Thus, while the prior attempts to create a style of "gallery exhibition" in Pisté simply did not fit the political and economic realities of the Pisté art world, a *concurso* format was logical and compelling within local cultural expectations and experience. It resolved the problem of the artisans' need for an economic incentive for which to work and functioned as the mechanism by which to ensure their participation. An additional carrot was the promise that five artisans and their prizewinning artwork would travel to the United States for a late fall exhibit. Not only did 50 artists register and comply with their commitments, but a number of artists who had traveled from cities an hour away had to be turned away on the morning of opening day.

Work was nonstop in the organization of collaborators who greatly assisted in the preparation. Arrangements were made with local businesses for prize monies and materials. The local Coca-Cola distributor donated beverages for sale as well as a 30-by-30-meter tent for an outside exhibit. Representatives from local groups—such as tour guides and businesses—as well as from regional institutions—such as Alfredo Barrera Rubio, then director of the state office of the INAH, and a curator from the state-funded museum of culture and arts—were asked to be judges. A local restaurant owner and dance professional organized the opening entertainment with live traditional music and a regional dance performance by a troupe of children that he directs.

In short, the three-night event was shaped into a form that abided by cultural norms and expectations. It was a success in the manner of non-political and non-religious social events that enact and substantiate "community." Success was dependent upon the articulation of the field school's goal of exhibiting the artwork as art with local conceptions of an exhibition as a handicraft competition. In an approximation of gallery style exhibition, the summer 1999 exhibit used pedestals and wall sections on which to place or hang artwork, as well as an elaborate system of lighting. This reterritorialization of the artwork—displacing it from the tourist market and reframing it as art—was the basis for a transformation of its local valorization. Yet the whole exhibit was culturally framed as a meaningful and relevant cultural event with music, prizes, and collaboration. Along these registers of collective belonging and identity, the event effervesced with renewed community spirit, self-appreciation, and good will amongst the diverse, and often antagonistic, sectors of Pisté. There is, however, a great risk in this type of format: If it were to become a routine, annual function, this form of event could ultimately re-inscribe the artwork as *artisanry* and not as *art*.

CONCLUSIONS

Experimental Ethnography in Pisté: Between and Betwixt

With the goal of positively affecting a modification in the valorization of the Pisté art, the ethnography developed a twofold strategy. First, it was necessary to extract the artwork from the tourist handicraft context from which it had emerged and from which its value was determined. Second, the reinstallation of the artwork into different contexts would contribute to a shift in the assignation of value as well as a change in its perception or reception, from ethnographic artisanry to aesthetic art. The key phrase is "could contribute," for the process of this change is a long and difficult road, as Mullin (1995) has analyzed in the transformation of Southwest Indian artwork from handicrafts to ethnographic curios to an art and aesthetic imbued with national values. In this case, it took the combined support of anthropological institutions whose sponsorship of competitions cultivated cults of the individual artist and wealthy art connoisseurs. Thus, the complicated shift in perception or reception is a triple-headed objective. Not only must the artisans themselves alter their understanding, but so must the social community in which the artisans or artists are embedded, in order that a whole series of other consumers (e.g., tourists, art critics, anthropological authorities, curators, state agencies, collectors, dealers, etc.) will be compelled to re-evaluate the artwork according to a different marketing structure of value.

Thus, in the project of experimental ethnography, fieldwork not only became the strategic means of establishing an art writing in which Pisté Maya art could circulate, but fieldwork itself was yet a third mode of art writing that entailed particular kinds of commentary, transcultural engagements, communication, and interaction. The question arises as to how we might measure the success of the research. In short, there is no adequate non-subjective way to gauge the success of the project in strict scientific terms. The immediate benefits or "social change" are intangible and immaterial—that is, they exist in the diverse form of attitudes, perceptions, ideas, and sentiments in Pisté. More concrete and quantitatively measurable manifestations may occur in the long run. Nonetheless, an important precedent of exhibiting and writing about the artwork in new ways was established and experienced in Pisté. Regarding the value, success, or failure of the ethnography as a social science betwixt and between pure or basic and applied or practicing anthropology, this question also requires time for answers to develop. In part, time is needed to bring the results and processes of this research into publication, and in part it requires the commentary and critique of other anthropologists. Nonetheless, the Ah Dzib P'izté' Project, as part of the Field School in Experimental Ethnography, contributed to the broader agenda of actualizing alternative practices of ethnographic fieldwork with the aim of creating and fomenting new communicative links and transcultural exchange between anthropology and the cultural communities in which it operates.[13]

Experimental Fieldwork: Between and Betwixt Pure and Applied Paradigms

Experimental ethnography as elaborated in this study of the Pisté Maya art world is a mode of fieldwork in which given, prior, and assumed knowledges are used and recirculated in fieldwork activities, dynamics, and practices. This recirculation of knowledge has the goals of actualizing an ethnographic process that has both (1) relevance to and for the communities in which research is conducted and (2) experiments with the very practices of fieldwork itself with the aim of theorizing and reconfiguring alternative forms of ethnography. The aim of such a reconfiguration is not, however, to displace either pure or applied research paradigms, but rather to contribute to the pluralization of ways of doing ethnography.

On the one hand, experimental ethnography has an affinity to applied anthropology. Research in the applied model tends to be governed by tangible objectives that can be generalized as having three forms: (1) effecting social change in a traditional community's relationship to modernity or modernization; (2) producing knowledge for use in the creation of governmental policy or to inform the political action of non-state collectivities; and (3) aiding communities or collectivities in rediscovering and revitalizing one or more aspects of their cultural traditions in the face of globalization, Western hegemony, or national modernities. Experimental ethnography locates the value of the anthropological intervention, however, not in the teleology of these objectified results (i.e., social change, policy or political action, or cultural revitalization) but in the process of fieldwork itself. The goal is not the application of knowledge produced in and through fieldwork, but the recirculation of knowledges that are already there in the sites of fieldwork. In this different model, the value of research lies with and in the actual dynamics of fieldwork; this is the primary locus where the real-world relevance and significance of this form of ethnography is to be measured, evaluated, and appreciated. To be sure, there are forms of applied anthropology that place primary value on the very dynamics of fieldwork itself and, thus, prioritize the intervention of research in the sites of fieldwork as a kind of in-situ problem solving. But again, the difference here between applied and experimental ethnography is the prior conception of a problem to solve in the first case. In this regard, experimental ethnography is less like applied anthropology and much more like the phenomenologically oriented ethnographies of certain dialogical approaches, theater anthropology, and strands of feminist scholarship.[14]

On the other hand, experimental ethnography has an affinity to pure or basic models of research because of its positive view of, exploration of, and contribution to theory and theoretical issues. Yet, the primacy given to the on-the-ground relevance of fieldwork in its very conduct and processes makes this quite clearly distinct from positivist and neo-positivist social sciences. "Knowledge" is not being "tested" *for truth* to produce facts by a determined structure of fieldwork procedures that processes this knowledge or these facts (by verifying, accumulating, and stockpiling). It is also distinct from other modes of ethnography inspired by theoretical traditions of sociocultural critique (e.g., Marxisms, feminisms, post-structuralisms, postcolonial discourse, etc.). The critical intervention of ethnography in those traditions ultimately targets an academic or popular audience quite displaced from the actual sites of fieldwork.

In this vision of experimental ethnography, fieldwork practices are being "recombined" *to explore their utility* in the recirculation of given knowledge in a relevant manner by the very activity of the exploratory bricolage. This exploration for utility is where a different notion of experimentality enters into play. Based on the etymological meaning of "putting out" (exo-) into danger or risk (peril), fieldwork itself is at peril and is a perilous locus of "failure" (e.g., shortcomings, inadequacies, partial results, etc.). Since, the subject and criteria of "failure" in all kinds of ethnography is a huge topic that must be reserved for a different occasion, note here that the experimentality of this emergent kind of ethnography is a kind of bricolage of fieldwork in which concepts, methods, techniques from various fields of art (e.g., scenography, museology, art installation, and performance arts) are recombined with the inherited methodologies of anthropology in both its pure or research and applied forms.

NOTES

1. The source of the soapstone was exhausted in the early 1980s. Pistéartisans then began to mix limestone, cement powder, and paint and to shape the mixture into blocks of different sizes that are then "carved" with a technique that is more accurately described as scraping. Since the artworks formed from this mix are sold as "stone" carvings, the field school labeled this medium *piedra pisteña* or Pistéstone. With the introduction of latex molding in the mid–1990s, artisans began to copy diverse handicrafts—not only locally made wood carvings but also foreign ceramic, stone, and wood handicrafts produced in other parts of México and Yucatán. Economically speaking, this copying is expedient as it cuts the cost of purchasing handicrafts from itinerant wholesalers and allows one to sell the "same" product, but in Pistéstone. Curiously, despite the fact that this medium is used for replica reproduction, it is nonetheless not marked by conservatism, as noted below. Instead, Pistéstone is a medium in which there is significant innovation and experimentation with designs, motifs, forms, and figures.

2. The Field School in Experimental Ethnography was funded by student support in the summers of 1997, 1998, and 1999. Support was also provided by a grant from the University of Houston in 1997. Major funding of the research program with the artists in the summer of 1999 in Pisté, and the cost of the artists' travel to participate in the December 1999 U.S. exhibition, was funded by a Cultural Studies Grant from the Fideicomiso U.S.-México, a funding agency sponsored by FONCA (México's national Fund for Culture and the Arts), Fundación Cultural Bancomer, and the Rockefeller Foundation. Costs of the exhibition and catalog (Castañeda, Armstrong Fumero, and Breglia 1999) were funded by support from Lake Forest College. These funding sources are gratefully acknowledged.

3. The choice of words to refer to this tradition, its objects, their producers, and the work of producing the objects from this tradition has political, aesthetic, cultural, and economic ramifications. Thus, where the analysis focuses on questions of how to categorize the work, the term "artwork" is used as a neutral term between "artisanry" and "art," "artisan" and "artist." "Artwork" has the added benefit of referencing one or more of the products, producers, and processes of production.

4. The three projects are The Chilam Balam Project in Memory and History, SELT or The School in Experimental Language Training, and the Ah Dzib P'izté' Project in Maya Art and Anthropology.

5. "Failure" or "inadequacy" is difficult to measure and gauge if the criteria for failure are in terms of the kind, quality, and amount of engagement and interaction that one seeks. In the conduct of fieldwork, if a procedure is inadequate, then a shift in procedures or objectives is quickly instituted. If this is not possible, then, after the fact of fieldwork, the writing of ethnography can convert all "failures" into processes that reveal significant dynamics, understandings, or experiences that provide compelling moral, cultural, practical, pedagogical, political, or other lessons that were learned by the ethnographer and are to be learned by the reader of the ethnography.

6. My first visit to Chichén Itzáwas at the age of eleven in 1972, when my parents made the overland drive to visit relatives and ruins in México and Guatemala. A picture my father took of my mother and me posed at the edge of the Sacred Cenote inspired me to return to this site for master's research in 1984 and 1985, for dissertation research from 1987 through 1989 and in 1991, and for postdoctoral research in the summer of 1992 and each summer between 1995 and 2001. Having already witnessed the phenomenon in 1988 and 1989, my pilgrimages to the spring equinoxes at Chichén began in 1993 and include return visits in 1995 and 1997 with Jeff Himpele (see Himpele and Castañeda 1997) and in 2001 and 2003. In 2002–2003 I returned to Yucatán to live in Mérida while teaching and conducting research with support from a Fulbright grant.

7. The related work of Bourdieu (1993) on "fields" and art is not explicitly used in this essay, but informs the general project and is discussed elsewhere (Castañeda n.d.).

8. See Canclini (1993, 1995) and Castañeda (1996, 1998, n.d.; Himpele and Castañeda 1997) regarding how the Pistétradition ambiguously fits into Canclini's analysis.

9. The concept of art writing is introduced by Carrier (1987) and discussed in relation to anthropology and ethnographic writing by Marcus and Myer (1995).

10. By way of this phrase, a contrast is made between the exhibitionary styles of Mexican handicrafts generally and those that are constructed with either "deep" displays or "back" regions or both, in which the same tourist art is exhibited and sold but with an aura of greater authenticity, value, antiquity, meaning, et cetera. Steiner's (1995) discussion of the African tourist art markets, which builds on MacCannell's borrowing of Goffman's concept of front and back stages, is an exemplary contrast.

11. The students working on the Ah Dzib P'izté' Project in 1997 were Carlos Arana, Fernando Armstrong Fumero, and Catherine Deane. Joy Logan, associate professor of Spanish at the University of Hawai'i-Manoa, was the field school co-director, and Edith Flores, a master's student in Spanish from the University of Houston, was the assistant instructor. Laurie Kovacovic, whose area was the ethnographic study of transcultural dynamics in the teaching of English as a second language to Pistéchildren and youth, provided fundamental assistance to the research with the Maya artists in both 1997 and 1998. Jennifer White and Ana Wandless, members of the research team on the history of Pisté, also contributed significantly to the art project in 1997 and, in the case of Wandless, in 1998. Armstrong Fumero returned to the field school in 1998 and 1999 and assumed the role of student director of the Ah Dzib P'izté' project. Sarah Saso, James Todd, and Hutan Hejazi-Martinez participated in 1999. Lisa Breglia, doctoral student in anthropology at Rice, was the assistant director of the field school in 1998 and 1999 and directly contributed to the art project, especially in terms of the joint installations of PistéMaya art and the Chilam Balam Project in Memory and History in 1998 and 1999 (see Breglia 2003). In Houston, sustained dialogues with Abdel Hernández have been crucial to think through all aspects of experimental ethnography. Hernández, Breglia, and Armstrong Fumero actively participated in the Lake Forest installation. All of these persons and others who participated in the field school process are deeply appreciated for their contributions.

12. The director, in the words of one local, is "folkloric" (Himpele and Castañeda 1997). This attribution derives from a long and complicated history of involvement in the community and is especially shaped by the friendships the director had established during his very public participation in the sociopolitical movement of 1989–1991 and its subsequent breakup, which included a return to old and new antagonisms between the once-allied factions of the town leadership (Castañeda 1996, 1998, 2003).

13. A note of acknowledgement: There are a great number of persons who directly and indirectly contributed to the process of the Ah Dzib P'izté' Project. I would like to gratefully thank all of the artists, artisans, authorities, and collaborators from Pistéand the community, especially Gilberto Yam, Rebecca Pat, and Victor Olalde. The second debt is to all of the field school participants, especially Lisa Breglia, Joy Logan, Laurie Kovacovic, Edith Flores, Fernando Armstrong, Ana Wandless, Jenny White, Hutan Hejazi-Martinez, Juan Castillo Cocom, and James Todd, without whom this would not be. Numerous colleagues, who have aided this project by providing me with the opportunity to present this material for dialogue and debate at their universities, are thanked for their generosity: Joanne Rappaport, Mark Leone, Ted Fischer, Luis Vivanco, Ruth Behar, Fernando Coronil, Bruce Mannheim, Mary Weismantel, Brooke Thomas, Oriol Pi-Sunyer, Lynnette Leidy, Ann Annagnost, Celia Lowe, Kathy O'Connor, Marvin Cohodas, Anne Pyburn, Rick Wilk, Claudio Lomnitz, Tom Cummings, Michelle Day, Geoff White, Ming-Boa Yue, Alfredo Barrera Rubio, Steve Mintz, Steve Tyler, and George Marcus. Funding agencies, especially the Fideicomiso U.S.-México are thanked and listed in Note 2. Chris Reed and Cynthia Robin are deeply appreciated for their critical aide and heartfelt companionship in the Lake Forest process. A special thanks to Tim Wallace for his friendship and support, as well as the invitation to collaborate with me on this and other projects.

14. See Mannheim and Tedlock 1995 and Tedlock 1983, 1995 for dialogical anthropology; Schechner 1985, 1988; Turner 1982, 1988; and Barba 1991, 1995 for theater anthropology; and Behar 1993, 1996; Stewart 1996; and Visweswaran 1997 for the feminist scholarship on ethnography. Significantly, the emphasis on process rather than product is also a part of certain movements in art, such as in action painting, conceptualism, and performance art or art installation (see Castañeda in press).

REFERENCES CITED

Armstrong Fumero, Fernando
   2000 Making Art in Pisté: Art and Experimental Ethnography in a Yucatec Maya Community. Master's thesis, Department of Anthropology, University of Pennsylvania.
Barba, Eugenio
   1991 Dictionary of Theater Anthropology. London: Routledge.
   1995 The Paper Canoe. London: Routledge.
Becker, Howard S.
   1982 Art Worlds. Berkeley: University of California Press.
Behar, Ruth
   1993 Translated Woman. Boston: Beacon Press.
   1996 Vulnerable Observer. Boston: Beacon Press.
Bourdieu, Pierre
   1993 The Field of Cultural Production. New York: Columbia.
Breglia, Lisa Catherine
   2003 Docile Descendants and Illegitimate Heirs: Privatization of Cultural Patrimony in Mexico. Ph.D. dissertation, Department of Anthropology, Rice University.

Carrier, David

1987 Artwriting. Amherst: University of Massachusetts Press.

Castañeda, Quetzil E.

1995 The Progress That Chose A Village. Critique of Anthropology 15(2):115–147.

1996 In the Museum of Maya Culture: Touring Chichén Itzá. Minneapolis: University of Minnesota Press.

1998 On the Correct Training of Indios at the Handicraft Market at Chichén Itzá. Journal of Latin American Anthropology 2(2):106–143.

2001 Approaching Ruins: A Photo-Ethnographic Essay on the Busy Intersections of Chichén Itzá. Visual Anthropology Review 16(2):43–70.

2003 New and Old Social Movements: Measuring Pisté, From the Mouth of the Well to the 107th Municipio of Yucatán. Ethnohistory 50(4):611–641.

2004 Art-Writing in the Modern Maya Art-World of Chichén Itzá: Transcultural Ethnography and Experimental Fieldwork. American Ethnologist 30(1):21–42.

N.d. The Authentic, the Hybrid, and The Unpopular: Alternative Modernities in the Maya Art World of Chichén Itzá. In Popularizing the Public and Publicizing the Popular in Latin America. J. Himpele and R. Albro, eds. Unpublished MS.

Castañeda, Quetzil E., Fernando Armstrong Fumero, and Lisa Breglia

1999 Ah Dzib P'izté': Modern Maya Art in Ancient Tradition. Exhibition Catalog. Lake Forest, IL: Lake Forest College.

Castañeda, Quetzil E., and Lisa C. Breglia, eds.

1997–1998 Monographs of the Field School in Experimental Ethnography. Unpublished manuscripts, The Open School of Ethnography and Anthropology (Pisté, Yucatán, México).

Clifford, James

1988 The Predicament of Culture. Cambridge, MA: Harvard University Press.

1997 Routes. Cambridge, MA: Harvard University Press.

Danto, Arthur

1964 The Artworld. Journal of Philosophy 61:571–184.

Errington, Shelly

1998 Death of Authentic Primitive Art. Berkeley: University of California Press.

Foster, Hal

1995 The Artist as Ethnographer? In Traffic in Culture. G. Marcus and F. Myers, eds. Pp. 302–309. Berkeley: University of California Press.

Garcia Canclini, Nestor

1993 Transforming Modernity. Austin: University of Texas Press.

1995 Hybrid Cultures. Minneapolis: University of Minnesota Press.

Greenblatt, Stephen

1992 Resonance and Wonder. In Exhibiting Cultures. I. Karp and S. D. Lavine, eds. Pp. 42–56. Washington, DC: Smithsonian Institution.

Hervik, Peter

1998 The Mysterious Maya of National Geographic. Journal of Latin American Anthropology 4(1):166–197.

Himpele, Jeffrey, and Quetzil E. Castañeda

1997 Incidents of Travel in Chichén Itzá. Watertown, MA: Documentary Educational Resources.

Hobsbawm, E., and T. Ranger.
  1985 The Invention of Tradition. Cambridge, UK: Cambridge University Press.
Kidder, Alfred V.
  1930 Division of Historical Research. Yearbook #29 (1929–1930). Washington, DC: Carnegie Institution of Washington.
Kosuth, Joseph
  1991 Art After Philosophy and After: Collected Writings, 1966-1990. Cambridge, MA: MIT Press.
Logan, Joy
  N.d. Transforming the Ethnography within Educational Pedagogy into Experimental Ethnography. In Monographs of the Field School in Experimental Ethnography (1997). Q. Castañeda and L. Breglia, eds. Unpublished MS.
Mannheim, Bruce, and Dennis Tedlock
  1995 Introduction. In The Dialogical Emergence of Culture. D. Tedlock and B. Mannheim, eds. Pp. 1–32. Urbana: University of Illinois Press.
Marcus, George E., and Fred R. Myers
  1995 The Traffic in Art and Culture: An Introduction. In Traffic in Culture. G. E. Marcus and F. R. Myers, eds. Pp. 1–54. Berkeley: University of California Press.
Morales Valderrama, Carmen, Ella F. Quintal Avilés, María Elena Peraza López, and Lourdes Rejón Patrón
  1992 Las artesanías del oriente de Yucatán: su proceso de cambio a partir de los setenta. In Memoria del Primer Congreso Internacional de Mayistas. Pp.316–337. UNAM: México DF.
Mullin, Molly H
  1995 The Patronage of Difference: Making Indian Art "Art, Not Ethnology." In Traffic in Culture. G. E. Marcus and F. R. Myers, eds. Pp. 166–200. Berkeley: University of California Press.
Peraza López, María Elena, and Lourdes Rejón Patrón
  1989 El Comercio de Artesanias en Chichén Itzá y Algunos Efectos del Turismo en la Region. Mérida: Centro Regional de Yucatán, INAH.
Peraza López, María Elena, Lourdes Rejón Patrón, and Julio Piña Loeza
  1987 La invasión de vendedores de artesanías en la zona arqueológica de Chichén Itzá, Yucatán. Boletín de Ecuady 14:17–30.
Pick, James B., W. James Hettrick, Edgar W. Butler, and Katsumi Kunakoshi
  In press Tourism in Mexico: Its Development, Dependency, and Spatial Patterns. In BALAS 2001 Conference Proceedings. J. Anderson and D. Dimon, eds.
Price, Richard, and Sally Price
  1992 Equatoria. London: Routledge.
Schechner, Richard
  1985 Between Theater and Anthropology. Philadelphia: University of Pennsylvania.
  1988 Performance Theory. London: Routledge.
Steggerda, Morris
  1941 The Maya Indians of Yucatan. Washington, DC: Carnegie Institution of Washington.
Steiner, Christopher
  1994 African Art in Transit. Cambridge, UK: Cambridge University Press.

1995 The Art of Trade: On the Creation of Value and Authenticity in the African Art Market. *In* Traffic in Culture. G. Marcus and F. Myers, eds. Pp. 151–164. Berkeley: University of California Press.

Stewart, Kathleen
1996 Space on the Side of the Road. Princeton: Princeton University Press.

Taylor, Lucien, and Ilisa Barbash, prods.
1993 In and Out of Africa. 59 min. Berkeley: University of California, Extension Center for Media and Independent Learning.

Tedlock, Dennis
1983 The Spoken Word and the Work of Interpretation. Philadelphia: University of Pennsylvania Press.

1995 Interpretation, Participation, and the Role of Narrative in Dialogical Anthropology. *In* The Dialogical Emergence of Culture. D. Tedlock and B. Mannheim, eds. Pp. 253–288. Urbana: University of Illinois Press.

Turner, Victor
1982 From Ritual to Theater. New York: PAJ Publications.

1988 Anthropology of Performance. New York: PAJ Publications.

Visweswaran, Kamala
1997 Histories of Feminist Ethnography. Annual Review of Anthropology 26:591–621.

Part 2

ANTHROPOLOGICAL ANGST AND THE TOURIST ENCOUNTER

WILLIAM A. DOUGLASS
University of Nevada, Reno

JULIE LACY
University of California, Davis

Informed by and critical of the anthropological critique of tourism, this work is a retrospective examination of one author's willingness to act as consultant to a financially motivated tourism-development scheme in the Basque region of Spain. Navigating between the Scylla of cultural commodification and the Charybdis of local agency and voice, the anthropologist's role in such a project is fraught with anthropological angst. We consider two critical works on Basque tourism that warn against such involvement, but in the end conclude that the decision must be made on a case-by-case basis. Key Words: tourism, essentialism, Basques, cultural authenticity, agency

The anthropology of tourism was born out of anxiety (Crick 1989). Unlike general tourism studies, in which the phenomenon is frequently analyzed on its own terms if not actively promoted, the stance of the anthropological subdiscipline was generally critical and moralistic from the outset. For those anthropologists with a romanticized (not to mention possessive) view of "their people," and a willingness to assume personal and professional responsibility for their cultural survival, tourism seemed inimical to the continuity of cultural "authenticity" (however vaguely defined). The danger could come from without (outside capitalistic entrepreneurs prepared to market a local cultural "attraction" globally), from within (those members of the local society disposed to package its cultural uniqueness for personal profit), or from the collusion of both.

NAPA Bulletin 23, pp. 119–134, ISBN 1-931303-22-3. © 2005 by the American Anthropological Association. All rights reserved. Please direct all requests for permissions to photocopy or reproduce article content through the University of California Press's Rights and Permissions website, www.ucpress.edu/journals/rights.htm.

In addition, there is the less altruistic yet related issue of anthropological professional territoriality. In discussing the anthropologist's self image, James Clifford notes, "we are not missionaries, colonial officers, or travel writers" (1997:64). Indeed, anthropologists often harbor a profound animus towards the very presence of such figures within the hallowed field site, perceiving them as sullying if not downright corrupting influences, pursuing self-serving agendas informed by less than perfect anthropological understanding and respect.

It is the missionary's stated purpose to effect change on her own terms. There is the further galling fact that she will likely outstay even the anthropologist, and thereby possibly gain superior knowledge of local cultural reality and the language in which it is expressed, if only to translate the biblical text in order to transfer Christianity more efficaciously. If, in a largely postcolonial world, the colonial officer is seldom an issue any longer, the travel writer remains, and is, for the *serious* anthropologist, the quintessential purveyor of shallow and sensationalized cultural narratives. Anthropologists' disdain and pain are exacerbated by the travel account's oftentimes greater appeal to its intended First World audience, as opposed to that of the anthropological study. Given that the purpose of the travel account is to exoticize its subject, while the anthropological study seeks to familiarize it, one can easily understand Claude Levi Strauss' pronouncement in the very first line of his classic work *Tristes Tropiques*: "Je hais les voyages et les explorateurs" [I hate traveling and explorers] (Lévi-Strauss 1955:13).

It is easy to cast even greater aspersion upon the tourist, who, by definition, is the most fleeting and hence most superficial of all possible visitors. Nevertheless, within the anthropological imagination, the tourist encounter can be rife with unique danger, particularly whenever the visitor transgresses the unwritten "look but don't touch" rule. Whether by example (the very conspicuous wealth and leisure of the tourist status) or actions (the expected-if-demeaning photo poses, gratuities, stentorian demands, officious comments, etc.), tourists are far from benign visitors. Indeed, it might even be argued that no two tourists ever experience the same attraction, since it is irrevocably altered by the tourist encounter (though the same can certainly be said for the anthropological one). In short, many anthropologists believe that over time popular "pristine" venues are likely to evolve into "touristed" or "touristy" ones—the pejorative euphemisms for "spoiled" or "ruined."

The initial anthropological angst regarding tourism is reflected in several essays from *Hosts and Guests*, edited by Valene Smith (1977). Indeed, Davydd Greenwood's article in that canonical volume, "Culture by the Pound: An

Anthropological Perspective on Tourism as Cultural Commoditization," is arguably the emblematic, most oft-cited expression of the malady. Greenwood's piece both describes and prognosticates darkly about the *Alarde* festival in the Basque town of Fuenterrabia (Hondarribia) in the Spanish Basque province of Gipuzkoa.

Ambivalence has also been one of the hallmarks within the literature of this particular subdiscipline. This is scarcely surprising, given that the anthropological concern with tourism studies more or less coincides time-wise with the deconstructionist critique of the anthropological enterprise per se. One of its most acerbic criticisms regards the discipline's historical role as the handmaiden of imperialism—i.e., that it acquired ethnographic understanding in tandem with colonial administrations, the better to control subject peoples' destinies. As noted previously, within the post-colonial world,[1] cultural tourism is regarded by some anthropologists as the thin edge of the wedge of unwarranted and unwelcome First World capitalist hegemony—hence the imagery of "commodified culture."

Arguably, at least for its critics, this penetration is tantamount to neoliberal neocolonialism, denunciation of which can be tantamount to personal assuagement of professional guilt over the discipline's collaboration in colonialism's previous incarnation. It should, however, be noted that this particular legacy predisposes anthropologists, to a greater degree than other analysts, to examine the genuinely dark side of tourism's moon. Whether underscoring such pernicious practices as sex tourism (Enloe 1989; Craik 1997), ecotourism's privileging of environmental concerns over human ones (Mowforth and Munt 1998), the enhanced control of "deviants" such as the homeless to avoid disconcerting tourists (Bird 1993), the dislocation of locals (particularly subalterns) for tourism development (Crick 1989; Pi-Sunyer 1982), and the demeaning and usually tenuous nature of tourism employment and its unequal benefits (Smith 1997), the anthropological criticism of tourism can be both trenchant and timely.

Not all anthropologists are unremittingly critical of tourism, however. One need only peruse the journal *Cultural Survival Quarterly* to appreciate the extent to which cultural tourism can be seen as the main viable economic alternative for many communities. To quote the introduction to the article "Will Tourism Destroy San Cultures?" of the Kalahari, "Tourism is often blamed for many of the problems faced by indigenous peoples the world over. The issue of tourism and culture is a difficult one, but the positive role tourism can play in cultural survival should be recognized" (Ioma and Thoma 2002:39).[2]

From such a position, it is but a small move to the next level, in which the anthropologist takes an active role in tourism development—a move justified by the belief that anthropologists can contribute their knowledge and skills to the positive configuration of productive futures for their anthropological subjects. One might even argue that there is a certain logical imperative for anthropologists to become involved. After all, our subjects have every right to embrace economic opportunity as they perceive it, and the current juggernaut of touristic development is unlikely to be slowed, let alone stayed, by the anthropologist's protests. To this we might add that the anthropological account is itself vulnerable to co-optation by promoters in their rhetorical creation of a particular people's touristic cachet. It is not just culture that is susceptible to commodification, but also the very anthropological knowledge regarding it. In this case, then, it may make sense for the anthropologist to assume some sort of positive proactive stance, rather than simply carping ineffectively from the sidelines. The concerned anthropologist simply no longer has the luxury of dismissing tourism out of hand by either ignoring or condemning it.

Nevertheless, the applied anthropological engagement with touristic development is scarcely unaffected by the discipline's legacy of angst and ambivalence. What follows is a case study of one anthropologist's personal and professional struggle with all of the foregoing issues when confronted with the invitation to become the paid consultant to a major tourist development.

THE ANTHROPOLOGIST AS TANTALUS

The problematics of the commodification of anthropological knowledge were brought home graphically to William A. Douglass, one of this article's co-authors, when, as former director of the University of Nevada-Reno's unique Center for Basque Studies, he was approached by a Los Angeles-based urban architectural firm to become its consultant as it responded to an international request for proposals issued by the provincial government of Gipuzkoa in the Spanish Basque Country. The proposed project regarded the town of Urnieta and the creation of a "City of Circus and Magic," a theme park that would incorporate state-of-the-art technology and an internationally renowned performing group to create a world-class attraction.[3] At the same time, the Urnieta project envisioned embracing certain Basque ethnic features, particularly its remarkable cuisine. In short, Urnieta sought to secure its niche within contemporary global culture while at the same time displaying positive features of Basque cultural heritage. Ideally, the project would be a marriage between entertainment and education—the effusive if elusive goal of most such designed-from-scratch theme park projects in the global tourist industry.

Douglass was asked to name his price: as an anthropologist, he was being invited to reach out for personal gain and professional recognition in exchange for the special knowledge he had gleaned from a lifetime of investigation in both the Basque homeland and the several Basque diasporas worldwide. Personal opportunity? Faustian bargain? Ethical dilemma or moral obligation vis-à-vis his possible hosts? After all, these hosts, or at least some of them, seemed actively disposed to commodify their culture and that of the rest of the Basques.

Nor was he impervious to the opportunity for converting esoteric research into an entertaining and, he hoped, educational portrayal of "Basquelandia." There were so many enchanting elements to play with when configuring one of Europe's most exotic peoples. The Basques' very origins remain a mystery to this day, tangibly reflected in the uniqueness of their language and certain anomalies in their genetic profile vis-à-vis those of other Europeans. The Basque homeland is central in the distribution of Europe's Upper Paleolithic cave painters and contains many important sites. Basques were the continent's first whalers and may have visited Terranova in that capacity before the first voyage of Columbus. The Basque Elkano was the first to circumnavigate the globe; Simón de Bolivar liberated South America. Some Basques served within the colonial elite of the Spanish empire (Kurlansky 1999), while others were the solitary shepherds of the flocks of the Argentine pampas and the American West. And then, of course, there is the contemporary David-and-Goliath struggle between Basque ethno-nationalists and the Spanish and French states. In short, for the fanciers of educational and entertaining theme parks, the plethora of cultural "stuff" provided by the Basques is of such magnitude as to make Disney envious.

THE ANTHROPOLOGIST AS SOLOMON

Douglass weighed the cautionary admonitions provided by the anthropological study of tourism within the Basque context. Two texts came to mind. The aforementioned Greenwood article argues that the attempt to convert Fuenterrabia's *Alarde* into a tourist attraction mangled it fatally. The Urnieta project did differ, however, in the sense that it presumably dealt with invention rather than reconfiguration of its tourist attraction. The other study to be pondered was Joseba Zulaika's *Crónica de una seducción* (*Chronicle of a Seduction*), a stunning exposé of the mutual seduction, rather than deception, whereby Thomas Krens, director of New York's Guggenheim Museum, and Basque authorities conceived and executed the Bilbao Guggenheim project. One of the lessons of *Crónica* is the capacity of outside forces to dictate to the locals the configuration of their tourist attraction. That is, rather than a true partnership of equals, the terms and conditions of the Guggenheim–Bilbao were essentially mandated to the Basques by the Guggenheim–New York. Paying the tab did not translate into genuine agency. That particular lesson could be quite germane to the Urnieta project, and it was not altogether farfetched that the consulting anthropologist could actually end up telling Basques how to portray their culture to the wider world—at least as configured in one theme park.

Greenwood's and Zulaika's works share many common elements. Both authors were outsiders of the self-appointed observer variety, which is to say that—unlike the Urnieta project's tantalized anthropologist—neither was involved by invitation in any capacity with the object of their analysis. Both were motivated to "speak out," as it were, against perceived abuses; that is, Greenwood claimed to be responding to a moral imperative (1977:131) and Zulaika's entire text has the tone of the investigative reporter's *cri de coeur* (entreaty of protest).

Each work also employs powerful rhetoric to advance its argument. In denouncing the town council's attempts to convert the *Alarde* festival into a touristic performance, Greenwood states,

> By ordaining that the *Alarde* be a public event to attract outsiders into the town to spend money, the municipal government made it one of Fuenterrabia's assets in the competitive tourist market. But this decision directly violated the *meaning* of the ritual definitively destroying its authenticity and its power for the people. They reacted with consternation and then with indifference. They can still perform the outward forms of the ritual for money, but they cannot subscribe to the meanings it once held because it is no longer being performed by them for themselves. [1977:136, his emphasis]

Zulaika begins his engrossing text with a quote from Thomas Krens:

> Seduction: that's my business. I am a professional *séducteur*. I don't earn money but I raise it, and I do it by seduction. I make people give me gifts of twenty million dollars.[4] Seduction consists in that people want what you want without you asking for it. It is a transference of desire. I am in a way the greatest prostitute in the world. [1997:11]

Both Greenwood and Zulaika are concerned with Basque cultural authenticity, although they differ in this regard in certain ways. Greenwood sees the threat in commodification (i.e., the demeaning of Basque culture *for* outsiders), whereas Zulaika perceives the danger in the configuration of a project *by* outsiders that ignored totally Basque cultural reality while siphoning off critical public funding that had formerly gone to the fomentation of Basque cultural expression (2001a:12). Furthermore, Greenwood declares the real *Alarde* festival to be already dead and its meaningless continuation doomed to ultimate failure (1977:137). Zulaika makes no such prediction for Bilbao's Guggenheim, but the book was published just prior to the museum's inauguration, and *Crónica's* unrelenting litany of the shadowy deal-making underlying the project seems to augur failure—indeed the book was read as suggesting such by many of the Guggenheim's proponents and opponents alike.

The two texts differ in another critical fashion. Greenwood's article is firmly within the modernist anthropological tradition—particularly in its holistic treatment of culture and its privileging of the little community study (cf. Greenwood 1989:181–183). Zulaika's text is thoroughly postmodern, including its format (which reproduces newspaper clippings, images, handwritten notes, dialogue, etc.). Zulaika's argument is bracketed by quotes from Baudrillard's article on seduction and excerpts from Beckett's *Waiting for Godot*, informed by the thought of Walter Benjamin, and situated within a sweeping discourse on power and art within the global culture of the new millennium. It is therefore all the more striking that a certain shared anthropological angst could bring two such paradigmatically distinct studies to a similar moralistic conclusion.[5]

Finally, the two texts are products of strikingly different periods within the short history of the subdiscipline of the anthropology of tourism. The Greenwood piece dates from a time in which the concern with tourism was tangential to anthropology's research agenda and that of its individual practitioners.[6] Conversely, Zulaika's text is the pure product of his research design, conceived and implemented a quarter of a century after Greenwood's fieldwork, and during a period in which the concern with tourism and its impacts has become increasingly central to the anthropological enterprise.

THE ANTHROPOLOGIST AS AUTHENTICATOR:[7]
A CAUTIONARY TALE

In underscoring their "uninvited outsider" status in Fuenterrabia and Bilbao, respectively, it was not our intention to level particular criticism at Greenwood and Zulaika. Indeed, with few exceptions, we anthropologists always invite ourselves to our informants' parties, as it were. This was certainly true of Douglass during his field studies of the Basque villages of Murelaga (Bizkaia) and Echalar (Navarra) (Douglass 1969, 1975). However, by embracing involvement and employment as the paid consultant in a tourism project, the anthropologist assumes an altogether different role—one with its own imperatives, ethics, and responsibilities. By way of illustration, we might review some of the anthropological dilemmas germane to the Urnieta project, posed as questions:

1. What exactly was Douglass being asked to authenticate? It seems clear that his potential employer was seeking configuration of "Basqueness" rather than that of Basque village life typified by Urnieta itself. It is therefore questionable whether the anthropologist's former field experience in similar Basque communities was all that relevant to *this* particular project.[8]

    The implication for the broader issue of the anthropological contribution to—versus criticism of—tourism is that configuration of a people's cultural reality or realities is not the same as that of a particular context's (community's, region's, state's) multicultural nature. It seems likely that the anthropologist is both more comfortable and competent when addressing the latter rather than the former. Amanda Mason's contribution to this volume is particularly illustrative in this regard. It was her role as consulting anthropologist to ensure that the full range of the multicultural spectrum, including the world of women, was included within an upstate New York community's depiction of its cultural heritage. She was not being asked to define "New Yorkerness."

2. Who was Douglass's potential employer? Clearly, the answer was the Los Angeles firm in its pursuit of a contract rather than Urnieta itself. That fact was likely to impose both restrictions and responsibilities upon the scope of his participation. At the very least he should suspect—indeed, expect—that securing the business and building the theme park would take precedence over concern with Basque "cultural authenticity" per se.

3. What value was Douglass expected to add? We suspect that there is no simple answer to this question. Certain terms were to be negotiated in advance, but would likely have been modified along the way as the project adjusted to the inevitable unanticipated snags and snafus. Clearly, the Los Angeles firm perceived a name value at the outset in being able to enlist the anthropologist as its authenticating consultant. That particular cachet might have been an enduring expectation

throughout the execution of the project. A likely critical issue would have become that of the authenticator's responsibility for the final product. Was Douglass expected to sign the Urnieta project's "Basque portrait"? Obviously, there was the potential that he would be more appalled than pleased by it.

DISCUSSION

In grappling with these dilemmas, Douglass's angst was partly professional and partly personal. The charge to define "Basqueness" had all the potential of careening him close to both the Scylla of the largely discredited (or at least unfashionable) concern with "national character" that once pervaded the subdiscipline of culture and personality studies and to the Charybdis of anthropology's current debate—and rejection—of essentialism. In truth, as Douglass is a self-confessed cryptoessentialist (Douglass 2000), this issue, while not entirely inconsequential, was not too worrisome to this particular tantalized anthropologist.

More difficult to reconcile were Douglass's doubts about his own motives—both professional and personal. With regard to his professionalism, Douglass was uncertain whether the invitation stimulated his anthropological gland or his egotistical one. It is, after all, flattering to be *asked*, particularly when one is the practitioner of a discipline characterized more by its academic than its practical reputation and track record. Once charged, however—indeed, possibly as one consequence of the charge—an anthropologist faces the danger of believing too completely in his or her status as the consulting "expert." While there has been anthropological team research, within the academy anthropologists are perhaps surpassed only by historians when it comes to solitary investigation. The joys and sorrows of our disciplinary "lone wolf" legacy have obvious implications as the consulting anthropologist seeks her level within a team effort characterized by a parceled-out yet integrated division of labor. Our pillared (and pilloried) penchant for "holism" does not necessarily translate into comprehensive expertise, let alone Solomonesque omniscience. It can just as easily lead to a special brand of arrogance vis-à-vis the other team members and one's employer.

Douglass was reminded of the response of another class of cultural authenticators who were faced with personal ambivalence over having sold their services. This reference applies to the art historians and critics in the employ of wealthy wannabe art connoisseurs. The Bernard Berensons worked for the J. P. Morgans, but retained some sense of superiority and personal worth by privately disdaining and ridiculing their employers' tastes (Strouse 1999:504–505). Should he accept the consultancy, Douglass resolved to become a largely uncritical team member, open to compromise with a positive spirit in the interest of realizing the common goal.

At a more personal level, Douglass had to weigh the value of devoting his energies to this particular project. The time commitment could prove considerable, and he, like most of his colleagues, was already tardy in meeting several previous commitments. The Urnieta project would obviously devolve within a tight time frame in which nonacademic deadlines could scarcely be avoided or finessed. The consultancy would therefore have to take precedence over the rest of Douglass's scholarly agenda, raising the ethical issue of even greater procrastination in other areas. Did the "intrinsic" worth of the theme park justify such concessions? After all, the parameters of the project precluded radical exploratory initiative. Parallels to the role of the consulting archaeologist in the environmental impact statement process came to mind.

There was also the issue of the scope of the consultancy. How would the anthropologist articulate with the rest of the Urnieta project's team? Douglass was reminded of A. F. Robertson's reflections on his anthropological consultancy with a team charged with addressing the future of Dal Lake in Kashmir (challenged by pollution and a shrinking surface area). Robertson had to overcome the perception of the other team members that "as an anthropologist I would be possessed by righteous indignation about the threat [of any recommendations] to the Lake dwellers, and would deny the interests of other Kashmiris, the state and central governments, not to mention the tourists" (1987:8). Furthermore, like every anthropologist, Douglass would bring his unique personal history to the table. The Mr. Hyde to his Dr. Jekyll was his background as a Nevada casino owner and former marketing director of its operation. In short, unlike most potential anthropological consultants to a tourist development, Douglass had considerable business experience in tourism. Cognizant of the fact that in his marketer capacity he would never have retained an anthropologist for marketing advice, he resolved to resist any temptation to opine in this realm should he accept the proffered consultancy. The danger of triggering the tripwires of other team members charged specifically with the marketing responsibility was palpable, and doing so would probably run the risk of compromising their cooperative spirit and openness regarding anthropological advice.

Finally, there was the not inconsiderable issue of recompense and the implications of accepting it. Douglass was being offered an as yet undetermined[9] fee in return for his involvement. In short, he was being invited to commodify *his* knowledge of Basque culture. Acceptance would raise several crucial questions regarding the nature of the anthropological enterprise. While less sensitive in some respects, the dilemmas echoed those inherent in the current debates among bioethicists over the very ethics of providing consultation to the health industry. Once knowledge is commodified it can easily become proprietary. This, in turn, can readily impede the free flow of information requisite for scientific inquiry, at least as organized within academia. Carl Elliott recently denounced bioethicists who have become "little more than eunuchs in the corporate harem." He stated,

> Perhaps the new breed of corporate bioethicists will be able to whisper an occasional bit of prudent advice in the sultan's ear. But anyone with a financial interest in being an adviser to the rich and powerful also has an interest in avoiding anything more serious than the occasional whisper. My friends who do this sort of corporate work assure me that they could give me many examples of the unethical practices their wise advice has eliminated or thwarted[10] if only their confidentiality agreements with industry would permit it. Perhaps. I only know that I have never read an industry-funded ethics article that is critical of the industry that funded it. [2002:37]

CONCLUSION

It is now commonplace to state that tourism is the world's largest industry, which is, of course, another way of saying that it is the planet's biggest business. In our view, this fact alone is a huge—indeed the main—source of ambivalence within the anthropology of tourism. Like its subject matter, the discipline of anthropology first cut its teeth upon precapitalistic primitive and tribal societies and subsequently embraced marginalized, often victimized, subalterns within the world capitalist system. As we have seen, Greenwood finds meaning to be incompatible with money and Zulaika begins his work by specifying the seducer Krens's shocking 20 million dollar demand as the franchise fee for the Bilbao Guggenheim. Tourist projects are conscious capitalistic development first and foremost; the issues regarding subalternity and cultural authenticity simply receive low priority within them, if any at all. The anthropologist who accepts a consultancy in cultural tourism with missionary spirit or crusading zeal, intent upon saving the developer and the subject culture alike from themselves, is not only naïve but likely embarked upon an unrelentingly disappointing and bitter journey.

However, it is not our purpose to engage in blanket condemnation of an active anthropological role in tourism development. To the contrary, we believe that the anthropologist can make at least two positive contributions to such projects. In certain contexts, her linguistic and cultural fluency might well facilitate communication and thereby minimize misunderstandings among all parties. Furthermore, the anthropologist has access to the growing literature on cultural tourism, and is therefore in a unique position to infuse knowledge of what has worked (and failed) elsewhere. In short, the anthropological skills in both intercultural translation and comparativism are potentially useful, and may even prove critical to the success of projects designed by outsiders hoping to portray local traditions.

Douglass agreed to be the consultant to the Urnieta project but was not hired by the Los Angeles firm. He was never told specifically why, although it seems clear that either his potential employer or Urnieta or both abandoned the initiative. There is no theme park in Urnieta, nor, to Douglass's knowledge, one currently on the drawing board. Douglass obviously reconciled his personal and professional angst in agreeing to become consultant to the Urnieta project, which is not to say that his motives were altogether clear. At no point did he allay his low-key guilt over giving priority to a new commitment that would further undermine his ability to meet more longstanding ones. Personal financial gain was simply of no consequence in the decision. Nor did he view it as the opportunity to attain "insider" status and access with a view toward future publication in tourism research (although that would have been likely). To the contrary, at least over the short term, the commitment promised to compete with his writing agenda. In the final analysis, Douglass just could not stand the thought of being left standing on the platform as the Basques' next Guggenheim train left the station! In this regard, he was acting out the vulnerability likely shared by most anthropologists regarding "their people." Once it seems inevitable that they are destined to become the objects and agents of cultural tourism, the anthropologist can either become the scold (and thereby end up simply left out of the loop), or, if invited, leave at least some brushstrokes on the cultural portrait.

In expounding in detail the personal and professional reveries of one anthropologist tantalized by a possible consultancy, it is our purpose to underscore the inherent ad hoc nature of the decision process. The issues range from the personal to the professional; the practical to the ethical. Becoming a paid consultant to a cultural tourism project is far more than simply accepting part-time, value-neutral employment.

NOTES

1. At the 2002 annual meetings of the American Anthropological Association, there was a session entitled "Legacies in Performance: Historical Ritual and Cultural Commodification" devoted to critical analysis of events comparable to the *Alarde*.

2. Indeed, Greenwood himself in the pages of this same journal revisited his commodification of culture thesis and allowed that, while he was still right about tourism's "destructive force" regarding the *Alarde*, in Haiti "touristic voodoo and rural voodoo activities coexist without apparent conflict," while for Bermuda's Black Club tourism is "a positive force in cultural revitalization and development" (1982:27–28).

3. The Los Angeles connection was more than simply fortuitous, since configuration of one of the world's most notable tourist attractions—the Guggenheim Museum in nearby Bilbao—emanated from that Olympian source of global culture, the concepts and services of architect Frank Gehry. It was as if the authorities of the ambitious little Gipuzkoan community were engaging in sympathetic magic designed to catch lightning in a bottle for a second time.

4. The amount required of Bilbao as the project's original franchise fee.

5. There is also the relative success of the two texts themselves. Here we might comment that they share the fate of having been read extensively, but vary greatly in their respective readerships. Regarding Greenwood's thesis, Dennison Nash, in his textbook *Anthropology of Tourism*, notes that the catch phrase of "culture by the pound" aptly characterizes the concern over the commodification of culture that "now serves as an important point of articulation with anthropological, sociological and other theories" (1996:24). Outside of academic circles, however, it is largely ignored. The text remains untranslated from English and so remains inaccessible to the majority of the Basque public. Conversely, the Zulaika text is untranslated from the Spanish original, and is therefore little known within the largely Anglophone field of academic tourism studies. At the same time, *Crónica* was enormously controversial and attained bestseller status within both the Basque and Spanish reading publics. Readers interested in shorter versions of Zulaika's argument may consult his recent English-language articles (2001a, 2001b). Finally, both Greenwood and Zulaika experienced certain misgivings or second thoughts about their texts. In the epilogue to the 1989 reprinting of "Culture by the Pound," Greenwood admits that his analysis was informed disproportionately by "moral anguish" (1989:183). Similarly, although he had never predicted the Guggenheim's future, Zulaika has clearly been sobered by its success (2001a:12–13).

6. While it is beyond the scope of the present essay to address it, "Culture by the Pound" ignores extant critical historical documentation, privileges a single possible interpretation of the *Alarde*'s contemporary status over other, equally or more plausible ones, and fails completely as prognosis. The *Alarde* is not only alive and well, but subsequent to Greenwood's prediction of its immanent demise it has emerged as a prime context within which Basques contest political and gender issues.

7. Nor is the treatment of authenticity restricted to its preservation within a particular cultural context. Another canonical work in the anthropology of tourism, Dean MacCannell's *The Tourist*, examines the issues from the perspective of the guest's quest for a genuine or authentic experience (1999[1976]:91–108). Indeed, in his view, tourism is but one dimension of a dialectics of authenticity that transforms "material relations into symbolic expressions and back again, while continuing to differentiate or multiply structures" (MacCannell 1999[1976]:145). For criticism of such modernity framed as the individual's quest for personal authenticity, compare Berman 1982 and Taylor 1991. Bendix (1997) discusses the many ways in which authentication of authenticity is a prime concern of the humanities in general.

8. His services in this regard might have been more appropriate for another Basque tourism project: the transformation of the village of Zerain (again in Gipuzkoa) into a kind of Basque Jamestown, Virginia. Faced with depopulation and, particularly, a youth exodus, Zerain refurbished its "typical" dwellings, revamped a closed, centuries-old iron foundry, and revived several cottage industries. Villagers of a thriving if self-consciously anachronistic community, adorned in typical folk dress, now welcome the visitors who observe the actual manufacture of the many products offered for purchase (Garmendia Lasa 1997). But, then, quite tellingly, the residents of Zerain felt no need to retain an anthropological consultant for *their* project.

9. For the potential consulting anthropologist, there is a certain lesson to be learned from Douglass's negotiation with the Los Angeles firm. Initially, he fielded the invitation with all of the ambivalence informed by the anthropological angst we have already considered. His life experience in hotel–casino tourism did not in the least shield him from such misgivings. He dawdled over the value of his services and dithered regarding the specifics of his charge. This no doubt came across to his potential employer as an academic's unwarranted (and certainly unwanted) ambiguity. Clarity would have better served both parties in the negotiation.

10. For an anthropological example of this same viewpoint, compare Robert B. Textor's discussion of the positive role that he played in influencing the business ethics of the Motorola Corporation (2002).

REFERENCES CITED

Bendix, Regina
  1997 In Search of Authenticity: The Formation of Folklore Studies. Madison: University of Wisconsin Press.
Berman, Marshall
  1982 The Ethics of Authenticity. Cambridge, MA: Harvard University Press.
Bird, Jon
  1993 Dystopia on the Thames. *In* Mapping the Futures: Local Cultures, Global Change. Jon Bird, Barry Curtis, Tim Putnam, George Robertson, and Lisa Tickner, eds. Pp. 120–135. New York: Routledge.
Clifford, James
  1997 Routes: Travel and Translation in the Late Twentieth Century. Cambridge, MA: Harvard University Press.
Craik, Jennifer
  1997 The Culture of Tourism. *In* Touring Cultures: Transformations of Travel and Theory. Chris Rojek and John Urry, eds. Pp. 113–136. London: Routledge.
Crick, Malcolm
  1989 Representations of International Tourism in the Social Sciences: Sun, Sex, Sights, Savings, and Servility. Annual Review of Anthropology 18:307–344.
Douglass, William A.
  1969 Death in Murelaga. The Social Significance of Funerary Ritual in a Spanish Basque Village. Seattle: University of Washington Press.
  1975 Echalar and Murelaga: Opportunity and Rural Depopulation in Two Spanish Basque Villages. London: C. Hurst and Co.; New York: St. Martin's Press.
  2000 In Search of Juan de Oñate: Confessions of a Cryptoessentialist. Journal of Anthropological Research 56(2):137–165.

Elliot, Carl
    2002 Brief. London Review of Books 24(23):36–37.
Enloe, Cynthia
    1989 Bananas, Beaches and Bases: Making Feminist Sense of International Politics. London:
        Pandora.
Garmendia Lasa, Elixabete
    1997 Zerain (1975–1997): Herri baten berpiztea. Unpublished MS. Eusko Ikaskuntzako
        Jakitez Programa.
Greenwood, Davydd J.
    1982 Cultural "Authenticity." Cultural Survival Quarterly 6(3):27–28.
    1989 [1977] Culture by the Pound: An Anthropological Perspective on Tourism as Cultural
        Commoditization. *In* Hosts and Guests: The Anthropology of Tourism. 2nd edition.
        Valene L. Smith, ed. Pp. 171–185. Philadelphia: University of Pennsylvania Press.
Ioma, Kxao Moses, and Axel Thoma
    2002 Will Tourism Destroy San Cultures? Cultural Survival Quarterly 26(1):39–41.
Kurlansky, Mark
    1999 The Basque History of the World. Toronto: Alfred A. Knopf.
Lévi-Strauss, Claude
    1955 Tristes Tropiques. Paris: Plon.
MacCannell, Dean
    1999 [1976] The Tourist: A New Theory of the Leisure Class. Berkeley: University of
        California Press.
Mason, Amanda
    2002 Negotiating "The Enemy Within": Making Theory "Real" in Tourism Planning.
Mowforth, Martin, and Ian Munt
    1998 Tourism and Sustainability: New Tourism in the Third World. London: Routledge.
Nash, Dennison
    1996 Anthropology of Tourism. Oxford: Pergamon.
Pi-Sunyer, Oriol
    1982 The Cultural Costs of Tourism. Cultural Survival Quarterly 6(3):7–10.
Robertson, A. F.
    1987 The Dal Lake: Reflections on an Anthropological Consultancy in Kashmir. Anthropol-
        ogy Today 3(2):7–13.
Smith, M. Estellie
    1997 Hegemony and Elite Capital: The Tools of Tourism. *In* Tourism and Culture: An
        Applied Perspective. Erve Chambers, ed. Pp. 199–214. Albany: State University of
        New York.
Strouse, Jean
    1999 Morgan: American Financier. New York: Random House.
Taylor, Charles
    1991 The Ethics of Authenticity. Cambridge: Harvard University Press.
Textor, Robert B.
    2002 Anthropology and Business Ethics: A Pilot Experience. Anthropology News 43(9):14–15.
Trilling, Lionel
    1972 Sincerity and Authenticity. Cambridge: Harvard University Press.
Urry, John

1990 The Tourist Gaze: Leisure and Travel in Contemporary Societies. London, Newbury Park: Sage Publications.

Zulaika, Joseba

1997 Crónica de una seducción. Madrid: Editorial Nerea.

2001a Tough Beauty: Bilbao as Ruin, Architecture, and Allegory. *In* Iberian Cities. Joan Ramon Resina, ed. Pp. 1–17. New York and London: Routledge.

2001b Krens's Taj Mahal: The Guggenheim's Global Love Museum. Discourse 23(1):100–118.

AN ANTHRO-PLANNING APPROACH TO LOCAL
HERITAGE TOURISM: CASE STUDIES FROM
APPALACHIA

MARY B. LALONE
Radford University

This article argues for the use of an anthro-planning approach in local-level development projects, focusing here on its use in heritage tourism development. Anthro-planning is an approach that infuses anthropological perspectives and methods into planning projects. The article starts by discussing some guiding principles for an anthro-planning approach derived from the author's experiences in planning regional heritage tourism–education sites. The emphases are (1) taking a collaborative or partnership approach that actively seeks public participation in the planning process and (2) extensively incorporating anthropological field methods into the project design. The article then provides some concrete examples by showing how this approach was applied in planning two cultural heritage parks for an Appalachian Virginia region. One case documents the planning of an Appalachian coal-mining heritage park while the other example focuses on development of an Appalachian farm heritage museum and park. Key Words: tourism, heritage conservation, Appalachia, anthro-planning, applied anthropology

Public anthropology—with its focus on making anthropology actively accessible for public use—dates back to Margaret Mead, and applied anthropologists have been directing their efforts toward collaborative work with the public ever since Mead's time. As we reached the end of the 20th century, the American Anthropological Association newsletter promoted public, applied forms of anthropology as a central theme of action for the 21st century (e.g., Lassiter 2001). One way in which anthropologists can reach out to the public is by putting their training to work for the benefit of local-level planning. This article answers the question: "What contributions to public planning can come from

NAPA Bulletin 23, pp. 135–150, ISBN 1-931303-22-3. © 2005 by the American Anthropological Association. All rights reserved. Please direct all requests for permissions to photocopy or reproduce article content through the University of California Press's Rights and Permissions website, www.ucpress.edu/journals/rights.htm.

an infusion of anthropological perspectives and techniques into the planning process?" The paper will discuss the merger of anthropology and planning, or anthro-planning, and the benefits of this approach. Here, I demonstrate the use of an "anthro-planning approach" and its potential for work with local institutions and the public in developing heritage tourism. The paper first presents some guidelines that come out of an anthro-planning approach. It then provides examples of how this approach was put to work to guide the initial development of two heritage park projects in Appalachia.

AN ANTHRO-PLANNING APPROACH

A cornerstone of applied anthropology is its community-based orientation. This orientation guides the applied anthropologist to design projects that plan "with" and "for" people, groups, and communities. The development literature is filled with case studies of culture change in which development was done "to" people without their input or participation, and without sufficient study and forethought of what the development impacts might do to existing cultural patterns and needs. Taking guidance from these lessons, an applied anthropological style attempts to take a more collaborative orientation, designing projects so that people and groups within communities participate more directly in the planning process. This approach is in contrast to one in which the planner or developer sees himself or herself as the professional expert who requires minimal need for consultation with laymen in the target population during project planning. Practitioners who merge anthropology with planning—in what I will call anthro-planning—seek information, input, involvement, and expertise from within the local community whenever possible. They advocate taking a partnership approach toward work with community groups. They see their roles more as organizers of collaborative planning efforts and synthesizers of collaborative ideas (see LaLone 1997a, 2001a, 2003b, 2005; Schang 1997).

Anthropology provides a second contribution to the planning process through its well-developed techniques for studying human behavior. The skills of rapport building, observation, participant-observation, interviewing, and focus-group research can be applied profitably in many aspects of heritage tourism planning, as will be described in the Appalachian case studies that follow. This body of techniques from anthropology contributes significantly to an anthro-planning approach, since the techniques are tools that aid the practitioner in studying people's behavior so the behavioral knowledge can be used to plan "with" and "for" people.

This paper focuses on cases in which an anthro-planning approach has guided the research and initial design of local heritage parks. I use the term "heritage park" broadly here to refer to a site that, with planning, becomes a focal point for heritage-based activities including education and celebration. The tract of land usually brings together differing combinations of the following elements: signage that provides heritage education, a visitors' center or museum, outdoor performance areas, benches where visitors can rest and appreciate beautiful settings, paths or recreation trails, perhaps picnic areas and living-history reenactment areas, and visitor comfort facilities such as restrooms and water fountains. The heritage park site may be as large as a Civil War battlefield or as small as a farmhouse museum on a couple of acres. The size is not the defining characteristic; it is the designed way in which the heritage elements are brought together at the site to provide a planned visitor experience. Thus, the term "heritage park" encompasses parks and places that go by varying designations ranging from historic sites to living history museums.

The development of heritage parks requires studying the literature on both park landscape planning and museum planning, since it often merges the best of both to create a combined overall experience for the visitor. But heritage park planning is not simply about designing spaces, it is about understanding the behavior and desires of the *people* who will visit those spaces and the *people* who live nearby (the guests and hosts). Herein lie the strengths of an anthro-planning approach—it brings anthropology's techniques for studying human behavior and its people-inclusive development style to the forefront of the planning process. A successful research design will use anthropological techniques to study the social, economic, and political patterns and groupings within the target community or region, and then will apply that knowledge in ways that seek representative, participatory involvement from the public. A wise research design will not only compile the culture history data, but also will use anthropological perspectives and techniques to identify the varying ways that a region's history might be perceived by different groups within the region, and then will work to synthesize those views in the heritage interpretation (cf. LaLone 2003b). A wise design will use observation and participant-observation techniques to study visitor behaviors and responses at comparable heritage park facilities, and then will incorporate that behavioral knowledge into the planning process. An anthropologically guided research design will look to the public as a valuable resource for information, and will use citizen input and participation in developing the heritage plan.

Each heritage site will be planned around local specifications and regional needs, but an anthro-planning approach suggests certain principles that guide the practitioner's work. The practitioner infuses each project design with research that seeks understanding of the human behavior patterns of guests and hosts, and finds ways to incorporate the public as collaborators in the planning process. I have coordinated a number of local heritage projects over the past ten years, and have come to recognize patterns in the approach that I use to guide my research teams' work on heritage park planning. Some of the principles and activities that I try to incorporate into each project are:

- Establish a cooperative partnership with one or more groups within the community or region as the structural framework for running the project. These can be institutional groups (e.g., municipalities or universities) and allied, formal, or informal groups of citizens associated with heritages, ethnicity, occupations, age groups, interests, or hobbies. Although the specific combinations will vary with the nature of each project, the idea is to identify groups who might have an interest or a stake in the heritage project and link them together in a broad-based and inclusive approach toward planning the project. The partnership should be a relationship based on a sense of mutual assistance or reciprocity, with clear benefits for each of the participants in the joint effort. The anthro-planner is the central point of the framework, acting as a networker, liaison, coordinator, and synthesizer, pulling all the inputs into a total plan.
- Study the cultural history, often using ethnographic interviewing and oral history sources, in combination with written history and archaeological data. While the research process may parallel traditional anthropological research, the object and outcome of the research are intended for applied uses. This added dimension means that researchers must be mindful of their target audiences. Often people will also encounter heritage education as viewers and participants in an immersive heritage tourism experience, such as viewer-participants of living-history reenactments (e.g., Civil War re-enactors). For this type of planning, as I tell my student research teams, it is most helpful for planners "to place themselves into the heads of the viewer-participants," to try to imagine how they would react to the total experience, and then to use that perspective to further guide the historical research.

- Provide opportunities for citizens in the host community or region to learn about the project and have a seat at the table in the planning process. This can be accomplished by such activities as (1) focus group interviews and (2) community meetings where citizen input can be gathered and incorporated into the planning. It is important to listen to arguments and ask for citizen ideas for smoothing out potential problems. Anthropologists know from experience that interviews work best in familiar, comfortable settings. Similarly, planners are well advised to use these principles when setting up focus groups and local community meetings. The structure of the meeting should be non-hierarchical, friendly, and informal. It should foster the feeling that citizens are working "with" the planners in a real participatory process rather than being told how things will be planned. Surveys and questionnaires can also provide citizen input. My research teams apply the ideas generated from citizen input in a major way, using the community members' ideas and desires to guide the planning of features for the heritage parks. For example, in one project we learned through a community meeting that citizens considered nature education to be a needed feature in the park. Taking its cue from the citizens, the team expanded nature-based educational components from a minor into a major element in the plan (LaLone 2000a). Community involvement is critical for a successful project, because sometimes planners forget that the community members are the people who know the heritage and cultural context best.
- Search out people—laymen as well as professionals—with certain specialties who can serve as key resource people to give further advice to the research team (comparable to the key informants used by ethnographers). Most planning projects benefit from knowledge and skills drawn from multiple disciplines. The presence of key resource people provides an additional skill set, access to a broader knowledge base, and a potential source of volunteer labor from within the host region. It also generates goodwill through inclusiveness.
- Approach the project site as an anthropologist, using observation and participant-observation on site to guide the design process. I instruct my team members to "walk the site," placing themselves into the minds and footsteps of potential visitors. Through their participant experiences and by observing others, they find the best views, decide where benches are best sited for visitor fatigue and enjoyment, decide on needed signage, and so on. I ask them to design and map out a total visitor experience, starting where the patron will enter the site and creating a flow pattern guiding the visitor from feature to feature around the site. Similarly, when designing museums and structures, they map out a flow pattern within the building,

a technique I emphasize with my team so that they leave the drawing board behind and work out the project specifics on the ground.

- Study visitor behavior at comparable heritage parks, applying that behavioral knowledge extensively in the planning and design of the new project site. First, research teams study the literature on visitor or tourist behavior.[1] Research on museum visitor behavior has generated guidelines for preparing signage, including recommendations for effective visual layouts, the length of text, and the height and placement of signage. Then, I use comparable heritage facilities as learning models. As part of the research process, I locate heritage park facilities similar to whatever we are designing and use site visits as experiential learning tools. My teams visit these facilities in order to observe how visitors act in those settings, what features work positively, and what aspects hinder visitor pleasure. I ask them to do participant-observation, sitting on the benches, hiking the trails, and examining the vistas to learn through viewing and sensory participatory experience. Back at the planning table, I instruct them to apply what they have learned experientially as they develop our own heritage park design.

Offered as a few guidelines, these methodological suggestions emphasize the ways in which ethnographic data-gathering can be structured in planning a community-based, tourism development project. My experiences indicate that building community collaboration is essential to this process. Given their experience with working with both clients and subjects, applied anthropologists are well positioned to take the lead in this kind of work. In the next section, some case studies of my work will provide specific examples of how I have put these principles and techniques into practice.

CASE STUDIES FROM APPALACHIA

I have been involved in local heritage tourism planning in the Appalachian region of the United States since the early 1990s. My first project involved working with a coal-mining town to develop ideas for heritage tourism as an alternative economic base when the mines closed (LaLone 1997a). Later, my applied work focused on assisting localities in heritage park planning (LaLone 2000a, 2000b, 2001a, 2001b, 2003a). The following discussion provides two case studies in which I used the "anthro-planning approach" described above while guiding student research teams in undertaking planning for two heritage parks in a region known as the New River Valley, located in the Appalachian Mountains of Virginia. In these cases, the consulting teams were composed of students taking my applied anthropology class at Radford University. The consulting projects had a dual purpose: to assist the region with heritage park planning while simultaneously serving as vehicles for experiential student field-work training. Each team was motivated by the knowledge that they were en-gaged in real-life planning for heritage facilities that would actually be used by the public. They aimed for professional-quality work conducted within a four-month research period. Each project resulted in a substantial consulting report that contained recommendations for heritage park development, written by the team and submitted to the groups or institutions that commissioned the work.

Both of these examples involve local-level heritage projects in which the audience is envisioned as being drawn largely from the local communities and surrounding Appalachian region. The intent was to design sites for heritage interpretation, education, and celebration, primarily meeting the needs of targeted audiences within the region. This is heritage tourism on a local scale, targeting two groups in particular: (1) heritage-education buffs, people who are interested in seeking out destinations that offer heritage-education learning experiences, and (2) families whose roots go deep in their heritage, who seek out destinations that commemorate and celebrate key elements of their family heritage.

When planning projects at the local level, practitioners may be well advised to limit their etic use of the term "tourism," since it may not mesh well with local or emic sensibilities. In these two cases, the sponsoring municipal and university institutions were the clients who set the parameters of the project by specifying what they wanted in their heritage sites: (1) low-key, (2) low maintenance, (3) non-commercial, (4) educational and (5) small-scale promotion of the key elements of the site's heritage claims. To them, the idea of "tourism" was something to avoid because it conjured up visions of large crowds of "outsiders" who might do more damage than good to their heritage and nature facilities. This produced an interesting challenge for the research teams. Although our research and planning drew positively from tourism literature and models, we had to be careful to avoid using the dreaded T-word with our clients.

Case Study I: Coal Mining Heritage Park

Coal mining was once a principal way of life throughout the Appalachian Mountains. Although the mines have now closed in many regions, including the New River Valley, the community values of diligence, perseverance, and hard work associated with the mining culture are something people are working to keep alive. A citizen-based coal-mining heritage association formed in the New River Valley in 1994, and I had been working collaboratively with the group on a project to document and publish oral histories of miners and their families (LaLone 1997b, 1998, 1999). As the oral history project was coming to a close, we recognized that one former mine site, in particular, had great potential for development into a coal-mining heritage park.

The Merrimac Mine dated back to the Civil War, becoming famous for supplying coal to the ironclad Merrimac in its sea battle against the Monitor. Later, the Huckleberry Railroad line was routed alongside the Merrimac Mine to start the coal on its trip from the Appalachian region to the coastal ports of Virginia. The mine reached its height in the early 1900s, but then closed during the 1930s Depression years. In the 1990s, the abandoned site of the Merrimac Mine sat midway along a newly built recreational trail known as the Huckleberry Trail, which followed the former railroad line. As hikers and bikers passed through the site daily, they were unaware that it had played such a key role in mining history because no physical structures or markers stood to tell the story of the mines and the once-dynamic mining community that stood nearby. Montgomery County, Virginia, owned the thirty-acre site, and although there were no plans to use the site at the time, the county planning office became intrigued by my offer to have my applied anthropology class serve as an anthro-planning consulting team to investigate possibilities for developing it into a mining heritage park.

The first step was to create the collaborative framework for the project. In this case, I developed it as a four-way partnership that linked my team with the community coal-mining heritage association, the county planning office, and the state archaeologist for our region. We all met at Merrimac in April 1999 to walk the site, develop the spirit of collaboration, and begin discussing the activities my team would coordinate over a four-month period in the upcoming fall semester. Soon, the partnership was extended to include collaborative associations with the Merrimac church, local elementary schools, and a nearby retirement community that felt a special attachment to the Huckleberry Trail.

We had a substantial amount of cultural history material to use in developing the heritage education aspects of the park. This included two volumes of oral histories, a history of the Merrimac Mine, an archaeological survey of the site, and maps and photographs of the Merrimac Mine and surrounding community provided by mining families. In addition, the team benefited by closely working with members of the mining association who could describe the cultural landscape of the Merrimac site and the sights, sounds, and activities of families living in the mining community. For example, Fred Lawson, a former Merrimac miner, described the layout and contents of the miners' houses and gardens, and worked with a team member to develop recommendations for rebuilding and furnishing a typical miner's house as one park interpretive feature. The team used the cultural history material to develop ideas for a museum, reconstructed buildings, and other elements of the park focusing on heritage interpretation. As a way of tying these elements together, they developed a plan for a self-guided walking tour which guided the visitor in a circuit around the park, with heritage education signage to explain the way of life and specific points of interest in the mine industrial complex and the adjoining mining community.

Community involvement and participation were central to the planning process. Working in collaboration with county planner Meghan Dorsett, we combined anthropological and planning techniques to develop an anthro-planning course of action. We organized two community meetings at the Merrimac meeting hall for the purpose of gaining citizens' input. The meetings were held in a culturally appropriate style, using food, music, and ample opportunity to visit with neighbors—techniques which created a relaxed atmosphere. Participants then broke into three focus groups to brainstorm ideas for (1) heritage education, (2) trails and recreational features, and (3) facilities and amenities. As the group discussions got underway, people became quite involved in generating ideas, voicing their concerns, and then suggesting solutions to deal with the concerns.

As another technique for public input, we developed a short questionnaire based primarily on open-ended questions, asking residents what features they would like to see included in a heritage park plan. This was mailed to all local residents, including members of the mining association. The meetings and questionnaire gained public awareness for the project and created a community-based set of potential ideas for park planning. To our delight, the project became a magnet for community participation. Mining families, school teachers, senior citizens, railroad buffs, residents living near the proposed park, and Huckleberry Trail recreational users became involved in the effort. Many volunteered their services as key resource people, providing the team with further input on targeted topics.

The techniques of observation and participant-observation also played important roles in the planning process. Members of the research team made site visits to two existing heritage parks (Explore Park in Virginia and the Beckley Exhibition Coal Mine in West Virginia) to study how those destinations handled park layout, signage, outdoor exhibits, reconstructed buildings, amenities, and parking. They studied the ways that they, and other visitors, used these park elements, and incorporated that knowledge into their own park design. At Merrimac, they walked the site, using their experiential responses to the landscape to guide their recommendations for the placement of trails, picnic areas, performance areas, a playground, nature education areas, and other features. As a result, Merrimac's site for the parking lot was selected, in part, so that it would be out of the sight lines of visitors enjoying natural surroundings while walking on the park trails.

At the end of the four-month process, we produced a consulting report with recommendations for developing a Coal Mining Heritage Park that would offer visitors a heritage education experience along with facilities for nature education, recreation, and family entertainment (LaLone 2000a). The report presented:

- An overall design for the park layout and recommendations for phasing in its development;
- Recommendations for mining heritage education through a self-guided walking tour, signage, outdoor interpretive exhibits, a replicated miner's house, a mining museum and visitors' center, and heritage-based educational activities such as archaeology camps to foster public awareness of site and heritage preservation;
- Ideas for a system of low-impact trails and a recreation area that included picnic shelters, a playground constructed with a mining theme, and an open-air pavilion for staging entertainment events;
- Ideas for nature-based education, including signage and a nature education center; and,
- Discussion of facilities and amenities needed to make the park user-friendly, including restrooms, drinking fountains, trail benches, parking, security, and accessibility for disabled and elderly visitors.

Throughout the process, our anthro-planning team functioned in multiple roles. In addition to our research role, we often found ourselves acting as rapport-builders and liaisons, enabling communication to flow between the various interest groups and the municipal planning office. In the end, our most important role was probably that of synthesizer, taking all the ideas collected from the community and merging them with our own research to create a park design and set of recommendations.

The plan impressed the Montgomery County Board of Supervisors, which adopted the plan to create the Coal Mining Heritage Park at Merrimac. The park's dedication ceremony was held September 9, 2000. At that point, my role as director of the consulting team was over. I have, however, been able to maintain anthropological input in a new role, as a member of the county advisory committee for the park. The initial development of the park fell to the county planning office, with Meghan Dorsett transferring the plans into action as funds were acquired (Dorsett 2002). Some of the early actions that she set in motion included construction of a bridge linking parking to the major trail and recreation area, collaborative work with the school systems to establish the park as an official Globe site for nature education, and development of the walking tour. The county parks and recreation office is now taking over future development of the Coal Mining Heritage Park, which has gone from plan to reality.

Case Study II: Selu Farm Heritage Museum and Park

My second example of heritage park planning moves the focus from coal mining to another aspect of Appalachian cultural history: its farming heritage. The Selu Nature Conservancy lies in a beautiful mountain setting above a meandering river. Selu focuses on nature education and hosts conferences at its retreat center. Also at Selu, located just inside the conservancy entrance, are the archaeological remains of an Appalachian farm. From the mid–1990s, the desire had been to reconstruct the farmhouse to serve as a 1930s-period farm museum, but progress had been slow in getting the museum project off the ground. In spring 2001, my team took on the consulting assignment of developing a conceptual plan and set of initial recommendations for the farm museum as a way of helping the Radford University Foundation, owner of the conservancy property, jump-start this venture. For the framework of this project, my anthro-planning team joined with Ricky Cox, the person designated to become the museum's director, to form a partnership. We then extended the partnership into the broader community by seeking assistance from civic groups and local resource people as a key part of the planning process (e.g., the American Legion, local retiree organizations, and interested individuals).

Originally, we were asked to examine possibilities for reconstructing the main farmhouse building to serve as a living-history museum. I broadened the project's scope beyond the farmhouse to cover the wider farmstead with its outbuildings and fields, and asked the team to investigate possibilities for a small heritage park containing the farmhouse museum plus a number of other visitor features. My strategy was to have the team develop a holistic design for a full heritage park visitor experience. The experience begins when the visitor leaves the parking lot and enters a visitors' center to receive initial information. The visitor then takes a walking tour around the farmstead, visiting the farmhouse museum, stopping at barns and other outbuildings, visiting the garden and fields, sitting down to relax at key vantage points, reading the interpretive signage along the way, and finally taking a trail that loops back to the visitors' center and parking lot.

One of the team members' first activities was to walk the Selu site, mentally placing themselves in the minds and bodies of potential visitors. Using participant-observation and observation of their colleagues' behaviors as primary design tools, the team mapped out a directed flow pattern that carried visitors from feature to feature around the site. Once again the team was guided by observing sight lines, recommending that the parking area and visitors' center be located out of sight of the farmstead in order to enhance the perception that visitors were stepping back in time, experiencing the farm as it was in the 1930s.

Oral histories and site archaeological data helped generate information about the farm and outbuildings and to suggest potential living-history re-enactment activities for the museum. Part of the team worked on generating ideas for the farmhouse museum, including its furnishings, exhibits, storage, and staff areas. Oral history interviews with people who lived in the farmhouse, and who could describe it and the farm life in the 1930s, provided much of the data used to develop ideas for the interior furnishings and exhibits. Ray Dickerson, who grew up on the 1930s farm, served as a special resource person. Using his memories and the archaeological data, we were able to locate the outbuildings, garden, hog pens, and fields, so that these could be included in the heritage interpretation of the entire farmstead. A geology team, Kim Knight and Julie Gilfus, then helped us transfer our plans into a map for the heritage park site.

We employed focus group interviews, developed a community questionnaire, and obtained the guidance of special resource people. These helped us tailor our project and guided us in obtaining community input and participation in the planning process. We developed a questionnaire to determine what features potential visitors would like to see at the heritage site. This was administered to sectors of the university and civic communities. Focus group interviews held with members of the local chapter of the American

Legion provided suggestions for amenities, heritage interpretative exhibits, and festivals. A school principal, a fire and rescue worker, a planner, and museum directors served as key resource people, providing additional input on issues of school involvement, safety, and museum planning. We also conducted research to identify likely visitor groups to target for educational marketing, plus civic groups that might assist and enjoy involvement through a volunteer staffing program. In team brainstorming sessions, we brought together all of the community members' suggestions and synthesized them into a set of recommendations for potential heritage interpretation activities and festivals.

As part of the planning process, team members made field visits to three living-history museums in Virginia to study models for living-history designs (this included the Frontier Culture Museum, Historic Crab Orchard and Pioneer Park, and the Settlers Museum of Southwest Virginia, as well as discussion of other models such as Williamsburg, Virginia). They learned from walking those sites and observing visitor behavior. They received advice from museum specialists on topics ranging from interpretation to the design of museum storage facilities. The team then applied all of these collective experiences, ideas, and considerations toward developing a plan for the museum and park. We prepared a consulting report (LaLone 2001b) for the university foundation containing a set of recommendations on the following topics:

- A plan for the full museum site, including the spatial layout of the site, outdoor exhibits and structures, a visitor orientation center, trails and benches, a self-guided tour, interpretive signage, and parking;
- Plans for replicating the original farmhouse to use as the main museum building, including recommendations for the organization of space and exhibits both within the museum farmhouse and in the outbuildings, and ideas for exhibits, interpretive activities, and staffing needs;
- Recommendations for necessary museum facilities, including restrooms, drinking fountains, and other conveniences that visitors require, as well as collection storage facilities, accessibility for the disabled and elderly, site maintenance, and security.

Our plan was received with enthusiasm, and the heritage site was officially named The Farm at Selu. Although my consulting role was over at that point, I was offered a place on the Selu Conservancy advisory board, which will allow me to continue providing anthropological input over the long run. The job of putting the plan into action has now fallen to Ricky Cox as museum director. The foundation acquired a grant for the farmhouse reconstruction, and building started in 2002.

Project Recommendations

These two projects focused on using an anthro-planning approach to develop the initial conceptual ideas and recommendations for heritage park layout, content, and design, as described above. We also conducted analyses of regional accommodations during our team planning. We felt that with two university towns in the region and the rapid growth in commercial and highway development taking place in the New River Valley, the hotel and restaurant infrastructure is already in place to handle visitors drawn from outside the region for heritage education experiences and to attend festivals at the two heritage sites. In both cases, we addressed marketing in a small way by recommending that the sites develop heritage park pamphlets that not only serve to guide visitors around the sites but can be carried away and passed on to others, generating publicity through word-of-mouth networks and targeted distribution.[2] These recommendations align with the parks' mission statements, which place primary emphasis on developing heritage and recreational attractions for local and regional audiences. In other words, these parks are designed for visitors who want locally accessible getaway experiences on weekends and vacations that allow them to relax, learn, and celebrate the Appalachian mining and farming ways of life.

CONCLUSION

Many practitioners will find themselves working with localities and regions on tourism and other planning ventures. The case studies from Appalachia and the guidelines presented here demonstrate the value of blending anthropological techniques and perspectives into the planning process to form an anthro-planning approach. The strengths of an anthro-planning approach, as shown in these cases of heritage tourism, are twofold: (1) the design ideas are derived heavily from the use of anthropological techniques to study human behavior in heritage tourism contexts, and (2) the approach emphasizes seeking out multiple forms of collaboration with the public to plan attractions intended for public use and enjoyment. The inclusion of community members in the planning process gives the public a voice and a stake in the development and success of local-level projects such as those involving heritage tourism. The Coal Mining Heritage Park and The Farm at Selu projects demonstrate how anthropologists can contribute to community-based heritage tourism projects that are planned "with" and "for" local populations.

NOTES

1. I find the museum studies literature on visitor behavior and fatigue to be particularly instructive.
2. I limited the scope to exclude marketing studies so that it would be feasible for the student consulting teams to produce their reports within the confines of a four-month semester class.

REFERENCES CITED

Dorsett, Meghan
    2002 Coal Mining Heritage Park. Montgomery County, VA: Department of Planning and Inspections. Electronic document, http://gis.montva.com/departments/plan/cmhp/cmhp.html.
LaLone, Mary B.
    1997a The Appalachia Tourism Project: Applied Anthropology in an Appalachian Coal Mining Town. In Practicing Anthropology in the South. James M. Tim Wallace, ed. Pp. 91–101. Athens: University of Georgia Press.
    1997b Appalachian Coal Mining Memories: Life in Virginia's New River Valley Coal Fields. Blacksburg, VA: Pocahontas Press.
    1998 Coal Mining Lives: An Oral History Sequel to Appalachian Coal Mining Memories. Radford, VA: Dept. of Sociology and Anthropology, Radford University.
    1999 Preserving Appalachian Heritage: A Model for Oral History Research and Teaching. Journal of Appalachian Studies 5(1):115–119.
    2000a Coal Mining Heritage Park, Montgomery County, Virginia: Study, Plan, and Recommendations. Report prepared for the Montgomery County Planning Office and the Coal Mining Heritage Association of Montgomery County. Radford, VA: Dept. of Sociology and Anthropology, Radford University. Electronic document published by Montgomery County, Virginia, http://gis.montva.com/departments/plan/cmhp/rucmhp/rutoc.html.
    2000b Wildwood Park: Nature, Heritage, and Planning Ideas. Report prepared for Pathways for Radford. Radford, VA: Dept. of Sociology and Anthropology, Radford University.
    2001a Putting Anthropology To Work To Preserve Appalachian Heritage. Practicing Anthropology 23(2):5–9.
    2001b The Selu Living History Museum: Recommendations for An Appalachian Heritage Education Center. Report prepared for the Radford University Foundation. Radford, VA: Dept. of Sociology and Anthropology, Radford University.
    2003a Farm Heritage and Community Park: Conceptual Plans and Ideas. Report prepared for the Montgomery County Parks and Recreation Office. Radford, VA: Dept of Sociology

and Anthropology, Radford University. Electronic document, http://www.radford. edu/~mlalone/NRVFarmHeritageParkProj.htm.

2003b Walking the Line Between Alternative Interpretations in Heritage Education and Tourism: A Demonstration of the Complexities with an Appalachian Coal Mining Example. *In* Signifying Serpents and Mardi Gras Runners: Representing Identity in Selected Souths. Celeste Ray and Luke Eric Lassiter, eds. Pp. 72–92. Athens: University of Georgia Press.

2005 Building Heritage Partnerships: Working Together for Heritage Preservation, Education, and Local Tourism in Appalachia. Paper presented at the Annual Meeting of the Society for Applied Anthropology, Santa Fe, April 8.

Lassiter, Luke Eric

2001 Engaging a Localized Public Anthropology. Anthropology News 42(2):7–8.

Schang, Sloan

1997 The Anthro-Planner: A Resource Guide Dedicated to the Successful Integration of Anthropological Methodology into the Urban and Regional Planning Process. Electronic document, http://www.geocities.com/Athens/Delphi/8651/index.html, accessed February 15.

APPLIED ANTHROPOLOGY AND HERITAGE TOURISM PLANNING: WORKING FOR THE WESTERN ERIE CANAL HERITAGE CORRIDOR PLANNING COMMISSION

AMANDA MASON
Western Erie Canal Heritage Corridor Planning Commission

Using a case study approach, this article demonstrates how applied anthropological research can be used in heritage tourism planning, specifically in regions designated by state or federal government as "heritage areas." The participatory nature of ethnographic research not only identifies the ideas, perspectives, and needs that are vital to an effective heritage tourism plan, it also brings together the individuals and agencies that will become actively involved in the implementation of the plan. This reduces the distinction between the phases of planning and acting and promotes ownership and involvement in the tourism strategy. Because of this, both the ethnographic research process and the data it generates are complimentary components of community-based tourism planning. Also discussed are some common issues that arise in heritage tourism planning, such as conflicting stakeholder desires for resources, community frustration or exhaustion with the planning process, and mixed definitions of the concept of "heritage." Key Words: tourism, applied anthropology, community-based planning, heritage, ethnography

INTRODUCTION

As an applied anthropologist working in heritage tourism development, I focus my research on the central goal of creating a regional tourism plan for a five-county area recently designated as a "heritage corridor." The tourism I am striving to generate should preserve heritage resources, benefit the local economy, serve resident needs, and avoid marginalization. Before the region can be

NAPA Bulletin 23, pp. 151–169, ISBN 1-931303-22-3. © 2005 by the American Anthropological Association. All rights reserved. Please direct all requests for permissions to photocopy or reproduce article content through the University of California Press's Rights and Permissions website, www.ucpress.edu/journals/rights.htm.

marketed to visitors, there needs to be local support, community pride, and a desire for tourism. The region must also have sufficient services, sites, and infrastructure, all of which should be developed not solely to support tourists, but also to improve local quality of life.

To accomplish this, I believe, it is first essential to establish appropriate resource management practices that transform resources into economically beneficial tourist attractions while preserving the heritage of the community, a heritage that is authentic and inclusive and a source of pride for local residents. A meaningful strategy for making the region tourist-ready must stem from an understanding of how resources are currently being used, defined, and managed. They must include the use of formerly untapped resources. Collaborative partnerships that are developed during the planning process are essential for implementing a coherent management plan. Ethnography is an incredibly valuable tool in determining contemporary uses and perceptions, making it a necessary first step for reaching the end goal of successful community-based and community-enhancing tourism. I have found, in addition, that the participatory nature of ethnographic methods and the anthropological understanding

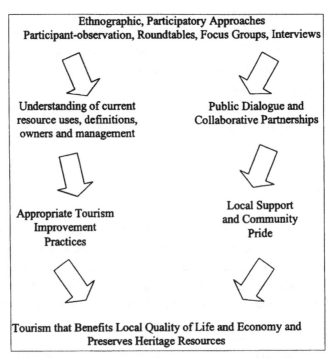

FIGURE 1.

of group dynamics are conducive to forming and maintaining needed partnerships.

There is much to be considered in regional tourism planning: notably, what types of tourism to plan, for what purpose, using what and whose resources, and with what type of management. For anthropologists in particular, each of these broad topics opens a Pandora's box of many more questions—questions concerning how to ensure that tourism is equitable, sustainable, and has a positive impact on the "host" community (Newby 1994). Tourism's impacts on culture, on the individual, or on the natural and cultural resources that are the collective property of future generations are all put into question. Successful anthropological research can avoid potential pitfalls by developing meaningful resource-management strategies that value the hopes and needs of local residents and prepare the groundwork for community-enhancing initiatives that will also serve as the basis for tourist attractions.

Both tourism researchers and anthropologists offer strategies for tourism development while highlighting the negatives associated with tourism in general. Tourism researchers work to define tourists and tourism types, marketing strategies, and destination management, and have recently been exploring community-based tourism development. Anthropologists have made contributions to the understanding of tourism's impact on the host community, the impact of travel on an individual, the power relationships in tourism developments, heritage and culture commodification, and a disregard for problems over authenticity and the ownership and interpretation of the past (Howell 1994). The challenge for those working in applied heritage tourism planning and development is to find the means to utilize tourism industry development strategies while being mindful of anthropological critiques of those strategies. This is particularly challenging since a large gap exists between those who do research and those working in the tourism industry. Indeed, the majority of working tourism planners I have met have no specific training or background in tourism as an academic field; rather, they usually have a sales and marketing focus. Although many of them recognize the need for change—that is, the need for stronger community involvement and regional cooperation, and a lessening of negative impacts on the environment or host culture—it is often not within their experience to tackle these issues.

In tourism development, anthropologists draw upon an existing body of theories and methods. With heritage tourism, for instance, studies discussing the tourist's desire for meaning or authenticity offered by MacCannell (1976) and Cameron (1998) provide useful insight. Having familiarity with and access to this knowledge base allows anthropologists to contextualize the efforts of the initiatives they themselves are working on. This context may be shared with both policy-makers and our co-workers, and its direct effects are perhaps best seen when it allows us to better understand and communicate with the tourists themselves. We can also make full use of our ability to come from an etic perspective, identifying interest groups as cultures, recognizing beliefs held by various stakeholders, and realizing how each group's beliefs, values, and behaviors affect its ability to communicate with other groups, especially as they value or ignore one another's input. The anthropologist must then rise to the challenge of taking these observations to a functional level by facilitating a dialogue between these groups.

I should point out that many of these roles are not specific to tourism, especially that of the facilitator. Rather, they seem common enough for all anthropologists who work in policy development, including planning and corporate or nonprofit management. Tourism development requires resource management, and those resources must be identified and assessed before policies can be developed for their future treatment. Nothing about this is simple. The first task—identifying tourism resources—is difficult because of the numerous resource types: natural, cultural, recreational, and historical, just to name a few. Practically everything becomes a potential or current tourism resource. The second task, assessing the resources, means determining current use, handling, and ownership, as well as past and anticipated or planned uses. The final task, determining policies for future treatment, requires perhaps the most work. The anthropologist must ask: Who is developing them? For what end? What principles or guidelines are contemplated? And with what authority, funding, or management will such policies be carried out? Almost always, a tourism resource will have multiple potential applications. Inevitably, different elements in the tourism industry will be in competition for that resource. An anthropologist can identify these conflicting demands, the groups that drive them, and the values behind the stakeholders, and use this perspective to help achieve balance among contending groups for resources.

CASE STUDY: APPLYING ANTHROPOLOGY ON THE ERIE CANAL

I work for a politically appointed planning commission composed of 18 members, all of whom are volunteers. The commission's purpose is to develop a management plan for The Western Erie Canal Heritage Corridor (WECHC).

FIGURE 2. Lift Bridge 5 over the Erie Canal in Fairport, New York.

This is a new, state-designated heritage area comprised of five western New York counties that were rapidly settled in the early part of the 19th century when the historic canal was an active commercial waterway. Since this canal was once the generator of economic development and social movements and ideas, it is seen as having the potential to do so again, but only through regional collaboration. Perhaps because it is particularly fitting in our situation, a common phrase at public meetings is "a rising tide lifts all boats." The planning commission hosts the meetings in order to gather together stakeholders from the five counties. My job is to locate, recruit, and facilitate a dialogue among these groups, in order to determine needs, issues, and current efforts, as well as to build a constituency.

I was hired shortly after the creation of the commission, so my first task was to understand the commission members' perspectives on a heritage corridor, what they wanted the project to accomplish, and what they felt were the regional needs of residents along the canal. At the same time, it was necessary to start educating the commission and staff, myself included, about other heritage areas, and about the New York state program in particular. In addition to doing some background research into existing heritage areas, I contracted the services of a practicing anthropologist,[1] a specialist in facilitation and business development, to program a retreat for the commission members. The goals of this first gathering were to provide an initial introduction between commission members and the project staff and to begin a visioning exercise for the heritage area. We also invited the members of a group of interested stakeholders working in the fields of tourism, heritage preservation, planning, and local politics who were responsible for establishing the heritage corridor.

A central theme from this retreat was that the heritage corridor should be used for regional revitalization. Economic development was the top priority for the group, or, as one participant put it, "to find a 21st century use for a 19th century creation." They felt this could happen by increasing tourism in the communities along the canal, rehabilitating and filling the key vacant buildings in the heart of the historic communities, finishing the recreational trail that parallels the canal, increasing boating use, and communicating the canal's significance to the region and the rest of the nation. Another theme that surfaced very clearly was that everyone in the room had been involved in a canal-focused revitalization project at least once before, and they were very determined to see concrete results from this effort. A few commissioners did not see the need for any additional planning or research, since what needed to happen was clear to them. Still, most agreed that a regional strategy had yet to be developed, and regional cooperation was seen as integral to getting enough political support to implement projects. It was also recognized as being important for "telling the whole story" of the western portion of the canal, and for offering a sufficient concentration of services to make the corridor a tourist destination.

Convinced the reason previous revitalization efforts had failed was due to a lack of community support, the commission's next step was to determine how to involve the public meaningfully in the planning process and to devise a method that would be different from earlier attempts to develop or revitalize the canal. On the one hand, this type of planning was intended to build partnerships for achieving the goals of the plan, and on the other, it would also uncover marginalized canal uses, heritage values, and needs. To accomplish this, we started a press campaign to get the word out that the area had been designated a heritage corridor, and began hosting open community meetings about the commission and its goals. We hosted one introductory meeting in each of the five counties in the corridor, and, at these, asked attendees to join a regional "task force" concerning one of five themes—recreation, education and interpretation, business development, revitalization, and tourism. Over the next four months, task-force meetings were held throughout the region, each bringing new participants together and producing lengthy lists of needs and ideas for improvements of the heritage corridor. To avoid any potential gaps between members of the planning commission and the residents and stakeholders, commissioners were always invited to these meetings, and often were asked to chair or facilitate them. I learned early on that no matter how accurate the data, if the commission does not feel involved, its relevance is minimal. For example, during four months worth of community meetings, we brought together over four hundred residents. However, despite frequent invitations to be in attendance, planning commissioners attended only two of the meetings. The commissioners' lack of involvement prevented them from fully understanding what was accomplished.

In retrospect, an additional problem with these meetings was that the commission and staff, myself included, were so focused on generating program ideas and defining needs that we failed to determine how all these things might be accomplished. In other words, we did not determine who would do all this work and how it would be funded. While these task force meetings were being held, we continued to hold commission meetings, also attended by members of the community, exposing the commission members to the variety and complexity of public interests in the corridor. This led them to request a "contemporary snap shot" of canal uses and interests in the region—what an applied anthropologist might call a rapid ethnographic assessment (Beebe 2001:xvi). To accomplish this, I set up a summer ethnographic research project, staffed by three anthropology student interns[2] whose job it was to understand current users and owners of the Erie Canal and its adjacent communities as identified by the legislation and the planning commission as potential heritage and recreational tourism resources.

A weakness of the task forces was that they were only comprised of people willing to attend meetings, so we doubted they were representative of all the issues and perspectives of residents, and they certainly did not involve any visitors to the region. For this reason, we decided anthropology could help, not only by observing canal users, but also by conducting conversational interviews with these users in a natural setting. Observational and analytical skills gained through anthropological training have helped with an understanding of the differences and similarities in these groups' concerns, focus, and cultures.

Much of our work entailed basic ethnographic methods of systematic participant-observation and multiple styles of interviewing. Our subjects were boaters, shop owners, tourists, cyclists, walkers, and others. The recreation task force had made it clear that boating was one of several recreational uses for the canal, but exactly how many other users there were, and which uses were more popular than others, was of interest. The interns and I also spent substantial time watching canal use, noting the numbers and types of trail and water users, talking to people in the canal-side parks, on the trail, and in boats. We conducted participant-observation in public parks and on the path along the canal, documenting canal uses. In addition, we experienced the tour activities available along the canal: hiking, jogging, biking, kayaking, canoeing, and taking boat cruises. We also worked with grassroots trail, heritage,

FIGURE 3. A historians' focus group at work on Erie Canal Heritage Corridor planning.

and community groups and sat in on government committee or commission meetings.

In addition to the what we recovered from the above activities, the ethnographic data generated by the conversational interviews and observations proved to be very useful information for marketing as well as determining potential developments of canal resources, such as improving the historic interpretation of certain sites, creating boat docks, canoe launches, and improving the Erie Canalway trail and adjacent parks. Observations of the canal, trail, and adjacent lands revealed that land-based uses were dominant in all of the key heritage sites, despite a policy and resource-management focus on water-based uses. Our observations showed that Erie Canal and adjacent trail or land use is heaviest in areas visible from homes, offices, services, and roadside parking. We believe this predominance is in some measure due to a lack of coordinated information about boating permits, docking and tie-ups, trail rules and access points, security, and accommodations. Most people, including visitors, rely on past experience or chance and do limited trip planning, as they have difficulty finding centralized information sources. When the interns showed tourists a few of the many tourism brochures and maps created by communities and travel agencies, people were impressed that such material even existed, but also noted, as one visitor put it, that "none of this stuff fits together." Some of the tourists we interviewed were frustrated by unpredictability of canal water travel and the lack of community coordination in providing adequate, quality services and accommodations. On the other hand, some tourists found the uneven level of services a welcome challenge that heightened the authenticity of their experience of the Canalway. Overall, however, conversational interviews conducted during these observations with tourists and regional residents suggested a need for improved access and distribution of information about available canal recreation, history, and contemporary ownership.

The team also decided a complement to the conversational interview and task force material was needed. Focus groups were used to clarify the list of issues and needs and to address three additional topics that no task force had been set up for: water quality, neighborhood, and agriculture. Both in focus-group interviews and on-site conversations, residents of the region had displayed concern for the water quality in the canal. In addition, members of local neighborhood groups felt the canal played a unique role in communities as a shared public space that has replaced the traditional function of a town center. The Canalway trail and adjacent parks are places to visit with neighbors and solidify community ties. Perhaps more than any other groups in the region, agriculturalists possessed strong heritage connections between their family land, ancestors, and the Erie Canal. It was the canal that brought their great-grandparents here, and the canal also shipped the products of their farms to markets worldwide. While the waterway has long been replaced by railroad and highway for transportation, it is still used to irrigate crops by many of the farmers adjacent to the canal. Discussions of contemporary irrigation use led farmers to indicate concern about a public trail running alongside their crops; they worried that their irrigation hoses and pumps might be damaged. There was also concern about liability among farmers who worried that the trail would bring trespassers who might be injured or exposed to chemicals during crop spraying.

Seven focus-group interviews were held to further explore the list of issues and to address the three additional topics that had no designated task force. The result of this work provided the commission with its request—a snap shot of canal activities, a set of regional concerns and desires, and an understanding of the visitors' perspective of the region. As the planning moves into more specific projects and locations, focus groups will remain an ongoing way both to gather information and to foster community involvement. Canal "buffs"—recreation and historian focused alike—are extremely proud of the canal and aware of its importance and benefit to the surrounding community, past, present, and future. Even the casual canal user often commented on its quiet and relaxing nature, and almost everyone enjoyed watching lock or lift-bridge operation and boats. A common sentiment among our interviewees was that even greater efforts needed to be undertaken to make the canal corridor an attractive destination for tourists, including canal bank improvements, trail development, signage, service creation, promotion, and historical studies. Residents and tourists that were aware of the canal's past, and current users, often regreted that more people did not share their enthusiasm, and felt that this could and should be changed. In addition, it is important to note that natural and cultural resource preservationists alike were hopeful that sustainable development would take place once people were educated about the importance of the canal, and that the tourism potential of these resources would also help protect them.

Common knowledge of the canal history is very limited. Historians involved with the planning commission and its staff suggest a lot of work be done in this area, including determining what is out there (documents, artifacts, surveying, etc.), making the information accessible to researchers, expanding interpretation, and tying multiple types of information to the canal—social, historic, geographic, geological, engineering, and economic, to name a few. The interpretation meetings that have been held have produced significant results, and regional, cultural, and historic associations are hopeful that these meetings will continue and expand.

Heritage tourism is an important and hoped-for source of economic development that, in some areas, has turned heritage interpretation into a political struggle for recognition. For instance, the cities of Buffalo and Tonawanda continue to argue over which one should be considered the official terminus of the Erie Canal. Originally, the canal ended in Buffalo; however, during intervening years of non-use, the city filled the canal in, making Tonawanda the present-day terminus of the active waterway. However, both communities adamantly maintain that they are the terminus, and feel the need to be recognized and publicized as such. This type of scenario has happened in other cases of heritage development, where competition has attempted to influence and perhaps jeopardize heritage interpretation (Turnbridge 1994). Other types of development, including housing, industry, and service-based entities are possible, and frequently mentioned by developers, planners, and residents. Promotion, consistency, and cooperation are essential to these activities. The constraints on development are linked with many difficult, inter-related, and perhaps unavoidable factors, including (1) the difficulty in obtaining building permits, (2) brownfields, (3) the fear that the canal's popularity is a trend that may end, and (4) the desire to bring in jobs and dollars without destroying

FIGURE 4. The Niagara Locks on the Erie Canal.

historic or natural resources. The creation of Local Waterfront Redevelopment Plans in many corridor communities is already addressing these needs; however, the need for a regional strategy is strongly advised. Our ethnographic research addressed these issues, and from the data of that research, the following recommendations were made to the Western Erie Canal Heritage Planning Commission (WECHPC):

- Expand and improve canal heritage interpretations;
- Continue discussions with residents, municipalities, and developers concerning site uses, community needs, waterfront standards, zoning, and smart growth;
- Promote "buy local" produce efforts and link agriculture to tourism;
- Conduct a regional marketing study;
- Ensure a unified, regional strategy for preservation and restoration of structures with a variety of tactics;
- Provide a broader view of how the resources work together;
- Make recreational information about the canal, trail, rentals, services, and clubs or organizations readily available and accessible;

- Promote the canal with local advertising to improve resident knowledge and use of the canal; and
- Have the WECHPC host a tourist–historian summit to improve communication between these two essential communities.

DEFINING A HERITAGE CORRIDOR

Despite its focus on "heritage resources," the heritage area's enabling legislation does not provide a definition of "heritage." The planning commissioners, stakeholder groups, and indeed everyone involved in this planning process created their own definitions of the term. During the beginning phases of our work, this did not seem problematic to my coworkers, but as a result of my anthropological perspective, I felt it was essential to ask how people defined their heritage, and what relationship the canal had to their heritage. I began some research to determine the feasibility of finding a shared definition. In many of our retreats, meetings, conversations, surveys, and focus groups the term *heritage* is usually treated as another term for *history*. Therefore, discussions about addressing one of the program's goals—interpretation—have focused on *historic interpretation*. Commissioners are facing economic decline in industry, jobs, and population. They try to equate heritage with "connecting residents to their past," "giving them a reason to stay," and, essentially, instilling a "pride of place" and familiarity with regional assets. I find it challenging to get those involved in the planning process to recognize the different ways they are using *heritage* as a concept. The participation of the residents in identifying their concept of heritage is an essential part of establishing policies and setting goals and principles (Herbert 1995). This task offers a strong role for anthropological skills in applied work, but also calls for academic attention to heritage as worthy of study.

One of the reasons anthropologists can recognize, study, and communicate these heritage definitions is because of our ability to contextualize our work within a larger framework. For instance, a definition of heritage would also assist in understanding the motivations for establishing a heritage area and its potential relation to public memory. Determining what defines a "heritage corridor site" will assist in defining its goals and its focus. Many of these site locations have suffered a rapid loss of industry and jobs. The Erie Canal Corridor area is located in what is referred to as the "rust belt." At a recent national conference featuring presentations from federal and state heritage areas, one speaker half-joked that when members of the community with which he was working realized that their former industries were dead and would now become themes for a heritage area, they were quite upset. "They were even more upset when they found out the new economic development strategy was to create a museum," he said. "Then they really thought their area was lost." We all must recognize that heritage tourism development in places like those in the "rust-belt" can only be one part of a larger program of economic development. When heritage tourism development is the main strategy, the effect is like placing a Band-Aid over a deep, festering sore (Boniface 1993).

Since heritage corridors are often placed in areas suffering from economic downturns, anthropologists as well as historians are faced with interesting questions concerned with public memory. If the heritage corridors currently sanctioned by the state and federal governments are in locations in need of economic development, will our public memory be focused on a loss of industry, environmental damage, and economic downturn? Will heritage corridors be increasingly used as an economic development strategy? Indeed, the participants at the conference mentioned earlier began to recognize patterns in their interpretive themes, such as the rise and fall of industry, agriculture, and labor movements. This realization had the presenters joking that they all must have hired the same consultants. The similarities in the descriptions and current experiences among the heritage areas also made them joke that perhaps they should consider adding the creation of a heritage corridor as a historic moment in their interpretive programs' storyline.

Inquiries into the use of heritage area designations suggest that these designations, while often criticized as being intended solely to develop a tourist destination, are missing the mark. Based on interviews and public sessions in this region, and explorations of the use of the term "heritage," it has become clear that residents also can and should benefit from this designation. For instance, in my experiences with the planning commission, the very act of planning, as orchestrated by the commission, brought together community stakeholders quite beneficially. Meetings, idea sharing, and networking were a part of the planning process. Therefore, tangible benefits resulted merely from the designations themselves and from the dialogue required either to receive the designation or to maintain it. (There are potential additional benefits that living within a heritage corridor might provide to community residents that are beyond the scope of my experience with the planning commission. These include improved recreational trails, roads, museums, and so forth. Further discussion of these are beyond the scope of this paper.) To achieve these immediate benefits in my work with the planning commission, I encouraged the commission to focus on ways in which the heritage resources of the area might be capable of serving multiple public needs in areas such as education, economics, and recreation.

Surveys and ethnographic methods employed in the area have helped determine how the resources are currently used and what suggestions both the users and resource managers have for their enhancement. Some exploratory data has shown that functional aspects of the resources—that is, the buildings, the canal, and the recreational trail—are of the most interest, especially to residents. The heritage, or history, is secondary. Learning about the past would add value to the experience of boating, cycling, or walking on the canal. In the case of one village, the heritage theme concept of the canal makes shopping, dining, living, or working in that space more interesting. This practice of "naming" streets, parks, and businesses after the canal also seems to help residents connect with their heritage by distinguishing the village from other places.

DEVELOPING SUSTAINABLE NETWORKS

Sustainability of planned initiatives is a heavily discussed topic in all kinds of planning fields, including tourism (Cogswell 1986; Garrod 1999; Murphy 1985). With the creation of this state heritage corridor comes an opportunity for regional initiatives. However, the existing overlap in resource management responsibility among local, county, and state planning offices, government agencies, and nonprofit organizations is confusing, blurring responsibility lines and hindering action from all of these groups. The majority of participants involved in the heritage area planning have been involved with canal resource plans in the past, and several are skeptical of the ability of any agency to implement a regional plan. Despite this skepticism, the WECHC Planning Commission has made significant contacts with heritage resource stakeholders during its first two years of work, and many of the suggestions given to the planning commission have already been acted upon. We have made frequent outreach to stakeholders; we have collected local and county planning documents, and have held scoping sessions with government agencies. Additionally, I and my group of ethnographers investigated what has been done in other canal development projects. We examined how the community perceived them, what roles members of the community took on as part of these development projects, with what motivations, and how successful they were in facilitating the formation of sustainable partnerships.

Public support is necessary both to secure funding and to establish partnerships to carry out initiatives. The ethnographic research process not only solicits important information, it also involves residents who will hopefully become advocates and resource managers themselves. Hosting focus groups, for example, brought together many people who, despite common interests, had been working independently and who have since built on and continued these initial networks—an added benefit to participatory planning. Many of the focus groups have revealed a distrust of planning procedures due to previous exclusion or a misunderstanding of the purpose or ability of the planning. Our experience suggests that community participation is essential if the WECHC's plans are to be implemented successfully. Implementation of the plan will require a strong base of constituents, implementers, and advocates (Murphy 1985). Indeed, aside from getting its plan approved by government, *work* is the next major hurdle for the commission. As it moves from planning to implementation, more funding is needed, but more importantly, planning participants must become active partners and not simply meeting attendees with advice and perspectives to share.

This is one reason that ethnographic methods (Hyland 1997; Van West 1996) for planning and interpreting heritage, which integrate action with academic thought, are essential. These methods ensure constituency building and provide a forum in which groups can collaborate on implementation strategies. Academically speaking, heritage is a dynamic, actively evolving and situationally defined way of locating or understanding oneself in the contemporary world. Community members often have a more static definition of heritage, and rather than seeing heritage planning as a collaborative effort that becomes a part of their own heritage—an effort in which the planning and the implementation will be participatory—they see it as being a way for them to voice opinions, concerns, and ideas. Citizens often believe politicians have development plans already prepared. They see the implementation as being separate from the planning process, and thus the job of the consultant.

A similar situation discussed in the literature is that community stakeholders sometimes feel it is the responsibility of the researcher or planner to be accountable for the projects on which they seek input (Brecher 1986). Due to this mindset, the planning commission must be very clear that it cannot be solely responsible for the implementation of the plan. The Erie Canal has already been the focus of several regional revitalization strategies, including a Canal Recreation Plan currently being carried out by the New York State

Canal Corporation, which owns and operates the statewide canal system, and an enormous regional effort to apply for and receive federal Housing and Urban Development funds under an initiative aptly named the Canal Corridor Initiative. Some of the people attending the meetings, roundtables, and focus groups held by the heritage area planning commission were also involved in the formulation of these past plans. They expressed impatience with "more" planning and with non-implementation of the former plans. Many felt they were repeating themselves, that we were "reinventing the wheel," and that any further discussion was a waste of time. Indeed, participants saw their role as just to help researchers research the project (Brecher 1986).

This is an unfortunate hazard in community-based planning. Often, community support must be shown in order for an organization to apply for funding. Community participants tend to expect that their suggestions will either be used or ignored, but that either way *some* kind of a project will happen. But funding doesn't always come forth, so plans that are developed as an application for funding are shelved. The next time potential funding comes along, these plans can be referenced, but new community support needs to be generated from what may have become a frustrated and exhausted community. Heritage resource management is dynamic and ongoing; it is not a static government commission overseeing historic sites and recreational assets, and it must have a strong focus on resident use, value, and enjoyment of the heritage resources. Thus, good heritage area planning should be participatory and should be followed by participatory implementation. Part of this strategy involves developing a sustainable effort that will be grounded in multiple institutions, organizations, and individuals.

Not only is community support essential to planning and implementation, but community cooperation is also necessary. Cooperation cannot be achieved unless the goals of individual stakeholders are understood and mutual terms are established. It is not unusual for one group within the stakeholding community to use heritage preservation as a means to "gentrify" areas by removing the "discomfort of undesirable social classes and their lifestyles" (Verrey and Henley 1991). Other groups may be very suspicious of such a group's motives in jumping on the heritage development bandwagon and be reluctant to support the project. Other stakeholders who favor heritage preservation may be anti-change and anti-development (Verrey and Henley 1991). Thus, the anthropological perspective, an effective means of examining underlying stakeholder motivations, is an important element in heritage work.

Underlying stakeholder motivations must be understood and used to implement a heritage resource management plan. Likewise, the underlying goal of
the heritage area creation—addressing regional needs—should also be valued.
This concept was well phrased by a member of the commission: "What works
for the local will work for the tourist." He was speaking from his experiences in
the small village of which he is mayor. There, efforts are made to keep downtown shops open and public spaces bustling with human activity. In this case,
shop owners, public festivals, and street signs are focused on one local theme:
the canal. These strategies work well for his village, which has one of the lowest commercial and residential vacancies in the region, a comparatively high
number of visitors, and an "honorable mention" listing in many travel guides.

What the mayor was also reflecting is the view held by many others on
this commission: that the focus should not be on the tourist, but first on the
residents of the heritage area. They suggest that addressing regional *residential*
needs may draw tourists and may also increase the quality of life of the region,
thereby encouraging investors to locate other types of businesses there. Further
exploration of the mayor's statement reflects the complexity of the actual planning being done by the commission—it is focusing not simply on tourism,
but on the economic health of the region and on developing meaningful ways
for residents to experience and celebrate their heritage. Since, as the mayor
points out, both residents and tourists are satisfied with the village, he finds his
village's policies to be very much in line with the overall efforts of the planning
commission. As an anthropologist, I also see the village as a good example of
successful tourism development, since it focuses on long-term community enrichment and celebration of its heritage rather than creating short-term tourist
attractions.

CONCLUSION

This focus on community enrichment by the commission has been facilitated
by ethnographic research. Few of the ideas generated were completely new to
the members of the commission. However, the rearticulation of the commissioners' own concerns by people throughout the heritage corridor validated
these concerns. This validation has reinvigorated the planning process. The
ethnographic data is building confidence in the plan's reality and has helped

to clarify the important issues, in addition to unearthing a communitywide concern for trail use and development. This perspective shift from boaters to hikers and cyclists is just one example of needed reprioritization of known concerns to more accurately reflect the desires of the community. Community members previously uninvolved in the planning also recognize this accuracy. Some of the people reading the draft plan are surprised at how many of the region's needs are addressed. As one village mayor wrote, "These are all important to the region. . . . Keep up the good work!" This response leaves me hopeful that we have created a meaningful management plan that meets the needs of the community and will lay the groundwork for good tourism.

A major role for anthropologists exists in both applied and academic tourism work (Howell 1994). Regional tourism planning requires the facilitation of many interest groups, a role that suits us well. The use of heritage for tourism and, as my example shows, to enrich and improve the lives of community members is a trend that anthropologists must continue to closely monitor. Heritage interpretation is highly informed by both ethnography and the reflexivity gained through anthropological training. Anthropologists have a critical role to play in helping local residents articulate their heritage concepts, encouraging participatory approaches, and helping residents gain confidence in making their views known to politicians. I am confident that anthropologists can continue to keep tourism developers "honest," applying a critical perspective to their work and encouraging their coworkers to do the same, while also monitoring the needs and effects of tourism, even as we ourselves work as the mediators.

NOTES

1. Judy Tso, applied anthropologist and principal of Aha Solutions, Inc.
2. From June to August 2001, two graduate students, Rosemary Riel (University of Maryland, College Park) and Pellegrino Luciano (CUNY), and one undergraduate, Aaron Tobler (Loyola University, Chicago), worked with the commission. They lived in the canal village of Brockport and conducted ethnographic research throughout the five-county heritage area.

REFERENCES CITED

Beebe, James
    2001 Rapid Assessment: An Introduction. Walnut Creek, CA: Altamira Press.
Boniface, Priscilla, and Peter J. Fowler.
    1993 Heritage and Tourism in "The Global Village." London: Routledge.
Bramwell, Bill, and Angela Sharman

1999 Collaboration in Local Tourism Policymaking. Annals of Tourism Research 26(2): 392–415.

Brecher, Jeremy
1986 A Report on Doing History from Below: The Brass Workers History Project. In Presenting the Past: Essays on History and the Public. Susan Porter Benson, Stephen Brier, and Roy Rosenzweig, eds. Pp 267–277. Philadelphia: Temple University Press.

Cameron, Catherine M., and John B. Gatewood
1998 The Quest for Numen at Historic Sites. Paper presented at the 97th meeting of the American Anthropological Association, December 2–6, 1998, Philadelphia, PA.

Cogswell, Robert
1996 Doing Right By the Local Folks: Grassroots Issues in Cultural Tourism. In Keys to the Marketplace: Problems and Issues in Cultural and Heritage Tourism. Patricia Atkinson Wells, ed. Pp 1–17. Middlesex, UK: Hisalrik Press.

Herbert, David
1993 Conclusions. In Heritage, Tourism and Society. David Herbert, ed. Pp. 212–221. London: Mansell Publishing.

Howell, Benita J.
1994 Weighing the Risks and Rewards of Involvement in Cultural Conservation and Heritage Tourism. Human Organization 53(2):150–159.

Hyland, Stanley
1997 Tourism in the Lower Mississippi Delta: Whose Field of Dreams? The Struggle Among the Landed Aristocracy, the Grassroots Indigenous and the Gaming Industry. In Tourism and Culture: An Applied Perspective. Erve Chambers, ed. Pp. 147–162. Albany, NY: SUNY Press.

Garrod, Brian, and Alan Fyall
1998 Managing Heritage Tourism. Annals of Tourism Research 27(3):682–708.

MacCannell, Dean
1976 The Tourist: A New Theory of the Leisure Class. New York: Schocken Books.

Murphy, Peter E.
1985 Tourism: A Community Approach. New York: Methuen.

Newby, P.T.
1994 Tourism: Support or Threat to Heritage? In Building a New Heritage: Tourism, Culture and Identity in the New Europe. G.J. Ashworth and P.J. Larkham, eds. Pp. 206–228. London: Routledge.

Turnbridge, J.E.
1993 Whose Heritage? Global Problem, European Nightmare. In Building a New Heritage: Tourism, Culture and Identity in the New Europe. G.J. Ashworth and P.J. Larkham, eds. Pp. 123–134. London: Routledge.

Van West, Carroll
1996 Building Blocks for New Economic Opportunities: National Register Projects at the MTSU Center for Historic Preservation. In Keys to the Marketplace: Problems and Issues in Cultural and Heritage Tourism. Patricia Atkinson Wells, ed. Pp. 1–17. Middlesex, UK: Hisalrik Press.

Verrey, Roberta, and Laura Henley
1991 Creation Myths and Zoning Boards: Local Uses of Historic Preservation. In The Politics of Culture. Brett Williams, ed. Pp 75–107. Washington, D.C.: Smithsonian Institution.

HOSTS AND HOSTS: THE ANTHROPOLOGY OF COMMUNITY-BASED ECOTOURISM IN THE PERUVIAN AMAZON

AMANDA STRONZA

Texas A&M University

For environmental anthropologists, ecotourism is an especially timely and practical topic. Increasingly, anthropologists are talking with conservationists, development specialists, tour operators, policy-makers, and local leaders about ecotourism and its impacts on local communities and ecosystems. This is good, as anthropologists are especially well suited to focus ethnographic attention on the general but critical question of what happens when people in host destinations near and in protected areas become involved in ecotourism. Do local "hosts" become etter stewards of wildlife, forests, and other ecosystems when ecotourism is introduced? If so, what is the process by which that happens, and what are the challenges along the way? This paper highlights various methods and insights gained during four years of research on a community-based ecotourism lodge called Posada Amazonas, located in Madre de Dios, Peru. As a joint business venture between a private company and a local community, Posada Amazonas represents a new standard for local participation in ecotourism. Here, members of the local community of Infierno work not only as boat drivers, cooks, and guides, but also as directors, owners, and decision-makers in the company. Learning and telling the story of Posada Amazonas ethnographically and from both sides of the partnership allowed me to move beyond a standard impact study of costs and benefits. Anthropological analysis entailed adding nuance to "the local community" and unraveling why people were or were not choosing to participate in ecotourism, and how their decisions were often related to social and cultural roles and perceptions. The ethnographic approach also led to analyses of processes and impacts—that is, how and why there were gains and losses in Infierno, in addition to what the changes were. Answers to these types of questions can have important implications for conservation, beyond calculating jobs gained or income earned. Finally, in addition to deepening the analysis of ecotourism,

---

NAPA Bulletin 23, pp. 170–190, ISBN 1-931303-22-3. © 2005 by the American Anthropological Association.

anthropologists can play important roles as cultural brokers between ecotourism partners, helping to facilitate communication across an array of perspectives and expectations. Key Words: community-based ecotourism, conservation, local participation, ethnography, Amazon

ANTHROPOLOGY AND ECOTOURISM

At first glance, tourism is hard to justify as a serious focus of anthropological study. In fact, tourism and anthropology seem to sit at opposite ends of at least a couple of spectrums. Whereas tourism has been called a series of "pseudo-events" (Boorstin 1969) and "staged cultural productions" (MacCannell 1976) in which authenticity lies in wait somewhere "backstage," and local people live as they "really are," anthropology is aimed at getting behind the curtain—cataloging, describing, and interpreting the most authentic of a society's "social facts." And while tourism generates glossy brochures and colorful stories that may or may not reflect any lived reality in a host destination, anthropology is instead intent on providing thick ethnographic description and accurate portraits of everyday life. Whereas tourism transports people to a liminal space in which social roles and responsibilities are abandoned or turned upside down, many anthropologists devote attention to the meanings and underlying structures of society—the "right side up," so to speak, from which a tourist might depart. But, as authors in this volume will attest, it is precisely because tourism can help bring into relief the differences between authentic and staged, structured and liminal, or traditional and invented that it is such a rich field of study for anthropologists.

For environmental anthropologists, tourism is an especially timely and practical topic. So much of the discourse about the loss of both cultural and biological diversity revolves around tourism and tourists, key protagonists in processes of globalization. Ecotourism in particular has moved to the center of debates about the impacts of encounters between "hosts and guests" in destination communities and ecosystems around the world. It has been touted as a "win–win" solution, a magic bullet for getting people to value intact forests and other ecosystems. In the Amazon, ecotourism has been shown to have a relatively low impact on forests compared to other activities such as hunting, logging, or agriculture (Borman 1999; Epler Wood 1998; Honey 1999; Wunder 1999). Some have argued that too much tourism, however—particularly if it is unmonitored and unregulated—can spoil natural areas, disturb wildlife, and lead to habitat conversion (Giannecchini 1993).

Given ecotourism's potential, it is no wonder that anthropologists are talking with conservationists, development specialists, tour operators, policy-makers, and local leaders about how best to implement ecotourism and then carefully measure its impacts. In fact, the concept and practice of ecotourism have received so much attention that the United Nations declared 2002 the "International Year of Ecotourism" and marked it as a time to take collective stock of the lessons learned. At the Ecotourism World Summit in Quebec, Canada, in May 2002, more than one thousand delegates from 132 nations gathered to assess the pros and cons of ecotourism for people and ecosystems around the world.

Though so many are focusing on ecotourism, I would argue that anthropologists have unique contributions to offer to the debates and analyses. For one, anthropologists are well suited to apply ethnographic attention to the general but critical question of what happens when people in host communities near and in protected areas become involved in ecotourism. More specifically, anthropologists can test whether and how widely held assumptions about the conservation benefits of ecotourism actually play out in the local setting. Do people in local communities become better stewards of wildlife, forests, and other ecosystems when they become involved as ecotourism hosts? If so, what is the process by which that happens? Are the new conservation behaviors prompted by changes in household social and economic activities; patterns of spending and saving; attitudes about conservation and resource scarcity; perceptions of wildlife (particularly the species tourists pay to see); or values or devaluations of local culture, ethnicity, and tradition? Few studies about ecotourism include such empirical data, either qualitative or quantitative. Those that do tend to focus on income and jobs, assessing economic changes brought about by ecotourism (e.g, Bookbinder et al. 1998; Lindberg 1991). Anthropologists can add new dimensions to the analysis, holistically assessing many other changes catalyzed by ecotourism and ultimately helping to discern what the local changes might imply for conservation.

ANTHROPOLOGIST AS CULTURAL BROKER

In this paper, I will describe the various methods, challenges, and insights I have experienced during anthropological fieldwork on the impacts of ecotourism in the Native Community of Infierno of Madre de Dios in the southeastern Peruvian Amazon. My goal for the past several years has been to write an ethnographic and holistic account of the initiation and development of a community-based ecotourism lodge called "Posada Amazonas," which was first conceptualized in 1996 and opened to tourists in 1998. Posada Amazonas represents an unusual experiment in ecotourism because it entails a joint business venture between a private company and a local community. Here, members of the local community of Infierno work not only as boat drivers, cooks, and guides, but also as directors, owners, and decision-makers in the company. They share the rights and responsibilities of ownership with Rainforest Expeditions, a private Peruvian tourism company based in the capital city of Lima. For its innovation as a partnership, its early economic success, and its proven concern for local participation, Posada Amazonas has received considerable media attention and won numerous awards from conservation and development organizations, including the "Equator Initiative" presented at the World Summit for Sustainable Development in Johannesburg, South Africa (2002).

In Posada Amazonas, I have found an ideal place to explore the ways in which local participation in ecotourism can—or cannot—improve chances for resource management and conservation. For my doctoral research (1996–2000), I used a case study format, relying on both quantitative and qualitative data gathered in interviews, written surveys, participant observation, and a range of participatory methods to record the ways in which ecotourism played out in the community of Infierno.

Throughout the research, I collaborated often with project managers from both the company and the community. My role as a cultural broker began to emerge, rather unintentionally, as I sought to communicate insights from my research—and, more basically, what I was doing—to the two partners. Often, I encountered points of disconnect between what actors on both sides of the partnership expected or wanted me to say, and what, in fact, I was learning. Exploring the divide between preconceptions and hopes about Posada Amazonas on the one hand and the ethnographic picture on the other became an important, if unexpected, part of my research. It also became my contribution as a practicing anthropologist to offer my data and insights to the company as the project itself was unfolding. In the following sections, I will describe the project and what I was doing in the field research, highlighting the points of disconnect—either between the company, the community, and me, or between the expectations for the project and the realities I was discovering.

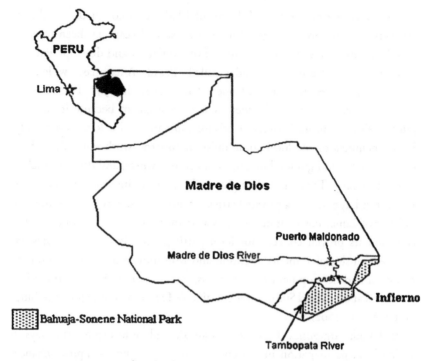

FIGURE 1. Department of Madre de Dios, Peru; Native Community of Infierno; and Bahuaja Sonene National Park.

CONTEXT: ECOTOURISM IN THE PERUVIAN AMAZON

The complex of thatched cabins with open views to the rainforest known as Posada Amazonas is located along the Tambopata River in the Department of Madre de Dios in southeastern Peru (Figure 1). The Tambopata River is a veritable lifeline of biodiversity that flows from the Andean slopes of Puno near Lake Titicaca and through the low foothills and terraces of the Amazon plain before feeding into the Madre de Dios River and ultimately draining into the Amazon River. Along its trajectory, the Tambopata passes some of the most species-rich communities yet reported on earth for birds, butterflies, and dragonflies (Gentry 1990; Foster et al. 1994). Conniff and Bensonsen wrote, "Biologically, Tambopata is one of the world's mother lodes. It is possible," they suggested, "in a good half-hour, to see more species in Tambopata than the Italian primitives dared put in their paintings of Eden" (1999:127). To add to this diversity, the three million hectare Department of Madre de Dios is important for conservation because it has one of the lowest human population densities in the entire Amazon basin. A "megadiversity hotspot" if ever there was one, Madre de Dios boasts three major protected areas: the Manu Biosphere Reserve, the Bahuaja Sonene National Park, and the Tambopata National Reserve.

Despite the enticing brochures that promise lands "teeming with wildlife," much of the fauna in the Amazon is well camouflaged and surprisingly difficult to detect. In most places, having a guide—preferably a local one—is essential if one is to see anything. Tambopata is an exception. Even first-time visitors with ill-trained eyes for tropical wildlife are likely to see a great number of species in Tambopata. In fact, a typical stay of four to five days in Tambopata holds the promise of glimpsing at least 30 pairs of large macaws, a family of giant otters, four or more species of primates, and several varieties of the region's most charismatic rodents, including capybaras and agoutis. Tapirs and peccaries are also quite common, and at least six or seven tour groups a year are lucky enough to spot a jaguar. Tambopata has always been especially popular among birdwatchers. Famously, it is the site of the world's greatest single-site bird list: more than 550 species in an area of 50 square kilometers (by comparison, 914 bird species have been recorded for all of the United States and Canada combined) (AOU 1998). Of particular interest to many visitors is the fact that hundreds of parrots and macaws congregate frequently at several local salt licks called "colpas."

Until as recently as 1993, Tambopata was little more than a hinterland compared to southeastern Peru's more popular destination, Machu Picchu. For years, only a small enclave of neotropical biologists and conservationists frequented the forests of Tambopata, and the options for tourists were minimal. Today, increasing numbers of international tourists are adding Tambopata to their regular itineraries, and at least in part because of the sheer diversity and relative visibility of wildlife, Tambopata has become a prime site for ecotourism development in the past decade. In 1987, Groom et al. (1991) estimated that 6,520 tourists visited Puerto Maldonado in 1987; by 1997, the numbers had more than doubled (MITINCI 1998).

THE COMMUNITY-BASED LODGE OF POSADA AMAZONAS

Since 1990, the number of lodges along a small stretch of the Tambopata River has increased from three to nine. One of these, the community-based Posada Amazonas lodge, is situated in the buffer zone of Bahuaja-Sonene National

Park (537,053 hectares), several hours by motorized canoe from the capital town of Puerto Maldonado. Featuring a complex of thatched, open-sided and traditionally designed buildings, the lodge includes five main cabins, each with six large guest rooms that can accommodate 60 guests. With an investment of half a million dollars and two years to build the lodge, Posada Amazonas is a luxury lodge by Amazon ecotourism standards. Despite its rustic design and remote location, the lodge emphasizes comfort and service, accompanied by specially tailored itineraries, gourmet buffet meals, and naturalist guides trained in both ecology and hospitality. The typical tourist is from the United States or Europe, has at least a bachelor's degree, and is in a higher income-earning bracket. In its first three years of operation, Posada Amazonas was booked solid, attracting 3,000 to 4,000 tourists a year who paid between $60 and $100 per night's stay. A typical itinerary includes climbing a 45-meter tower that offers birds-eye views of the canopy, hiking forest trails, visiting a "colpa" frequented by macaws and parrots, visiting a local subsistence farm, and floating along the edges of an oxbow lake on a large catamaran, searching for giant otters and numerous bird species.

But Posada Amazonas warrants attention not merely because it is in the middle of a biological hotspot or because it has had success drawing boatloads of birdwatchers. Nor does it necessarily merit extra attention because it is located in the territory of a local Amazonian community, Infierno (Figure 2). Rather, what makes the lodge of special interest is the fact that it is co-owned and managed by the eighty or so Ese'eja Indian, riberenho, and Andean families who make up the community. This local ownership of Posada Amazonas came by way of an innovative partnership. In May 1996, the members of Infierno and the private company, Rainforest Expeditions, signed a legally binding contract to begin building and co-managing Posada Amazonas. Calling their joint venture the "Ke'eway Association in Participation," the partners agreed to split profits—60 percent to the community and 40 percent to the company—and to divide the management 50–50. A critical tenet of the agreement was that community members should be actively involved in the enterprise, not only as staff but also as owners, planners, and administrators. Further, they should join Rainforest Expeditions in making decisions about the future of the company and in providing services for tourists. The partners also agreed that after 20 years, the entire operation—the lodge and everything in it: short-wave radio, furniture, kitchenware, power generators, et cetera—will automatically belong to Infierno, and the community will have the choice of either continuing to collaborate with Rainforest Expeditions or taking over as proprietors and

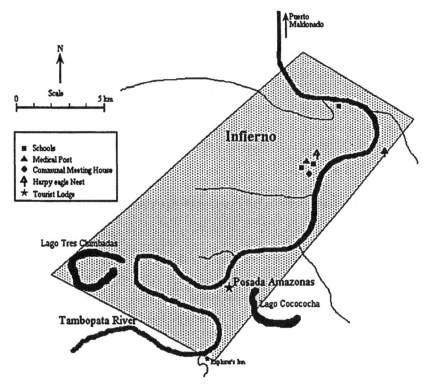

FIGURE 2. Communal Boundaries of the Native Community of Infierno, on Tambopata River.

managers. Meanwhile, the company oversees the day-to-day operations, hiring and training community members to assume increasing amounts of responsibility.

As long as they remain partners, the members of Infierno are obligated to maintain an exclusive contract with Rainforest Expeditions. No one from the community can strike a deal with a competing company to build a second lodge, nor can any individual independently create an additional ecotourism project within communal territory. Also, outside visitors must seek permission from the association before using ecotourism infrastructure in the community, including the lodge itself, trails through the forest, the catamaran in the oxbow lake, and the canopy tower.

Each partner has brought different resources and skills to the project. The company has offered financing, market savvy, experience in the logistics of transport and food service, trained personnel, knowledge of the preferences of Western tourists, and, perhaps most basically, an immediate demand in the form of several boatloads of tourists. The community has supplied labor, local knowledge of wild flora and fauna, title and access to ten thousand hectares of communally owned forested land, and, importantly, an indigenous identity that has already been used to boost the lodge's marketing appeal. The community also boasts a variety of the relatively observable, accessible, and photogenic wildlife species that are so important to the ecotourism experience, including giant otters, macaws, and, during the first year of the project, a pair of nesting harpy eagles—the largest birds of prey in the Americas.[1]

PRACTICING ANTHROPOLOGY BETWEEN HOSTS AND HOSTS

I began the research in May 1996, the same month the Native Community of Infierno signed the 20-year contract with Rainforest Expeditions to launch their ecotourism joint venture. Because of the fortunate timing, I was able to collect and analyze my data as part of a natural experiment. Rather than completing all of the field work in one extended visit to the study site, I collected data four times over a period of 13 months over four years. In the first field season, when the lodge was little more than an idea, I conducted a stakeholder analysis, which I will describe in greater detail below. In the second field season, as the lodge was being built, I collected baseline data on people's household economies and on their values with regards to ethnicity, culture, and tradition as these related to tourism and conservation. In the third field season, when the first group of tourists arrived, I returned to ask the same questions I had asked in previous years, in addition to some new questions. Finally, in the fourth year, when the lodge was fully functional and people were beginning to focus on other concerns in the community, I returned to work in an applied capacity, leading focus groups and workshops to envision needs and priorities for the future. Since completing the research, I have joined with community leaders in Infierno to share and compare lessons learned in Posada Amazonas with other community-based lodges in Ecuador and Bolivia.

When I began the fieldwork, I was questioned on numerous occasions about my role, my ethics, and my objectives. Some people suspected that I was a spy for Rainforest Expeditions and that perhaps my research would unabashedly favor the company. In *The Anthropology of Tourism*, Dennison Nash has found that many anthropologists refuse consulting possibilities with tourism companies for reasons like these. He notes a common assumption that "by getting into the tourism business one opens up the possibility of being 'bought' by one's employer and, hence, the establishment" (Nash 1996). I had not been hired by the company—no one was paying me—but I did share my findings and insights with both the company and community, and that aroused suspicion. To compound the concern that I had been "bought," I was perceived as biased because the owners of the company had been my good friends for several years prior to the joint venture. Particularly in my first year of research, my abilities to remain relatively impartial and objective as a scholar were challenged.

Despite the suspicions, the fact that I collaborated with both the company and the community presented several practical advantages. In particular, my role as an insider made me privy to the company's financial records and archives, as well as to many candid conversations in staff meetings. Had I been more of an outsider, especially one opposed to the project (as many observers were), perhaps these privileges would have been curtailed. I imagine in such a case the research might have been slanted toward the hearsay, rumor, and marketing propaganda that surrounded the project. Instead, I tried to build the analysis on all aspects of the project: not only the published success stories produced for the public, but also the private discussions about the dilemmas and problems the project was facing from the beginning.

Also, as an insider, I was able to gain access to the lodge and its clientele on a daily basis. I observed the project not only from the perspective of a visitor, but also from the viewpoint of the owners, administrators, accountants, personnel managers, guides, cooks, waiters, housekeepers, and boat drivers. I accompanied people in their homes and farms in the community, and then I joined them in the lodge, watching and talking with them as they interacted with tourists, and paying special attention to how they were coping with their dual responsibilities, both in the lodge and as members of the community. In other moments, I accompanied the tourists on their activities and in the lodge, surveying them formally and informally about their opinions and impressions of what they seeing, and sharing with them what I was learning.

Though I was involved in many of the inner workings at Posada Amazonas, in many ways my role in Infierno was similar to that of a tourist. Though I lived in the community for weeks and months at a time, I was always more of an outsider in that setting than an insider. I was forever conscious then that I was very much a part of what I was trying to understand—that is, the changes in Infierno brought on by tourists and other outsiders. Often, I felt I was in a hall of mirrors, watching the interactions between the locals and the visitors, while, at every turn, catching my own reflection. Many times, I would introduce myself to tourists, explaining that I was an anthropologist writing an ethnography about community-based ecotourism. Invariably, someone in the group would laugh, a bit self-consciously, and ask, "So, you'll be watching me?" Well, yes, I often thought, but I'll be trying to watch all of us, myself included.

I found, not surprisingly, that few people admitted to the status of "tourist." Most preferred the idea of a traveler, or one who is more intent than others on exploring the real world—MacCannell's backstage—behind the fake façade. I remember a couple of guests in particular who flatly denied the "tourist" label. They were backpackers who passed through Tambopata in 1996, stopping for the night in Infierno's central commons (the area with the communal meeting house, the school, and the soccer field in Figure 2). The president of Infierno at the time, a young Ese'eja man, was a bit taken aback that the visitors had set up camp in the center of the community without prior notice. He waited for them to awake the next morning before approaching to question their plans. Politely, he asked how they'd slept ("Were you cold?"), and then gently informed them that Infierno was a private community—all tourists should check with the project office in Puerto Maldonado, or, alternatively, consult with the native federation, FENAMAD, for permission to stay. Obviously offended, one of the women crawled out of her tent, finished twisting the lid back on her Nalgen water bottle, and explained in broken Spanish, "Oh, but we're not tourists. We were just passing through for the night."

ANTHROPOLOGIST AS BAROMETER

There was also some uncertainty about who I was as an anthropologist and what I could achieve. At times, the company thought it useful to use me as a barometer of general sentiment in the community. They would ask, "How are things going? What does 'the community' think and feel about the lodge?" After all, I was living there, sharing meals with people—shouldn't I have my finger on the pulse of the community? Though anthropologists have been known to claim entire communities as "theirs," I knew I could not represent the diversity of opinion about Posada Amazonas in Infierno. The community extends over nearly ten thousand hectares on either side of the Tambopata river, and regardless of geographic spread, I simply could never capture the full range of perspectives. People were always changing their minds, and different sectors within the community—men and women, young and old, indigenous and riberenho and Andean—generally perceived and engaged in the project in fundamentally different ways.

I had learned this in the first year, when I conducted a stakeholder analysis (Grimble and Chan 1994) and tried to understand how ethnicity, gender, age, resource use, and geographical location within Infierno correlated with varying opinions about the ecotourism project and varying levels of involvement with Rainforest Expeditions. For this type of analysis, I interviewed members of Infierno as well as representatives of outside organizations about their hopes, concerns, and conflicting agendas surrounding the cooperative agreement between the community and Rainforest Expeditions. In focus groups, I used a series of hand-drawn posters to characterize various development phases of the tourism project and to serve as launching points for discussion.

What I learned from the stakeholder analysis was that conflicts outside the community, usually on the part of people who sincerely wanted to help Infierno, often intensified conflicts within the community rather than providing much guidance. For example, tour companies that were vying for the same "socially responsible" ecotourism market had the members of Infierno asking, "Who should we deal with?" Nongovernmental organizations (NGOs) were competing, too, over the role of who should advise the community in dealings with Rainforest Expeditions. The members of Infierno seemed generally open to working with any group willing to offer support. However, once they became enmeshed in the political relations among stakeholders outside the community, they were resigned to taking sides. The result was that outside relations were replayed and then intensified inside the community.

FOMENTING PARTICIPATION

In my role as cultural broker between the community of Infierno and Rainforest Expeditions, I often encountered points of disconnect between what people expected I would say or do as an anthropologist and what I was in fact able to contribute. A first point of disconnect was on the issue of participation.

My intent in the first year was to carry out exploratory research with the applied task of helping to coordinate a process of participatory planning among the members of the community, Rainforest Expeditions, Conservation International, and other NGOs involved in the project as advisors. Essentially, the company wanted to be sure that people in the community knew about the project. The first thing I learned was that the community's vote to sign the

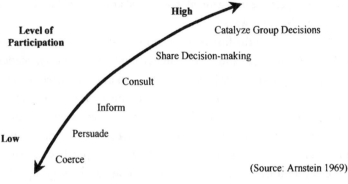

FIGURE 3. Ladder of Participation.

contract had been unanimous—but in fact many people were either ill-informed or, as in the case of most women, completely uninformed. The company also wanted to give people the chance to decide whether or not and how they would like to participate in the project.

Faced with this reality, all of us involved with the project had different strategies for fomenting participation. Figure 3 from Arnstein (1969) shows different strategies for fostering local involvement in a project. Especially in the first year of Posada Amazonas, the company saw me—the anthropologist—as a resource for going house to house and getting people to participate. Their strategy for how I might do this was somewhere between "persuade" and "inform." In fact, I *was* going house to house for interviews, but my concern was to ask for opinions about the project and to encourage people to weigh for themselves the costs and benefits of getting involved. In my mind, the best way to foment participation was somewhere between getting people to "share in decision making" and "catalyzing group decisions."

UNDERSTANDING PARTICIPATION

Another point of disconnect between the partner hosts and me was how to define participation. All of us—the community, the company, and I—were concerned about participation, but for different reasons. For the company, "participation" was little more than a means to fill labor needs. Especially in the beginning, as they were building the lodge, they literally needed enough hands to haul equipment, lumber, and appliances up steep and muddy riverbanks, to nail down thousands of floorboards, blaze several kilometers of trails through the forest, and collect enough palm fronds to weave together nearly 20,000 panels of roofing thatch. The details were endless, down to the last handmade towel rack. Coordinating all this labor required both leadership and a significant investment of time away from people's farms, forests, and families.

When the lodge opened, so too did many new opportunities for getting involved. Everyone talked about participation. Who was participating and who wasn't participating? Did some people have an unfair advantage over others? Were some people earning more or less than others? Who determined who got to participate and in what ways? In my mind, the importance of participation was as much conceptual as practical. I was less worried about getting hammers in people's hands as I was about encouraging people to think critically about tourism, reframe their relationships with the company, and gain a sense of ownership over the lodge.

For many people, the idea of participation was altogether confusing. Never before Posada Amazonas had they been invited to participate actively in a project of such magnitude. So often in the past, the responsibilities of conceptualizing, planning, and decision-making for any kind of development project had been left to outsiders. People had little experience in being architects of their own plans for change, and they had even less experience building from the ground up a luxury ecotourism lodge with hundreds of thousands of dollars of capital investment. Without firsthand experience, people felt limited in their ability to contribute. Compounding the lack of experience was a general complacence about social roles. Many felt uncertain about how to treat the company as a partner rather than as an employer. In fact, this new kind of interaction was a leap for both sides. In the initial months of the joint venture, the owners of Rainforest Expeditions were accustomed to lining people up in rows and delivering lists of things to do. The intention of acting as equal partners was there, but neither side was prepared, either practically or psychologically, to deal with the other on such progressive new terms. It would take time, and yet the company needed the community to get involved. It wasn't just a noble social experiment; it was a new kind of business model, built on the very real need to have active participation of the people of the community.

WHO PARTICIPATES?

As everyone grappled with the issue of how to foment participation, we discovered another point of disconnect on the question of *who* should participate and *how*. I found we needed to pay attention to the heterogeneity of needs and priorities within communities, as well as to different kinds of participation. Not everyone in any host destination will participate equally in tourism. Some people may join directly, interacting with tourists on a regular basis as guides or performers, while others may become involved only behind the scenes, working as support staff or as wholesalers of foods and supplies. People differ also in terms of how much time and energy they can invest in tourism: some will work as full-time wage laborers; others will contract their labor occasionally, or earn cash only through the sale of goods. Others will choose not to participate at all.

The expectation for Posada Amazonas, especially from the perspective of outsiders, was that participation would broadly lead to economic benefits and could be summed up as cash earned or employment gained. But, as an anthropologist, I observed and perceived participation and its impacts in Infierno more holistically. Participation in this community-owned lodge became more than just income and jobs. There were and are many ways to participate in Posada Amazonas, including joining the Ecotourism Committee, a community "board of directors" created to meet regularly with Rainforest Expeditions, as well as many others, and I was interested in all of them. As a method, I created an index derived from several kinds of indicators to measure whether a person was deeply involved in ecotourism, a little bit involved, or not involved at all. These included different scores for level of interaction with tourists (e.g., high for guides, low for artisans), percent of income earned from tourism, whether or not a person was part of the Ecotourism Committee, et cetera. With this index, I was able to make "participation" an ordinal variable rather than a simple binary variable. Every person and household I interviewed in Infierno had a score from 0 to 18, low to high participation, which could then be correlated with many other economic and social variables collected in interviews to generate quantitative analyses or to be described in qualitative, ethnographic fashion, characterizing changes brought on by different kinds of participation in ecotourism.

With attention to such differences, I discovered that gender was a key variable that determined who participated in tourism (see Swain 1995). With the descriptive quantitative analysis of participation scores, it was easy to see that virtually no women were represented in the "high participation" end of the index, at least not at the beginning of the project. This is not surprising, as gender roles in Infierno assign women as responsible for childcare. It was very difficult for women to work at the lodge—which is far upriver from people's homes—and also attend to their gender-based responsibilities at home.

But with ethnographic data, more details about important changes prompted by gender-biased participation in ecotourism became clear. Especially in the first year of the project, most of the women had no plans to get intensely involved, but situations in their households were changing nevertheless. Though women were not clearing trails, debating the bylaws of the agreement, or participating in guide training, they were affected by the project, often through the participation of their spouses. If their husbands or older sons were involved in the project, that meant there would be new constraints on men's time for farming and other productive activities.

Changes for the men certainly implied subsequent shifts in women's responsibilities. Women whose husbands and sons were involved were generally spending more time alone as they maintained the household. In addition to their normal chores, which included a full day of washing clothes in the river, cooking, caring for young children, and keeping chickens and other small livestock, several women also became responsible for attending meetings in their husbands' stead, working on the farm, and selling produce in Puerto Maldonado. For every man who became involved in tourism, there was a woman who was taking on more and more responsibilities in the household, essentially becoming a single head of household.

Not only were women doing more, they were also doing different *kinds* of things. Maria, a woman who later began to work at the lodge herself, first became involved when her husband took on the position of community coordinator. In the first months, she often cooked for groups of men who were involved in planning or building the lodge. Even *what* she was cooking changed: her family no longer relied on food they had produced, but rather on food they had purchased (or had been purchased for them by Rainforest Expeditions). Also, there was new income available to purchase new clothes and medicines and new items for the household, such as cooking utensils, plastic food containers, radios, or even, in a couple of cases, battery-operated televisions.

DEFINING SUCCESS

As more and more people did begin to get involved, including women, the definitions for "successful" participation also varied. For many community members, success per se hardly mattered. They seemed focused on *limitations* rather than on what they could achieve. Leaders were mainly concerned about potential new conflicts in the community and about how tourism might favor some over others. The general question was not "What can we achieve?" but rather "How are we getting along?"

I encouraged people to pursue small but concrete and locally initiated goals—such as getting organized to pool resources and purchase a two-way radio. This approach was based on a philosophy of self-determination and the need to build organizational capacity within the community so that people could negotiate for themselves and plan their own future. This entailed learning to gather ideas and concerns from their neighbors and families, transforming these ideas into proposals for support, however small, and then learning to deal confidently with politicians and NGOs to negotiate for their needs.

While the company supported small-scale ideas, they also encouraged larger projects, including a $50,000 World Bank initiative to promote handicraft production. Our different definitions of success emanated from our broader visions. I was thinking about the need for autonomy and social sustainability; the company was thinking about getting things done, preparing their community partners to become better businesspeople (e.g., taking risks, cost-benefit planning for the future, etc.), and ultimately ensuring a good return on their investments. As a profit-making enterprise, they could ill afford to think like an NGO and give priority to notions of self-determination over practical needs for efficiency.

COMMODIFYING CULTURE

Aside from the issue of participation, the company and I disagreed substantively on the role of culture in Posada Amazonas. The company was eager to promote culture as an added attraction. Here, again, they hoped to have an anthropologist who could help push this through—referring again to the "persuade" level of participation. As anthropologists are known to "deal in" culture, some in the company thought my presence would be helpful in identifying and "rescuing" Ese'eja ethnic identity. Rather than helping objectify and showcase for tourists certain features of indigenous culture in Infierno, I perceived the contribution I could make as quite different.

Early on, there was a great deal of attention on Posada Amazonas and, by extension, on the community. Over the course of research, I encountered seven anthropologists, five biologists, four filmmakers—including the BBC and Discovery Channel—four volunteers, and six NGOs—all in one community with 80 households. Other anthropologists carrying out research in the community joined me in expressing concern about how so much attention might affect how culture in the community was being interpreted, represented, and exploited for profit, as well as who would be making decisions about such matters. Specifically, we encouraged community members in Infierno to consider how displaying aspects of their culture for tourists might challenge local meanings. This was a subject of great anthropological interest, beyond the need to put more "local color" in the brochures. Because Posada Amazonas is a locally managed tourism project, people in Infierno were becoming not only the subjects of brochures but also active participants in determining what was being said and depicted about them.

This became especially apparent to me one afternoon when I was showing a small stack of photographs to Diego, a young Ese'eja man who had been deeply involved in the tourism project from the beginning. One of the photographs in the stack portrayed Gustavo, an Ese'eja man in his 40s, dressed in a traditional tunic called a *cushma,* clutching a bow and arrow, grinning slightly, and gazing directly into the camera. Diego studied the picture for a few moments, and then, holding it up for better perspective, declared, "This will be great for the brochure!"

I was immediately taken aback, for I had not once considered using the photograph for a brochure. Though I could see that it was a provocative image, it was one that Gustavo had requested I shoot for his own use, not for public consumption. Later, I thought about Diego's comment, and how much it revealed, in so few words, his consciousness of public image, his awareness of tourists' desire for a "real-looking" Ese'eja, and his knowledge of the fact that Infierno had become a place to be seen and, in that way, consumed. I realized also that not everyone in Infierno perceived things in the same way Diego had, and perhaps that was precisely the point: Diego had been involved in tourism from the beginning, and his involvement had already somehow influenced his sense of self and his desire to project the "right image" to tourists, one that would be perceived as ethnically authentic and adorned with the appropriate accoutrements of Ese'eja culture.

As an ethnographer, I perceived that my contribution to Posada Amazonas was to characterize these kinds of changes in Infierno rather than to do what the company hoped, which was to help market culture. Often my conversations with both sides entailed asking people to consider what culture and ethnicity meant for them and why. Do some people have "more culture" than others? What does it mean to be Ese'eja or riberenho (a riverine person) or Andean, and why are some of these characteristics perhaps more interesting to tourists than others? These types of discussions were invariably rich and animated, and, after just one year, we could all see more conscious planning about how to manage the community's cultural resources for tourism.

CONCLUSION: MEDIATING BETWEEN HOSTS AND HOSTS

As I describe all the points of disconnect, I'm afraid I might be making the case against the brokering role of anthropologists in ecotourism projects. But in fact my experience practicing anthropology between Infierno and Rainforest Expeditions proved both effective and enlightening in several respects. For one, learning and telling both sides of the story, especially through ethnography, allowed me to reveal the whole story of Posada Amazonas, beyond just the economic costs and benefits of ecotourism. This meant unraveling why people were choosing to participate in ecotourism or not and how their decisions were often related to social and cultural roles and perceptions within the community, as opposed to a mere lack of understanding. The ethnographic approach also forced me to include analyses of process, in addition to impacts—that is, how and why there were gains and losses in Infierno, in addition to what the changes were. Answers to these types of questions may ultimately have more important implications for conservation than do the more unidimensional analyses of jobs gained or income earned.

In the case of Posada Amazonas, process-oriented analyses helped define the concept of "participation" and clarify the usefulness or difficulty or confusion participation presented for different kinds of actors in the project. The process-driven, ethnographic approach also added nuance to the idea of "the local community," highlighting the ways in which diverse sectors within the group perceived, reacted to, and defined success differentially. The holistic assessment extending beyond economics also focused attention on issues surrounding the commodification of culture, and how it could and should be represented (and by whom) in the setting of Posada Amazonas.

Finally, in some ways, my role as a mediator between the two hosts helped to create a level of transparency and openness in the working dialogue between them. As I pointed out differences in their perspectives and expectations, each side gradually learned more about the other, and the partnership actually seemed to gain strength rather than becoming debilitated. When I pointed out disconnects between what was being said, done, and felt, the company was able to gain greater insight into its own actions and into those of the community, while the members of Infierno also began to affirm that their partnership in Posada Amazonas represented a new kind of development, one in which they stood on equal ground with their partners, despite so many economic and social differences with Rainforest Expeditions. In time, as more and more local communities become involved in ecotourism operations, the role of mediator, sometimes played by anthropologists, will be able to add new understanding to such partnerships.

NOTE

1. A Google search for "Posada Amazonas" reveals a huge number of links to tour companies promoting this ecotourism destination, usually accompanied by many pictures of local flora and fauna.

REFERENCES CITED

Arnstein, S.R.
    1969 A Ladder of Citizen Participation. American Institute of Planners Journal 35:216–224.
American Ornithological Union (AOU)
    1998 The AOU Checklist of North American Birds. Maclean, VA: Union.
Boorstin, Daniel J.
    1961 The Image: A Guide to Pseudo-Events in America. New York: Harper and Row.
Borman, Randy
    1999 Cofan: Story of the Forest People and the Outsiders. Cultural Survival Quarterly 23: 48–50.
Epler Word, Megan
    1998 Meeting the Global Challenge of Community Participation in Ecotourism: Case Studies and Lessons from Ecuador. Working Paper No. 2. Washington, DC: The Nature Conservancy.
Foster, Robin B., Theodore A. Parker, Alwin H. Gentry, Louise H. Emmons, Avecita Chicchon, Tom Schulenberg, Lily Rodriguez, Gerardo Lamas, Hernan Ortega, Javier Icochea, Watler Wust, Monico Romo, J. Alban Castillo, Oliver Phillips, Carlos Reynel, Anderw Kratter, Paul K. Donahue, and Linda J. Barkley
    1994 The Tambopata-Candamo Reserved Zone of Southeastern Peru: A Biological Assessment. RAP Working Papers 6. Washington, DC: Conservation International.
Giannecchini, Joan
    1993 Ecotourism: New Partners, New Relationships. Conservation Biology 7:429–432.
Gentry, Alwin H.
    1990 Four Neotropical Forests. New Haven: Yale University Press.
Grimble, Robin, and Man-Kwun Chan
    1995 Stakeholder Analysis for Natural Resource Management in Developing Countries: Some Practical Guidelines for Making Management More Participatory and Effective. Natural Resources Forum 19:113–124.

Groom, Martha A., Robert D. Podolsky, and Charles A. Munn

   1991 Tourism as a Sustained Use of Wildlife: A Case Study of Madre de Dios, Southeastern Peru. In Neotropical Wildlife Use and Conservation. J. G. Robinson and K. H. Redford, eds. Pp. 393–412. Chicago: University of Chicago Press.

Honey, Martha S

   1999 Ecotourism and Sustainable Development: Who Owns Paradise? Washington, DC: Island Press.

Langholz J.

   1999 Exploring the Effects of Alternative Income Opportunities on Rainforest Use: Insights from Guatemala's Maya Biosphere Reserve. Society and Natural Resources 12(2): 139–149.

Lindberg, Kreg

   1991 Economic Policies for Maximizing Nature Tourism's Contribution to Sustainable Development. Washington, DC: World Resources Institute.

MacCannell, Dean

   1976 The Tourist. 2nd edition. New York: Schocken Books.

Ministerio de Turismo (MITINCI)

   1998 Madre de Dios 1994–1997:Arribos y Pernoctaciones de Extranjeros en Establecimientos de Hospedaje, Segun Nacionalidad. Lima, Peru: Oficina de Estadisticas.

Nash, Dennison

   1996 Anthropology of Tourism. New York: Pergamon.

Swain, Margaret Byrne

   1995 Gender in Tourism. Annals of Tourism Research 22:247–266.

Wunder, Sven

   1999 Promoting Forest Conservation through Ecotourism Income? A Case Study from the Ecuadorian Amazon Region. CIFOR Occasional Paper No. 21. Bogor Barat, Indonesia: Centre for International Forestry Research.

   2000 Ecotourism and Economic Incentives: An Empirical Approach. Ecological Economics 32(3):465–479.

KEEPING THE PEOPLE IN THE PARKS:
A CASE STUDY FROM GUATEMALA

TIM WALLACE
North Carolina State University

DANIELA N. DIAMENTE
Universidad del Valle de Guatemala

No settled family or community has ever called its home
place an "environment." None has ever called its feeling
for its home place "biocentric" or "anthropocentric." None
has ever thought of its connection to its home place as
"ecological," deep or shallow.... the terms themselves are
culturally sterile.... the real names of the environment are
the names of rivers and river valleys; creeks, ridges, and
mountains; towns and cities; lakes, woodlands, lanes,
roads, creatures, and *people.*

WENDELL BERRY
Sex, Economy, Freedom, and Community, page 34, emphasis
added

*Ecotourism is seen as a mechanism by which environmental conservation can be
promoted and attained. Nevertheless, nature conservation NGOs do not really
understand that ecotourism has unforeseen consequences. Anthropologists can be
good mediators between the conservation NGOs and the communities that are
the targets of their ecotourism projects. This paper describes a case study in which
the authors were indirectly consultants for The Nature Conservancy in Guatemala
and the manner in which they served as a social conscience for the NGO. The
authors also served as assistants in developing a collaborative network for tourism
projects that have had direct benefits both in the short run and in the long run for
the communities participating in those projects. The conclusion drawn from the
case study is that applied anthropologists can play a significant role in mitigating
the negative economic effects of conservation projects that are designed mainly
to help wildlife rather than people. These anthropologists may also have a role in*

NAPA Bulletin 23, pp. 191–218, ISBN 1-931303-22-3. © 2005 by the American Anthropological Association. All
rights reserved. Please direct all requests for permissions to photocopy or reproduce article content through
the University of California Press's Rights and Permissions website, www.ucpress.edu/journals/rights.htm.

helping local communities benefit from the ecotourism development efforts of nature conservation-oriented NGOs, which are often found as part of the requirements for receiving funding from their donors. Key Words: ecotourism, Guatemala, conservation, participatory development, NGOs

INTRODUCTION

I was a teenager the first time I ever thought of a concept of "the environment." It happened when I started seeing "Do Not Litter, $200 Fine" signs along major highways and the early interstate road system. The next time I thought about it was during the Lyndon Johnson administration when Lady Bird Johnson, the First Lady, was the promoter of an anti-billboard campaign along interstate highways. I wondered what the big deal was, since I actually enjoyed seeing crazy signs to break up the monotony of driving long distances. Then came Earth Day, and soon there was a whole generation of people who had a strong commitment to environmental protection and conservation. Well, now I am nearing my sixth decade, and environmentalists are as active politically across the globe as they are here in the United States. On the other hand, for Diamente, a 20-something graduate student in anthropology, "the environment" has always been a basic concept and one widely accepted by most U.S. citizens. In the last thirty or forty years, there has been a proliferation of special NGOs whose sole purpose is to "protect, defend, and conserve" the environment. Now there are the Sierra Club, the Wilderness Defense Fund, the World Wildlife Fund, and The Nature Conservancy, to mention only a few. Anthropologists, too, are environmental activists, and the American Anthropological Association has a large, relatively new section called Anthropology and the Environment. I myself am the listowner of a listserve called Ambientnet (ambientnet@lists.ncsu.edu), an outreach tool of the Society for Applied Anthropology's Environmental Anthropology Topical Interest Group.

The concern with the environment is paralleled by the historical growth and development of nature parks and national parks as well as the global expansion of tourism beyond the core to the periphery of Western and Central Europe and the United States and Canada. The concept of the "park" was invented in the West (Harper 2002:11), but it is the U.S. concept of "national parks," exemplified by the institutionalization of the National Park Service, that is most emulated in developing countries (Brechin et al.:16). The underlying motivation for the first parks was the conservation of what had been seen as rapidly diminishing natural resources (forests, wildlife, etc.).[1] In rural, usually remote "wilderness" areas, humans are perceived as the fatal factor in the demise of our ecosystems (Marks 1984:4–5), so the concept of "parks without people" was born. In the United Kingdom, parks are seen quite differently as serving the economic interests of local people, but it is the U.S. model that has been most widely diffused. In the developing world, the primary concern of environmental NGOs is, as it is in the United States, conservation of what are thought to be scarce and dwindling natural resources.

In many places around the world, natural resources are threatened by numerous factors, including the threat from enormous population growth and the lack of technology to make more efficient use of those resources. Madagascar, an island with incredibly unique and diverse wildlife, is a clear example of the very rapid loss of primary forests that may hasten the demise of many unique species of flora and fauna. In an attempt to assist in slowing deforestation, USAID funded several major environmental conservation projects in the 1990s, one of which was the Ranomafana National Park Project (RNPP) initiated by Patricia Wright, a physical anthropologist and MacArthur Foundation Fellowship winner now located at SUNY-Stony Brook.

I visited Ranomafana for five weeks in 1992 as an agricultural marketing consultant. RNPP was an ecotourism project that depended on the successful introduction of a national park for lemur protection. At that time there were about 30,000 Tanala and Betsileo peoples who were living on the periphery of Ranomafana National Park and depended on forest products for their survival. For generations they had relied on the forests for subsistence, but now they were required to stay out of the park and were sometimes arrested for activities using forest resources, such as chopping wood, hunting animals, harvesting crayfish, et cetera. The project hired an agronomist and an ecotourism expert to help develop the park and provide assistance to local people. Furthermore, it was expected that income from working in ecotourism, chiefly as park guides, would be a principal substitute for the locals' loss of access to forest resources.

At the time of my visit, there was little direct economic benefit to local residents from tourism. Most of the income generated came from the project administrators, workers, and scientists (Wallace and Diamente 2002:10). The few ecotourists who visited the local parks usually stayed in the park itself and did not lodge in local hotels or eat at restaurants run by local residents. A small number of local residents worked as guides, but they earned more from selling national tourists the fern tree pots they made from endangered trees inside the park. A recent ethnography by Janice Harper (2002:211–12), who worked in a Tanala community near RNPP, concludes that the payoffs to Tanala have been very few, and that indeed the local residents may be worse off today than before the project started.

The point is that economics, ecotourism, and conservation may be related, but they don't always go together well. Anthropologists must be the voice of conscience when conservationists want to use tourism to justify projects that might have negative impacts on local residents. Jin Igoe (2004) recently published an excellent ethnography of national parks and conservationism in East Africa. In one telling passage (Igoe 2004:320–31), he reports that one community-based conservation project he studied, ironically called "Good Neighborliness," did not have the support, for a variety of reasons, of the local Maasai community. Nevertheless, in spite of local resistance to the project, the project directors and tour operators all insisted that the project should go forward regardless, leading to a paradoxical position in which a community-based project forged ahead without community support.

Environmental conservation and ecotourism development should take into account the needs not only of the international and national communities but also of the local people. This is an important reason why the anthropological perspective is an essential element in national park development projects. Within this context, anthropologists do three things very well: (1) they help environmental NGOs maintain an awareness of the importance of including local people in conservation planning, (2) they help local people become involved in the planning process, and (3) they translate environmental concepts employed by the local people so they can be incorporated into site conservation plans.[2] Also, anthropologists bring with them a transcultural perspective in which an understanding of how cultural patterns work in one context helps to understand how cultural patterns could work in other cultural contexts. Another element of anthropological investigation is its preoccupation with the well-being of local people and with the cultural transformations throughout historical advancements.

A CASE STUDY: THE NATURE CONSERVANCY AND THE PARKS IN PERIL PROJECT

In this paper, using an example from Guatemala in which we recently participated, we suggest a model by which anthropologists who study in tourism can work with conservationists to help ensure that the development process includes participation from local residents and reflects local environmental concepts and attitudes toward tourism development. The NGO that developed this project in Guatemala was The Nature Conservancy, which received its funding from USAID. The Conservancy has been in Guatemala for some years, working in the northern forested areas of tropical Guatemala, Mexico, and Belize with varying degrees of success (Beavers 1995). In 2002, the Conservancy decided to direct some of its resources in its "Parks in Peril" program toward a long-term conservation project in the heart of the Mayan highlands west of Guatemala City.

Guatemala's western highlands are characterized by a series of tall, forested volcanoes formed by relatively recent geologic events, including one about a million years ago that produced Lake Atitlán. Located in the Department of Sololá, the lake bed is a collapsed crater about 800 feet below the surface and is surrounded by jagged-edged volcanic remnants as well as more recent volcanoes, some of which are still active. Also, the slopes of these highlands are home to the largest indigenous population in Central America (Herlihy 1997:217). About 56 percent of Guatemala's modern population are descendants of the ancient Maya, and Sololá has one of the highest concentrations of Maya people in the country. The region has seen rapid population growth in recent years, but it is also one of the poorest regions of the country. The beauty of the lake, the mountains ("la Cordillera Volcanica"), and the surrounding countryside has long attracted Guatemalan and international tourists alike. Thus, expensive tourist hotels and restaurants in some of the towns around the lake exist side by side with very modest dwellings of native Maya. In the eyes of the Conservancy, the combination of poverty, growing population, and international and domestic tourism have put the health of local wildlife and flora in jeopardy. Mayans, on the hand, regularly engage in their own kind of conservation practices (Hornback 2004) and often see themselves as stewards of the environment (Winkler 2001).

In January 2002, I arrived in Guatemala on a Fulbright to teach a course in applied anthropology and a course in the anthropology of tourism. In addition, I was to lead an ethnographic field school for anthropology and ecotourism students from the Universidad del Valle de Guatemala (UVG), my sponsoring university, and to undertake a small research project at Lake Atitlán. One morning shortly after my arrival, I was introduced to Edwin Castellanos, director of the UVG Environmental Studies Center (Centro de Estudios Ambientales). Dr. Castellanos asked me to join his group of UVG researchers in a subcontract to the Conservancy to produce an assessment of the

FIGURE 1. At 800 feet in depth, Lake Atitlán is the deepest freshwater lake in Central America.

status of native flora and fauna of the Lake Atitlán National Park. The central focus of the research was to find ways to counter the actual threats to the ecological biodiversity of the Lake Atitlán watershed, and in particular to the southwestern side of the lake, which appears to have had less tourism activity and growth than the other side. My role as a tourism expert in the project was a relatively small part of the overall schema. My responsibility was to "develop an assessment of the potential of ecotourism as a conservation-related income source" (UVG 2002:49) for the Mayan people of the southwestern side of the lake—the area that has the greatest amount of natural and secondary growth forests and thus, potentially, the greatest amount of new ecotourism projects. North American students and a Guatemalan student from the UVG were to assist in data gathering for the project.

ECOTOURISM AT LAKE ATITLÁN THROUGH THE ANTHROPOLOGICAL LENS

Whereas The Nature Conservancy approached the ecotourism component of the project with its "nature first" ideas, we found that it would be unfortunate, if indeed impossible, to ignore the human and cultural elements of the environment. After all, the "environment" includes not only nature but also the individuals—both local residents and visiting tourists—who interact with and utilize nature and who together create a community. As anthropologists, our greatest concern engaged this broader definition of community when considering the terms of reference set out by the grant. In general, the Conservancy grant requested an assessment of the state of tourism development on the southeast side of Lake Atitlán, while keeping the ideals of ecotourism as goals for the all-too-near future. However, we quickly discovered the urgency of many social, ecological, economic, and cultural issues that need to be addressed prior to developing new ecotourism sites in the area.

The Conservancy proposal envisioned a three-year project moving from a diagnostic phase to a site conservation—planning phase to the project's implementation phase. We were in the thick of the field school and our research when we were asked to provide suggestions for projects for the year-two phase of the grant. Certainly, this forced us not only to think beyond the work that we had been able to accomplish by that date, but also it required that we review what the grant had set out to do in this first phase of the project. The original funds set aside for the tourism research component had already been cut by two-thirds, so we were quite concerned that we did not have enough resources to do a thorough assessment, let alone enough data to prepare for projects in the second year. Nevertheless, the principal investigators at the Conservancy insisted we should forge ahead with a much-scaled-back "background research" study that would "help them to focus and better manage" their development projects. They also made the assumption that we, the foreign anthropologists, with very little funding for research resources, would be capable of determining what the local people needed to improve their socioeconomic situation vis-à-vis ecotourism. In spite of the limitations, we were able to produce a set of recommendations for year-two projects. Several of these were implemented, as we will discuss later.

The original thrust of the ecotourism component of the project set out to investigate the conditions of tourism, the principal actors in tourism or related to it, and the potential for new sources of income from tourism within each of the six communities of the pilot area. However, the Conservancy seemed to hint that we should search for potential ecotourism development areas in places outside the Maya communities—primarily in the heavily forested areas of the Mayan municipalities and on lands held by private chalet owners. The southwestern side of the lake is much more forested than the northeastern side due to the great height (above 3,000 meters) of its three volcanoes (Atitlán, Toliman, and San Pedro). Their steep slopes at higher elevations make farming more difficult. The southwestern side also has a larger area of land covered by coffee trees. The northeastern side has more maize and vegetable farming and thus fewer trees.

As anthropologists, we were aware of the possible issues, obstacles, and dangers associated with targeting tourism development. We made sure to keep our eyes and ears focused on the members of the communities and to examine what tourists actually do when they visit the region and how their visits interconnect with the lives and activities of the local residents. The indigenous Mayan peoples have a history of caring for their land, and the Lake Atitlán region is certainly not an exception. Even though rapid and vast population increases have caused stresses on the land and the ways in which the people care for it, all aspects of the land—its water and forests—remain sacred elements of the culture. Nevertheless, a number of additional social and environmental factors have damaged or might one day endanger the rich biodiversity of the region. These factors form the basis for The Nature Conservancy's concerns.

In this respect, the Conservancy's intentions are good. Seeing ecotourism as ideal, its goals are for more tourists, more local participation, better environmental education and awareness, and thus increased benefits for the people and the land. Unfortunately, the equation is not that simple. The lack of proper training in tourism management, the lack of institutional support for tourism entrepreneurs, and the inability to effectively provide widespread security for ecotourists in rural areas cannot be overlooked or solved very easily.[3] Moreover, the forests where these new ecotourism destinations were "supposed" to be concealed more than the numerous *Costumbrista* spiritual sites of the people.[4] Not long ago, in the 1980s, they were the hiding places, battlegrounds, and graveyards of very many people during the most violent years of Guatemala's civil war. Still today, there are stories that not even the forests will tell and dangers that neither TNC nor any anthropologists truly could foresee. Therefore, the ecotourism component of this project could only be provided by following the notion that ecotourism means exploring to all ends, leaving no ground untouched, or moving deeper into forested land with hopes of "preserving" its biodiversity. After all, what was once pristine can all too quickly become poisoned. Ecotourism development, as we saw it, should be aimed at taking advantage of the biodiversity and beauty of the lake in places where there were already possibilities.[5]

In our study, not only did we try to estimate the potential for ecotourism development, but we also evaluated current levels of infrastructure and of institutional and community support for more tourism. In addition, we interacted with project leaders frequently to make them aware of the need to be careful in drawing conclusions before we more fully understood how the proposed conservation projects and tourism development plans would impact local communities. Even though there are few destinations where planning actually has preceded development, it is essential that ecotourism development, as experts agree, is well planned and involves a high level of local participation before initiating tourism businesses. We wanted to produce a report that addressed the conditions necessary for successful and sustainable ecotourism development and that would also support environmental conservation on the southwest side of Lake Atitlán. Ecotourism can only be viable when it completes its dual mission of providing local economic benefits while helping to protect and conserve the ecological environment (Whelan 1991:20).

One major problem for future ecotourism plans was the lack of safety and security for tourists who planned to hike trails in forested areas between and above the towns in the study area. Since the end of Guatemala's 30-year civil war in early 1997, there has been a rise in ambushes of tourist buses and private vehicles, armed robberies, lynchings, and kidnappings (Gonzalez Arrecis 2004). The large number of tourists around Lake Atitlán makes them attractive targets. During our stay, two tourists were relieved of all their possessions by two armed men as they walked along a trail from one town (Santa Cruz) to another (San Marcos La Laguna). In January 2004, three tourists traveling with an armed guide were confronted by four machete-wielding, pistol-toting thugs. The guide fled after he shot at and missed the robbers, leaving the three tourists to be robbed of everything they carried (from the website of the U.S. Embassy in Guatemala).

Although The Nature Conservancy wanted us to investigate specific ecotourism projects that might be undertaken by private Ladino[6] and Mayan entrepreneurs, early on we came to the conclusion that so little was known about tourism at Lake Atitlán that we needed to reorient our research along more diagnostic lines. The more familiar we became with the Conservancy perspective, the more we began to realize that it assumed the local residents themselves were the main threats to the biodiversity of the region. Despite the presence of several excellent ecologists on the Conservancy staff, it seemed to us that they failed to recognize in the grant proposal that local people had been living in this environment for centuries and that they had probably worked

FIGURE 2. The Maya make discreet use of their land, but tourists need hotels.

within a time-tested system of checks and balances involving the nature of the region. On the other hand, the Conservancy did assume that "modernization" was bringing with it unforeseen consequences that might negatively affect the environment. To its credit, the organization also hired a UVG graduate student in anthropology, who in turn recruited six volunteer anthropology undergraduates from the UVG to research the ways local residents use forest resources in their daily lives. However, we faulted the Conservancy on three accounts: (1) they did not provide sufficient funds to hire a team of professional anthropologists to do the research, (2) they generally were uninterested in investigating local concepts of ecology, and (3) they did not allocate enough time to establish the rapport with locals that would provide the basis for in-depth ethnographic reporting. To compensate for this, we provided logistic support and mentoring for the undergraduate volunteers to help them gather and process the data more effectively.

Another thing that the Conservancy overlooked in their proposal was the idea that tourism itself may be a cause of negative effects on the environment. For example, around the lake are nearly a thousand vacation homes, locally referred to as *chalets*, built by largely absentee Ladino and foreign landowners

(Petrich 1999:88).[7] Most of the chalets are precariously perched on craggy promontories on the steep slopes of the mountains that rise from the lake. Add this to the fact that there are more than 100,000 tourists that visit the shores of the lake each year. Between the potential erosion caused by the chalets and the waste generated by the tourists, not to mention the cultural effects caused by tourist demands, there is the potential for dramatic effects on the local environment. Nevertheless, The Nature Conservancy focused on local people and their relationship to environmental harm and not on the tourists and chalet owners and their potential for damaging the environment. As anthropologists, we both believed that it was our responsibility to refocus the Conservancy perspective on tourism and the environment while still fulfilling our contractual responsibilities. In light of our concerns about this proposal, we developed the following objectives for our part of the research:

1. Investigate the strengths and weaknesses of current and potential tourism destinations and activities in the Lake Atitlán area, focusing on the capacity and flexibility of regional tourism in order to modify and create better tourism development for the pilot area;
2. Identify key actors in tourism within the pilot area; and
3. Determine strategies to strengthen institutions related to tourism development in the pilot area.

FIELDWORK

The fieldwork part of the study began at the start of March 2002 with the permanent presence in Panajachel of one of the authors (Diamente) and visits three times per week by the other author (Wallace). During this time we initiated contact and communication with the principal actors in tourism in the Atitlán region and arranged the logistical foundations for the arrival of the North American and UVG students at the end of May. They were to work on a series of rapid analyses of touristic elements in the Atitlán region. Meanwhile, Diamente, with the assistance of Wallace, began a rapid analysis of the impacts of tourism and ecotourism in the six communities of the pilot area. Until the end of May, Wallace concentrated on the training of UVG students, maintaining contact with the North American students, and compiling a bibliography relevant to the topic, with reference to previous tourism studies in Atitlán. On May 24, the students arrived at the lake and moved in with local families in the pilot area. In addition to these 17 students, six additional UVG anthropology students worked on the collection of data in the human use and management of natural resources.

From the end of May until July 6, the students carried out their fieldwork using ethnographic methods such as participant-observation, informal and semi-structured interviews, and other participatory methods to create a research project on a tourism topic. They finished their preliminary reports prior to leaving the Atitlán region, and we incorporated their findings into our final report. Throughout the seven-week term of the field school, we held classes in ethnographic training for the students and managed the research projects while continuing our own ethnographic research (systematic observation and interviewing) for the project in the six communities in the pilot area.

The anthropology and ecotourism students from Guatemala and North America who participated in the field school contributed greatly to the research activities and data collection associated with the grant, in addition to designing and completing their individual research projects. Although we did not specifically assign any of the activities, with the possible and loose exception of activity 4 below, the students did volunteer valuable information that aided in carrying out the required research. With their help, we were able to carry out the following associated activities to accomplish the original objectives of The Nature Conservancy project:

1. Identify key actors such as local residents, guides, private business owners, NGOs, government and private leaders—all who have or have had initiatives in tourism;
2. Compile and review previous studies on tourism in the Lake Atitlán area to ground the fieldwork and to complement it with the necessary information;
3. Carry out a rapid analysis of the ecotourism and tourism elements in the six municipalities of the pilot area;
4. Carry out a rapid ethnographic analysis of cultural and environmental impacts of actual tourism in order to investigate more carefully the type of problems that exist and to better determine the actions that can be taken both to abate the negative impacts and to augment the beneficial impacts;
5. Compile data for GIS maps in order to visualize the distribution of actual and future tourism resources; and,
6. Determine strategies for training workshops for individuals employed in tourism services, such as tour guides and transportation workers such as bus and van drivers and ferry boat captains.

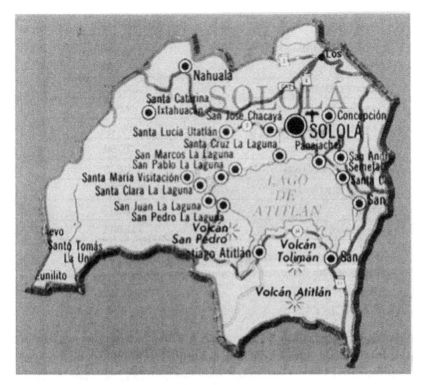

FIGURE 3. Communities around Lake Atitlán, Guatemala.

The six communities within the pilot area of this study were San Marcos La Laguna, Santiago Atitlán, San Pedro La Laguna, Santa Clara La Laguna, San Juan La Laguna, and San Lucas Toliman (see Figure 3). These communities differ along a number of lines. Not only do they vary in size, population, economy, and degrees of development, but they also are made up of three different Mayan ethnic groups. Santiago Atitlán, San Pedro, and San Juan are predominantly Tz'utujil, while San Lucas and San Marcos are mainly Kaqchikel. The majority of Santa Clara residents are of Quiché language and culture. Also, given the varying locations around the lake, each town exhibits a unique potential for ecotourism related to its contiguous natural environment.

Figure 4 shows the distribution of tourists in the study area; for comparison purposes, it also shows the distribution in the town of Panajachel, the gateway town to the tourist attractions of Lake Atitlán. Only three of the six

COMMUNITY	NUMBER OF INTERNATIONAL TOURISTS 2001–2002
Santiago Atitlán	54,750
San Pedro La Laguna	29,000
San Marcos La Laguna	10,950
San Lucas Tolimán	2,560
San Juan La Laguna	1,825
Santa Clara La Laguna	210
Total:	99,295
Panajachel	141,000

FIGURE 4. Estimated number of tourists visiting the study area in comparison with Panajachel, 2001–2002. (Some tourists visit more than one community during their stay.)

communities (Santiago, San Pedro, and San Marcos) receive a considerable amount of tourists, although all of them manifest a certain degree of potential for development. On the other hand, both San Juan La Laguna and, to a lesser degree, Santa Clara La Laguna express interest in ecotourism development but do not see any considerable amount of tourism at the present. San Juan has the advantage of neighboring San Pedro, and therefore some tourists take day trips or hike through the town. However, few find the women's weaving cooperative or the talented painters (see http://www.artemaya.com), for example, since its minimal attractions are not well developed as of yet. Similarly, Santa Clara, a mountain town and the only one not bordering Lake Atitlán, does not have much to offer in terms of attractions to the scarce tourists that happen to pass through, though the denser vegetation in the higher elevations above the town has been designated as the location for a canopy tour.[8]

All of the towns lack a sufficient foundation upon which to build, but San Pedro is the most prepared for more ecotourism development. In Figure 5, we have listed the distribution of touristic services among 12 communities on the shores of Lake Atitlán. The table shows that the gateway town of Panajachel has most of the tourism services and that, with the exception of San Pedro and Santiago Atitlán, there is not much substantial tourism activity at the present. Part of The Nature Conservancy project's goal is to increase the amount of tourism in the less touristed areas by developing ecotourism attractions. We concluded that

Population and Available Services	Santiago*	San Lucas Tolimán*	San Pedro La Laguna*	San Juan La Laguna*	Sta Clara La Laguna*	San Marcos La Laguna*	San Pablo La Laguna*	Sta Catarina Palopó	San Antonio Palopó	Sta Cruz La Laguna	Panajachel	TOTAL
Population (1999)	29,380	21,629	9,508	8,880	6,837	1,685	6,195	2,065	12,015	3,453	10,584	
Hotels	5	5	14	4	2	8	0	4	1	4	54	101
Restaurants	20	10	22	6	3	10	3	5	2	3	97	176
Internet cafés	0	1	5	0	0	0	0	0	0	0	6	12
Spanish schools	2	0	8	0	0	1	0	0	0	0	4	15
Art galleries	17	0	3	1	0	0	0	3	0	0	5	29
Handcraft stores	45	3	6	4	0	0	0	6	3	0	213	280
Bike, kayak, diving rentals	1	0	4	0	0	0	0	0	0	2	6	13
Museums	1	0	0	1	0	0	0	0	0	0	2	3
Tour guides	6	1	20	0	0	0	0	0	0	3	36	67
Travel agencies	0	0	0	0	0	0	0	0	0	0	12	12
TOTAL	96	20	82	15	5	19	3	18	6	12	437	

FIGURE 5. Distribution of tourists and touristic services in Lake Atitlán, Guatemala. Asterisk (*) indicates communities within the study area of The Nature Conservancy project. (Source: Tim Wallace y Daniela N. Diamente, Ecoturismo en el lado Suroeste del Lago Atitlán: Informe Final, Proyecto Los Volcanes, Panajachel, Julio, 2002.)

ecotourism would not prosper in the short run without significantly enhancing security and developing a strong network of local entrepreneurs who were prepared financially and administratively to enter the business. Furthermore, we worried that ecotourism would not provide a large, steady amount of tourists to support new businesses. Finally, we thought it somewhat counterproductive to encourage more tourism when one's goal is to reduce human impact on an already fragile ecosystem, especially if one starts with the assumption that local residents are the principal threat to that ecosystem. For these reasons, we wrote our final report in such a way as to encourage entrepreneurship training, institutional, and community-strengthening projects.

In the next section, we would like to describe two of six communities in which we and our students were working. This brief ethnographic description may help in giving the reader a better understanding of the nature and variety of tourism in these communities, as well as the challenges facing ecotourism development and conservation projects in the study area.

San Pedro La Laguna

In the last ten years, the community of San Pedro La Laguna has become the third most visited destination around the lake, after Panajachel and Santiago Atitlán. And although more tourists visit Santiago, San Pedro has far more overnight guests than any other community except for Panajachel. Tourists like San Pedro because the residents have a live-and-let-live philosophy toward tourists that allows them more freedom of action—more breathing room to relax and enjoy the scenery. Also, many of the tourists are of the backpacker type and are seeking a less expensive, more "authentic" experience. Although authenticity is in the eye of the beholder, and one can vigorously debate which community is the most authentic, San Pedro has a welcoming feel to tourists. In addition, it boasts a growing number of hotels and restaurants that cater to the backpacker tourist. Finally, San Pedro today features about fifteen Spanish-language immersion schools that cater to a diverse tourist client. San Pedro also has the best trail to the top of the local volcano (Volcán San Pedro), which is the least difficult mountain to climb of the three in the region. In next section, we describe what it is like for a tourist who is discovering San Pedro for the first time. Perhaps this account will help the reader better understand the tourism issues that are confronting this town and others like it.

FIGURE 6. San Pedro La Laguna is the fastest growing ecotourism destination around Lake Atitlán.

San Pedro La Laguna: a Mini-Ethnography We arrived in San Pedro by boat from Panajachel, as most tourists travel there, and immediately we were approached by a number of men who insistently offered their tour guide services, just as they do to every boat that docks at the main pier, every hour, every day. Having visited on several occasions already, we knew the routine of "No, gracias," to say to them, as well as to the ubiquitous bread ladies and children, and to the indiscreet "What ya smokin'?" as we passed by the tourist hangouts and up the hill to Big Foot Excursions Travel Agency. This one travel agency in town acts more as an outdoor adventure guide and doubles as a nonprofit reforestation project. Whether tourists want to rent kayaks, bikes, horses, or climb the volcano, they can arrange it. And so we set out with a group of students on a gorgeous, clear morning to "conquer" the top of volcano San Pedro.

Feeling a bit like cattle, we all piled into the back of an oversized pickup truck and headed up the curvy gravel road to the start of the hiking path. First, we passed through the bustling center of town in front of the large, simple Catholic church and its statue of Saint Peter (San Pedro), and it became obvious that this town had become a center for regional commerce. The tourist part of town along the shore, with its winding sandy paths that reveal a variety of international restaurants and cafes, hostels, and language schools, seemed a world away. And all of that faded as we ascended the base of the volcano together.

Crossing through corn fields and criss-crossing through rocky and sparsely forested areas, we huffed our way up the mountainside, stopping to rest quite often. To whom did these sloped *milpas* (corn crop fields) belong, anyway? And how do they feel about all of these tourists tromping through their source of food, income, and life? These thoughts ran through our minds while we intensely concentrated on foot placement, and exhaustion crept in. At the halfway mark, after two hours of hiking and an extended rest, only the more daring and determined half of the group proceeded. While Wallace had to accompany the sensible persons, Diamente pushed on and upward through thickening forest. Although I remember the surroundings to be beautiful, in between grasping vines to pull ourselves up and quite often slipping on the muddy precipitous trail, it was difficult to appreciate the biodiversity that encircled us. Unfortunately, this seems to be the case with most mountain climbers, since the achievement of reaching the peak supersedes the beauty one treads through to get there.

As if the stress of the climb were not tiring enough, being responsible for anything that could have happened drained us. We could not help but worry about someone injuring himself, or, even worse, someone else wanting to hurt us. It is no secret that tourists have been assaulted and robbed on this very volcano, as well as in numerous other areas of the Lake Atitlán region. There is no need to look farther than the U.S. Embassy's homepage to learn of the latest misfortunes. And yet, despite what have become urban legends that prevent some concerned tourists from partaking in such amazing activities, we kept them in mind and took the advice of so many to only venture into unfamiliar territory with a trained local tour guide. We requested three. Just how indispensable a guide is, not only to machete away at the trail and lead the way, became terribly obvious as we finally reached the peak. With a clearing up ahead, and success in mind after four arduous hours, I could not believe that the lead tour guide suddenly ran ahead, out of sight. Dumbfounded, I inquired why he did such a thing when he returned after a few brief moments to lead us up to the lookout. "I had to make sure no one was waiting for us," he simply replied. As my eyes grew wide, he added, "Just a few days ago, when we got up here, there were a group of thieves waiting who then robbed the tourists of all they had." Clearly, some stories take longer to disseminate, if they ever do. This one I decided to keep to myself for the moment, as everyone else seemed awestruck by the magnificent beauty of the view and the incredible sense of self-gratification. The view truly made all the pain and soreness for the following days worth it, at least this time.

In a community meeting a few weeks later, the leaders of Vivamos Mejor, a local NGO and a partner in The Nature Conservancy project, asked us to share some of our data on tourism to help promote their ideas. They wanted to create a project to improve the climb of the volcano San Pedro and possibly to construct a geology museum as part of the plan. We told our story, whose point was that security, or rather a lack thereof, was a major issue and needed to be a community concern. The work that Vivamos Mejor is trying to initiate, together with interested members of the community and municipality, has two aims: (1) increasing the income and benefits of tourism for local residents, and (2) recognizing and conserving their rich natural environment. Our concern for safety, along with facts on the quantity and rapid growth of tourism development in the town, helped put this project into perspective. At the very least, it served as yet another reminder of the need for a strategic development plan that would strengthen security for tourists, improve infrastructure, involve more local actors, and initiate an environmental education program for both children and adults, possibly through the museum project. At the close of this meeting, everyone agreed that the volcano is one of their attractions with the greatest ecotourism potential and that steps need to be taken to take advantage of and protect the resources they have. What remained to be decided, and that which is still in process, is what those steps will be. The basic goals are always the same: increased benefits for locals, tourists, and the land. Our question for them remained: How can the incentives to conserve and care more for the land be encouraged and communicated to both local residents and tourists?

Maybe the people of San Pedro will be able to direct their attention to this question and others after all. Since this first meeting, members of the community representing various sectors have formed a tourism committee that will be working directly with the municipality and Vivamos Mejor. With technical support from experts with Vivamos Mejor, they have drawn up plans both to improve and expand the climb of the volcano as a tourist attraction and also to address the necessary issues, including security. In fact, in a recent telephone call I learned that with the help of one of my students from the field school in 2003, the trail improvements have been completed, a tourist information building at the start of the trail has been constructed, and the guides have been retrained to begin working with the expected large numbers of tourists.

Santiago Atitlán

The community of Santiago Atitlán receives the largest number of tourists in the study area, second only to Panajachel around Lake Atitlán. However, very few of the tourists stay more than a few hours. This is reflected in the fact that this city of 30,000 Tz'utujil Maya has only four hotels, only two of which have accommodations geared towards an international clientele. Nevertheless, Santiago has many attractions. It has a vivid culture, well-known artists and wood carvers, a famous and tragic history, and a stunning location at the base of Atitlán and Toliman volcanoes that faces the bay on the other side of San Pedro volcano. Its historical importance as the ancient capital of the Tz'utujiles at Chuitinamit (as yet unrestored) is as significant as its more recent history during the civil war years. Given the presence and support of the guerrillas in the surrounding mountains, the violent years had a tremendous impact on the community. The Atitecos (residents of Santiago Atitlán), however, accrued international fame for their resistance and perseverance against the Guatemalan army, especially when they united and successfully expelled the military in 1990 after a protest that resulted in tragedy for Atitecos. To commemorate the event, they constructed the "Parque de la Paz" (Park of Peace) on the site where 13 Atitecos were murdered during their protest against the local military regime. Today, the site serves not only as a sacred place and reminder to the local community but also as an informative site of cultural and historical tourist interest.

In addition, the Catholic church, its renovated (and syncretic) altarpiece, and its colorful, crowded traditional celebrations during Holy Week serve as tourist attractions. That is to say, if there are three things that one must visit when in Santiago, as one resident claimed, "They are the Parque de la Paz for history, the Catholic church for tradition, and the notorious Maximón (a key icon in contemporary nativist religious beliefs) for Atiteco culture." The religious life of Atitecos plays an important role in the community and has become a tourist attraction for its "costumbre" traditions and, more than anything, for the infamous, venerated, revered wooden statue of Saint Simon or "Maximón." In fact, the first thing tourists hear when they step off the docks, or anywhere within the town, is "Maximón," as tour guides—often small children—offer their services. Tourists visit the *cofradia* (religious brotherhood often associated with syncretic Mayan-Catholic rituals) where Maximón resides

FIGURE 7. The Maya have adapted to change for centuries, and their customs attract tourists.

for a year at a time to witness ceremonies or make an offering of cigars, alcohol, or money, all of which are much appreciated and expected by the members of the *cofradia* that keep the decorative, wooden-masked figure company.

Inevitably, on the way to any of these three tourist attractions, a tourist passes through "Calle Gringo" where one can purchase an almost overwhelming abundance of weavings, carvings, paintings, and an endless number of other souvenir-type artworks of the Atitecos. We discovered a number of issues during our research, such as the social and economic consequences of local competition and children in tourism, directly related to this street alone (see Reyes 2002 and Castro 2002). Despite the high level of day tourism in Santiago, few tourists actually stay for more than a few hours, an occurrence that reduces the amount of income from tourism. On the other hand, Atitecos find tourists to be a very mixed blessing and, according to many of my students who have been housed in Santiago, they appear quite happy to see the last boatload of tourists leave for Panajachel. It is also well known around the lake that Atitecos are not very open to tourists and newcomers. Surely it is difficult to appreciate the biological and cultural diversity that the area embodies in this short time, which both resembles and

FIGURE 8. This rescued hawk is one of the main attractions at the Butterfly Farm of the Atitlán Nature Reserve, a local private venture.

generates the lack of interest, awareness, and activities in the natural and cultural environments.

Santiago is also very important for The Nature Conservancy project because it has one of the largest forested areas in the Lake Atitlán watershed. Most of the forested area is located on Atitlán and Toliman volcanoes, and the mayor of Santiago is the steward for most of it because it is considered community land. He alone is authorized to permit its use, whether it be for cutting trees for firewood or for permitting ecotourism ventures. At the present time, there is almost no local support for developing ecotourism activities—or really any tourism activities—beyond Calle Gringo. The Conservancy would like this to change, but has not had much success in getting the municipality's cooperation.

By contrast, the mayor of San Pedro La Laguna and his municipality have been very supportive of new tourism and ecotourism products. In part, this is due to coffee's recent and dramatic failure as an income-generating venture, which makes tourism look pretty good as a means to generate income for local residents. Another reason is that Vivamos Mejor has cultivated close working ties with the mayor of San Pedro and other community allies. Atitecos, on the other hand, have a broader array of economic activities on which to depend for their livelihood, and though they are anxious to sell their crafts to tourists, they don't want them around for too long. Vivamos Mejor has not been able to develop a strong working relationship with the Santiago municipality and has not spent much time cultivating relationships there. One result of this difference between the two municipalities is that most of the Conservancy efforts have been concentrated in the area of San Pedro. It is hoped that Atiteco attitudes will change over time, but we believe that this change will not occur quickly, if at all, without a more concerted, better-funded, community-based marketing scheme.

CONCLUSION: THE NATURE CONSERVANCY PROJECT, ECOTOURISM, AND CONSERVATION

To determine the ecotourism potential of any area, there needs to be an extensive study in order to locate and develop a tourism destination that complies with all of the many requirements described above for a successful ecotourism project. The limitations of this study did not permit an adequate evaluation of the many sites in the area with possible ecotourism potential. Moreover, aforementioned regional and local barriers block the development of such sites—including a lack of security, land-ownership conflicts, a lack of infrastructure, attitudes that tourism brings more trouble, and a low level of community participation. This is not to say that some of these ecotourism suggestions could not be developed. Rather, it is yet another reminder of the complexity of the situation.

As witnessed throughout the six communities, a number of intricate issues need to be addressed and resolved prior to pursuing The Nature Conservancy's original wishes to create ecotourism destinations. From our standpoint, the next, most important steps were to involve the community more in the decision-making process and to provide training opportunities for individuals who wanted to work in tourism either as guides or as partners in small businesses. We believed that it was more important to work with local Maya residents rather than chalet owners in part because they ought to be the ones to decide the degree to which their lands, their forests, and their towns would be impacted by new tourists.

As the second year (2003) of the Conservancy project began, Diamente was contracted as the local coordinator of the second phase (i.e., the phase devoted to designing implementation projects). She became the only social

FIGURE 9. Guatemalan anthropology and ecotourism interns prepare for a PowerPoint presentation to women of San Juan La Laguna who are starting a traditional medicinal plant tour program.

scientist officially employed by the Conservancy project (which may reflect the lower priority The Nature Conservancy placed on applied ethnographic involvement). On the other hand, we chose to conclude that the Conservancy had come to recognize the importance of having at least some anthropological perspective in the overall project. Unlike so many anthropological diagnostic studies, our work from the first year would have a continuing follow-up.

Our first concern was to communicate the data we had learned to members of the different communities in the study area. Our second concern was to involve more local residents in community development. Furthermore, we also strongly recommended a series of training seminars for local tourism entrepreneurs, and especially for women, because they carry out the bulk of the craft production and sales. We also suggested several smaller tourism development projects targeted at the average Maya family household level to spread the benefits of tourism more widely. Throughout most of 2003, Diamente was heavily involved in the development and implementation of environmental education materials and training that stemmed from the first phase of the project. Wallace returned in May 2003 with another group of

North American and Guatemalan anthropology field school students and, in addition, he taught a practicum for a group of UVG ecotourism students. The work of these students was particularly productive in getting community involvement in tourism development projects. The students produced:

1. A tour package of traditional medicinal practices for the benefit of local San Pedranos;
2. A coffee tour for small-scale San Pedro coffee producers;
3. A boating and fishing tour package working with local San Pedro artisanal fishers;
4. A self-guided tour for ecotourists visiting San Juan La Laguna;
5. A series of marketing workshops for San Juan midwives and San Juan weavers;
6. A guided tour of the famous Tz'utujil archaeological ruins of Chuitinamit through work with a local Atiteco historical society;
7. A thorough, qualitatative pre-study of Panajachel tourism service providers to assist them in long-range planning;
8. An analysis of the level of local support for several planned ecotourism attractions in Santa Clara La Laguna; and
9. A tour history and culture tour package for the developers of a local San Pedro museum.

Clearly, by the end of our stay in early August 2003, we had accomplished much of the agenda we had hoped for at the end of 2002. Moreover, we had left an indelible impact on the Conservancy project. Although we both had to return to work back in the United States, several of the Guatemalan students were now well placed to continue affecting the direction of the Conservancy project. Even more importantly for us, the director of Vivamos Mejor was so impressed with the work of our students and with Diamente's work for The Nature Conservancy that he hired one of the UVG ecotourism students, Maria Isabel Lambour, as the full-time staff person for a newly opened San Pedro La Laguna office, where she is now perfectly located to influence local policy and provide constant support to local residents venturing more deeply into tourism work. Another student, working directly with a different NGO, Fundación Solar, returned to San Juan La Laguna for her thesis work to complete a thorough local tourism development strategy for the community and to provide more training workshops for craft vendors. In summer 2004, Wallace returned again with another group of U.S. and Guatemalan students, this time with even more support from Vivamos Mejor, to help them with the next phase of development of ecotourism projects. We also began to work in communities beyond San Pedro and San Juan to develop the basis for community support for sustainable ecotourism projects.

Without the anthropological lens that we brought to this particular case in Guatemala, it was questionable whether or not ecotourism development around Lake Atitlán was going to include one of its fundamental components: the people. Since the departure of Diamente, one of the UVG project directors told us that The Nature Conservancy has not employed any more social scientists, nor have they been interested in any more social components to their program. On the other hand, much of that role has been taken up by other NGOs, especially Vivamos Mejor and, to a lesser extent, Fundación Solar. Both of these organizations have fought to bring in a social component in spite of the opposition or indifference from their international donor collaborators (e.g., The Nature Conservancy). So, even though we have not changed the Conservancy orientation, we were able to make what appears to have been a sufficient effort to ensure that local voices are heard, consulted, and brought into the discussion on a permanent basis.

There were two key pieces to this project: (1) the anthropologist–university connection, which contributed tremendous expertise and knowledge (e.g., ethnography) at low cost, and (2) local participation. The addition of locally trained university students had both short-term and long-term benefits. In the short run, the Guatemalans were able to kick-start community efforts on local projects, and, in the long run, these same students will be able to apply the skills and attitudes they have learned here to other settings. Still, local participation is key to the success of any ecotourism project regardless of its location, but especially when it involves the land, a river, or any element of the environment that people call their community or their home. As we become more aware of and concerned for our environment, we must not forget that we all, wherever we may reside, are part of the earth beneath our feet. In this case, our applied ethnographic endeavors helped to remind others that we must keep the people in the parks because *they* were there before *we* could call them anything other than what *they* have always known.

NOTES

1. See Lofgren 1999 for a history of the development of the concept of parks and wilderness.
2. See Stonich 2000 for an extended example.
3. There have been a number of reports of tourists robbed on trails by machete-wielding thieves.
4. *Costumbre* is a syncretism of traditional Mayan practices and mediaeval Catholicism. Since the 1950s, the rapid increase of support and participation of various Protestant churches (i.e., Evangelical)

has influenced the religious practices of the people, although many remain loyal to Costumbre tradition. This traditional Maya cosmovision centers itself around ritual and ceremonial aspects. The best example of this is seen through the presence and active role of the *cofradias*, religious groups that have incorporated their Maya-Tz'utujil identity in the practices of the Catholic church of Santiago Atitlán.

5. The head of AMSCLAE, the Lake Atitlán Water Authority, told us of several instances where tourists hiking in mountain terrains left the existing trails for sightseeing and trampled on endemic flora unique to Atitlán and disturbed Mayan sacred sites.

6. Ladino is equivalent to *mestizo* (mixed Indian-Iberian ancestry) in other highland Indian regions of Latin America. In Guatemala there is a strong racial divide between Ladinos and any other ethnic groups. Ladinos have held the dominant social, political, and economic power in Guatemala since the start of the Colonial period.

7. We were told by a local architect that he has built vacation homes for international tourists who only visit the lake once every four to five years.

8. The canopy tour is a series of cables connecting five to six tall trees high in the canopy. Tourists swing along the cable from one tree stand to another. Ostensibly the tour is to observe the forest at the canopy level, but in fact most tourists are attracted to the thrill of sliding along the lines high above the ground. The tour opened in late 1994.

REFERENCES CITED

Beavers, John
    1995 Community Based Ecotourism in The Maya Forest: Six Case Studies From Belize, Guatemala and Mexico. Guatemala City: The Nature Conservancy.
Berry, Wendell
    1993 Sex, Economy, Freedom and Community. New York: Pantheon Books.
Brechin, Steven R., Patrick C. West, David Harris, and Kurt Kutay
    1991 Resident Peoples and Protected Areas: A Framework for Inquiry. *In* Resident People and National Parks: Social Dilemmas and Strategies in International Conservation. Patrick C. West and Steven R. Brechin, eds. Tucson: University of Arizona Press.
Castro Miron, Pamela
    2002 El Turismo y los Niños Vendedores de Santiago Atitlán. *In* Tourism and Its Consequences: Reports from Lake Atitlán, Guatemala; Vol. 7, Final Reports from the 2002 NCSU Summer Ethnographic Field School in Guatemala. Tim Wallace, ed. Pp. 13–18. Raleigh, NC: Department of Sociology and Anthropology, North Carolina State University.
Gonzalez Arrecis, Francisco
    2004 Nuevas Políticas de Seguridad para Turistas. Prensa Libre, November 19.
Harper, Janice
    2002 Endangered Species: Health, Illness and Death among Madagascar's People of the Forest. Durham, NC: Carolina Academic Press.
Herlihy, Peter H
    1997 Central American Indian Peoples and Lands Today. *In* Central America: A Natural and Cultural History. Anthony G. Coates, ed. Pp. 215–239. New Haven, CT: Yale University Press.

Igoe, Jim
  2004 Conservation and Globalization: A Study of National Parks and Indigenous Communities from East Africa to South Dakota. Belmont, CA: Thomson-Wadsworth.
Marks, Stuart
  1984 The Imperial Lion: Human Dimensions of Wildlife Management in Central Africa. Boulder, CO: Westview Press.
Petrich, Perla
  1999 Historias, Historia del Lago Atitlán. San Pedro La Laguna, Sololá, Guatemala: Casa de Estudios de los Pueblos del Lago Atitlán.
Reyes-Cortes, Beatriz
  2002 Race, Tourism, and Santiago Atitlán: The Effects of Social Inequalities in the Attitudes of Cofrades. *In* Tourism and Its Consequences: Reports from Lake Atitlán, Guatemala; Vol. 7, Final Reports from the 2002 NCSU Summer Ethnographic Field School in Guatemala. Tim Wallace, ed. Pp. 90–98. Raleigh, NC: Department of Sociology and Anthropology, North Carolina State University.
Wallace, Tim, and Daniela N. Diamente
  2002 Estudio de Ecoturismo en el Lado Suroeste del Lago Atitlán: Informe Final. Panajachel, Sololá, Guatemala: The Nature Conservancy.
Whelan, Tensie
  1991 Ecotourism and Its Role in Sustainable Development. *In* Nature Tourism: Managing for the Environment. Tensie Whelan, ed. Pp. 3–22. Washington, DC: Island Press.
Winkler, Katja
  2001 Uso y Manejo de la Biodiversidad en Dos Comunidades Tz'utujiles. Guatemala, Fundacion Solar.

Part 3

MORE THAN NATURE: ANTHROPOLOGISTS AS INTERPRETERS OF CULTURE FOR NATURE-BASED TOURS

PALMA INGLES
University of Florida

Anthropologists have much to offer as interpreters of cultures for tourists traveling to remote areas of the world. Often advertised as ecotours, group travel is now being offered to areas of the world that are still considered off the beaten path. With more and more travel taking place in the form of organized, guided tours, the anthropologist is in a prime position to educate travel companies and tourists concerning the populations with which they come into contact while enhancing the experience for both the tourists and the host populations. Colorful brochures advertise tours that will have a range of naturalists to guide the tourists through the natural environment in a chosen destination. Rarely do tours advertise that they have anthropologists to help tourists learn more about the local cultures. This paper explores the benefits of hiring anthropologists as tour guides for nature-based tours, using examples from the Amazon. Key Words: tourism, Amazon tourism, indigenous tourism, tour guides, South America

INTRODUCTION

An ad in the Wall Street Journal said, "See the Amazon, the largest rainforest in the world! See nature at its best, more species of flora and fauna than anywhere else on the planet." If you want to see the Amazon, there are numerous travel companies ready to sell you a trip to the magical jungle or to almost any other remote, exotic location around the world. Often advertised as ecotours, group travel is now being offered to areas of the world that are considered off the beaten path. Most of these trips emphasize the exotic animals, birds, or

NAPA Bulletin 23, pp. 219–233, ISBN 1-931303-22-3. © 2005 by the American Anthropological Association. All rights reserved. Please direct all requests for permissions to photocopy or reproduce article content through the University of California Press's Rights and Permissions website, www.ucpress.edu/journals/rights.htm.

plants that tourists will encounter, but less often do they highlight the local people who inhabit the area of destination. Colorful brochures advertise tours that will have a range of naturalists to guide the tourists through the natural environment in a chosen destination. Rarely do tours advertise that they have anthropologists to help tourists learn more about the local cultures.

Today the common wisdom is that tourism is now the largest industry in the world. In the last few decades, remote locations of the world have been opened up to almost anyone with the time and money for travel. Even when the natural environment of an area is its main selling point, the place may have local populations that could be impacted by the actions of the visiting tourists. These cultures may or may not willingly share their environment with outsiders. If the host–guest encounter is positive, conducted in an ecologically sustainable way that allows the local population an opportunity to make some income off of the encounter, then tourism to remote areas has the potential to be of benefit to the people who live there.

In looking through a multitude of travel literature and websites over the last seven years, I have noticed that very few organized tours use anthropologists as guides. Often advertisements for nature tours or ecotours do not mention the local people whom tourists are likely to encounter on their trip. Is there a role for anthropologists as interpreters of culture in areas that specialize in nature tours? Places of interest to nature tourists today are often in developing countries where people continue to make their living off the land and where locals may depend on some of the same nature-based resources that the tourists have come to see. I believe there is a role for anthropologists to work within the tourism arena, working to educate and guide tourists, as consultants and analysts, and in conducting studies concerning the impact of tourism on a given area. In contrast to the narrow environmental focus of ornithologists, botanists, and other naturalists, anthropologists are generalists who take a more holistic approach to studying the environment. Who can describe local cultures better than an anthropologist who has worked with communities in the region being toured and knows the lifestyle of the people who live there?

ANTHROPOLOGISTS AND TOURISM

If organized nature-based tours target areas where humans share the landscape with the flora and fauna, why are they less likely to hire anthropologists as guides along with the naturalist guides? For over seven years, I have been working as a guide for tours in the Amazon, where I also studied the impacts of tourism on four villages that host and entertain tourists. When I first inquired about working as a tour guide, companies were reluctant to hire me as an anthropologist, even though I had already worked in the Amazon for a few years in pursuit of my doctorate degree. I was told that tourists visiting the Amazon wanted to know about plants and animals, not about the people. After convincing one company that I also knew a fair amount about the plants and animals, I was able to get my foot in the door and started guiding trips on tour boats in the Amazon. However, for the first few tours, I was listed in the company brochures as a biologist. Eventually, my Ph.D. in anthropology, coupled with my knowledge of local communities in the area, became a good selling point for the tour companies I worked for, so they became more comfortable with listing me as an anthropologist.

Traditionally, much of the study of tourism by anthropologists has focused on the negative impacts caused when tourists from the developed world come into contact with people in developing countries (Cohen 1988; Desmond 1999; Graburn 1982; Mansperger 1995; McLaren 2003). Other anthropological studies have tried to describe or classify tourists by certain typologies (MacCannell 1989; Smith 1989). As Chambers (2000) points out, most anthropological research on tourism has until recently lacked inquiries from the perspective of the local populations who serve as hosts. This may be due in part to the nature of foreign travel; until the last 20 years, most tourists only traveled to urban areas in the developed world. Now that more travelers are seeking experiences in developing areas of Africa, Asia, and Latin America, it becomes more important to understand the nature of travel to these regions and the impacts of tourism on the local people.

As the world's populations become more intertwined, and as tourism continues to be a major economic factor for many developing nations, it is important to study impacts of tourism in remote areas. Anthropologists may be able to offer valuable insight into the ways in which local cultures are impacted by tourism, and aid in designing tours that will allow tourism to benefit local populations and aid in the education of travelers.

Anthropologists have much to offer when working with the industry of tourism as guides, researchers, consultants, analysts, and policy makers. A key element in tourism is the tourist. Without tourists, there would be no tourism industry. With more and more travel taking place in the form of organized, guided tours, the anthropologist is in a prime position to educate the travel companies and the tourists concerning the populations with which they come into contact, enhancing the experience for both the tourists and the populations being toured.

WORKING WITH TOURISTS

When I first started working tours in the Amazon, I was somewhat skeptical of the idea that the local people benefited from having their world viewed by outsiders, and I thought I could make a difference. The tour companies with whom I worked led tours on various sizes of boats that traveled along the Amazon River in Peru and Brazil. In Peru, I worked with an American-owned company that had been conducting tours in the region since 1965. During a one-week tour, passengers lived on a midsized boat and took several excursions each day by smaller boats to go birding, forest hiking, and piranha fishing. Tourists visited small local villages where they toured schools, visited shamans, viewed agricultural production areas, and had the opportunity to see how villagers live in a typical small village along the river. They also visited indigenous tribes who dressed in traditional dress, performed traditional dances, and sold handicrafts when the tourists visited.

After working as a guide for several trips, I became interested in studying the impacts of tourism in the Amazon, especially on the indigenous villages that hold title to their land and continue to live at a sustainable level by producing crops for household consumption and the market and by fishing. After viewing the dances they performed for the tourists, I wanted to know whether the dances were really based on traditional dances or if they were contrived for the tourists, what the locals thought about their own performances, why they participated, and what benefit they received by hosting tourists.

Being familiar with the anthropological literature on tourism, I was inclined to believe that these people were selling off their own culture in a contrived way in order to make a little money. I wanted to know if they found it demeaning to dress up in the traditional dress that their ancestors had stopped wearing over a century before, whether they found of this type of host–guest relationship intrusive in their daily lives, and what impact their work with tourism was having on their livelihood strategies, culture, and use and preservation of resources. I designed my doctoral research to help answer each of these questions.

What I found from my ethnographic research was that these villages embraced tourism as a way to increase household income, since they were paid by the boat company for performing traditional dances and they could sell handicrafts directly to the tourists. I also found that tourism was helping to preserve some aspects of their disintegrating traditional culture. By continuing to use traditional elements of their culture for tourist entertainment, they are keeping traditions alive as their communities face new challenges brought on by the development that leads to cultural change. Further, money from tourism was aiding indirectly in the preservation of the natural resources of the area by providing the villages in my study with an alternative to increased slash-and-burn agriculture to increase household income (see Ingles 2001).

While I was conducting my research in the villages, I continued to work as a guide for tours on a regular basis. Since I was now armed with in-depth knowledge of local villages, more tour companies were willing to hire me as a guide. This gave me an opportunity to interview tourists (n = 86) on what they thought of their experiences in the Amazon, their motivations for travel, and what they had learned from their experiences. Most of the tourists interviewed said that they had originally come to see the Amazon due to the exotic flora and fauna found there. They also wanted to see the largest rainforest in the world before it disappeared due to development and continued overuse of resources. Very few tourists originally embarked on their journey to experience the local cultures. However, most people surveyed at the end of their trips said that even though their original motivations for traveling to the Amazon did not include local populations as part of the equation, the experience of visiting local villages, including visits to the indigenous tribes, were among the top highlights of their trip.

In subsequent tours on which I served as an anthropologist–guide, several tourists mentioned that they thought more tours to remote areas should include anthropologists that could educate the tourists on the lifeways of the local people. Often, tours of villages in the Amazon are short in duration, usually ranging from one to two hours in length, leaving the tourists with many unanswered questions concerning the cultures they have visited. Although foreign naturalists who serve as guides for organized tours in the Amazon may have in-depth knowledge of the flora or fauna, in my experience they know much less about the ethno-botany or ethno-biology of a region, or how local people survive and interact with their environment. They may not convey to the tourists how the local people are part of the environment, and that the local culture is built around adaptation to where they live.

Some naturalists view humans as competitors for the natural resources or as inconsequential in the tourism experience, and may believe tours in the Amazon are best conducted where there are no local populations. This is unfortunate for the tourists, who miss out on a well-rounded experience that includes humans as part of the landscape. When possible, especially on large ships that employ several guides at the same time, it is ideal to have a mix of naturalists and anthropologists to aid in making the tour an unsurpassed experience for the tourists. A naturalist guide is usually in a better position than an anthropologist to talk about the various species of plants and animals in the area being toured and to relate those species to other species around the world. On the other hand, anthropologists can help the tourists gain a greater appreciation of the cultures they are viewing. By discussing with tourists beforehand what they will be seeing when they visit a local village, anthropologists can help tourists understand more about the local culture, which can lead to a greater understanding of the culture and a better host–guest interaction. Many tourists will have a better appreciation of the diversity of the cultures with which they are interacting if they know more about them, thereby avoiding an ethnocentric interpretation of the culture.

There is ample opportunity for anthropologists to work in an applied manner with issues of tourism. In my work in the Amazon, as a guide and researcher, I have found that since I work with villages that serve as hosts and with tourists who visit the villages, I can be a valuable liaison between the companies that operate the tours and the villagers who act as hosts. I have been consulted by the operators of the tours regarding the interaction between hosts and guests and on ways to improve the experience for both groups involved. My research in four Amazonian villages, coupled with my guiding experience, helps me to be aware of potential questions and problems that may arise as people from different worlds come into contact with one another for a limited encounter, and I can work to help negate such problems.

I advise tourists on what to buy or trade for from the villagers, with special emphasis on the need for avoiding any handicrafts made with non-renewable resources such as bird feathers, animal skins, or animal teeth. Once educated, most tourists are happy to comply, and many of them admittedly would not have otherwise considered the potential depletion of natural resources when choosing what to buy. Many tourists welcome an opportunity to interact with local populations, but they want to ensure that what they do will not have a negative impact on the community. They will often consult me on issues such as how to make a donation to a local school or clinic, whether it is okay to give candy or money to the children in the community, and whether it is okay to take photographs or go inside peoples' homes when invited. While some tourists charge ahead and do what they want to do on their own, others depend on the guides who are familiar with the cultures for guidance.

The tour boats that I work with in Peru have Peruvian naturalists on board who grew up in the forest and have an extensive knowledge of the flora and fauna as well as the people. Many of the local guides continue to educate themselves through extensive reading and through working with other naturalists and anthropologists who escort groups of tourists. By working together on a daily basis to design the itinerary, we can jointly design the best programs for the tourists and devise ways to have a minimal impact on local cultures. The knowledge that I lack on the flora and fauna of the area is easily compensated by the in-depth knowledge these guides have of the local environment.

Many tourists who visit the Amazon prepare themselves for their trip by reading as much as they can about the Amazonian biosphere before their tour, and they start their tour expecting to learn more about their own topics of interest. Some tourists are well versed in various natural elements they will be experiencing, and they reinforce their existing knowledge and add to it by interacting with the naturalist guides during the tours. It is less frequent that tourists have much prior knowledge of the communities and cultures they will be visiting. They may not understand how dependent Amazonian cultures are on the natural resources in their area or the consequences of human actions on the local environment.

Anthropologists have the opportunity to explain the place that local people have within the environment, and they can also help tourists gain a more holistic understanding of the area being toured. While the naturalists can introduce tourists to the natural environment, they may not consider that tourists are also intrinsically curious about how other humans live. In the past, I have suggested unscheduled stops in villages or small towns where tourists can visit a local grocery store or go dancing at a local bar at night. In this way, they have an opportunity to interact with local people on a different level than they do when they visit small villages that regularly receive tourists. Most tours to the Amazon strive to be educational for the tourists. They are designed to help tourists learn as much as possible about the plants, animals, environment, and people of the largest rainforest in the world. I believe that tourists benefit most by having a range of guides with different expertise when touring places such as the Amazon.

BENEFITS TO TOURISTS WHEN ANTHROPOLOGISTS ARE GUIDES

When tourists venture outside their own cultures, they may not understand or appreciate what they are seeing. Some tourists who visit the Amazon have never before been in a Third World country. They may immediately view the villagers as people to be pitied due to the lack of infrastructure and the nature of their houses, or view the way of life for the locals as primitive, without merit. I use this opportunity to explain the complex knowledge that Amazonian people have concerning plants and their medicinal uses, the life cycles of the animals of the forest, and the use of natural resources—the rich cultural knowledge that these people possess. I also explain that, for many Amazonian people, life in a small village in the forest is preferable to life in a bigger community or city. In the tropical forest, people can usually produce enough food to eat; they can fish, find supplies needed for the construction of their houses, have access to relatively clean water, and live a fairly peaceful life. The Amazonian environment has led to the development of many rich, diverse forest cultures. What may appear bleak or poverty stricken to a foreign tourist is a way of life that has fostered generations of people who have lived and thrived in an adverse but unique environment for generations.

On one trip in the Brazilian Amazon, I worked with an American botanist who had spent years working with plants from the Amazon but was new to guiding tourists. He had an excellent knowledge of Amazonian plants, but his lectures were considered tedious and pretentious by many of the tourists. Although he could easily identify the genus and species of many of the plants, he did not relate how the plants were used by the animals or people of an area. His lectures were the type that would be typical for a graduate taxonomy class in botany, without any of the fascinating anecdotal examples of how the plants had been used by local populations through the ages. He eagerly discussed how botanists from the United States were working in the Amazon to identify plants for potential medicinal use, without mentioning the long history of medicinal plant use by the shamans and other indigenous people in the Amazon. Although most of the tourists were open to learning more about plants in the Amazon, they wanted this knowledge to be presented at a level they could retain and appreciate, relating to what they were seeing in their travels. I was often asked for a simpler description of the plants and of their specific uses. I used the Kayapo Tribe as an example of a group who have a use for the majority of plants in their environment, most of which they have classified according to the various uses they have as medicines, food, construction materials, fibers, etc. I have observed that as tourists learn about the ethno-botanical use of plants they have a greater appreciation of the forest people and of the knowledge locals have of their environment.

Two of the indigenous groups that I worked with in Peru were descendants of people who were born in Colombia and brought to Peru in chains as slaves during the rubber boom. They have had a very sad but fascinating history due to their encounters with the rubber barons, which started in the late 1800s. Today, when tourists visit their villages, they may be very unaware of the dark past these people have survived and the torture they endured. In 2001, I worked as a guide for a mid-sized ship making its annual two-month tour in Peru and Brazil along the Amazon. I presented a lecture where I discussed the history of these people and their abuse by the rubber barons. The particulars of these tribes, and the slavery involved with the rubber boom in general, were not well known by most of the tourists. As I gave descriptions of the numbers of Indians dislocated, enslaved, or killed during the rubber boom, many of the tourists were almost brought to tears. The lecture led to a long discussion of the rubber era, with very in-depth questions and answers concerning this time in the recent past. Although some of the naturalists had previously mentioned the rubber boom, they mentioned it only within the context of the money and the luxurious lifestyle it provided for the rubber barons. The devastation of the local cultures had not been mentioned by other guides in previous discussions concerning the rubber boom. During research for my doctorate, I had interviewed some of the elders of the tribes who had been moved from Colombia to Peru and enslaved for collection of rubber in the 1930s. As a result, I was able to give the tourists a good description of what life was like for the slaves of the rubber boom during that time—a description that would not have been provided by the naturalist guides.

As I have stated above, I believe that tourists benefit most when guides with a variety of expertise are hired. It may be years before major tour companies regularly hire anthropologists as well as naturalists for tours. Without anthropologists, tour companies continue to focus on the natural environment as if no humans lived there. Although many naturalists from the United States have done research in the Amazon area, quite often they have had very little contact with local populations and may not understand the culture or how humans relate to the environment in a given area.

Anthropologists and environmentalists continue to debate issues surrounding the creation of nature reserves (Beavers 1995; Ceballos-Lascurain 1996;

Harrison and Price 1996; Whelan 1991). Many environmentalists advocate the complete removal of humans in an area slated to become a reserve, seeing humans as only mass consumers of the environment, not as an integral part of the biosphere. In some cases, removing humans from an area has only proved that they actually helped protect the trees and animals from being overexploited by outsiders (see Beavers 1995; Wells et al. 1992). As local governments in developing countries work to create more reserves to protect wildlife and to lure the tourists' dollar, plans often evolve that exclude people from the area to be protected (Brandon et al. 1998). However, tourism venues can be created that both benefit the local populations and protect the natural resources (see Ceballos-Lascurain 1996; Healy 1994; Ingles 2001; Kemf 1993; Zeppel 1997). Anthropologists may be able to offer help in creating nature reserves for tourism by working with reserve developers to help find ways that local populations can remain in the area and increase their household incomes by working with tourism while at the same time using the resources in a sustainable manner.

Naturalists may convey to tourists the idea that humans in nature are bad for the environment and that it is wasteful for humans to kill animals or harvest trees. The challenge for the anthropologist is to help tourists understand the resources local people need and the reasons why they kill animals for food or cut down trees to grow crops. Anthropologists can help the tourists understand ways in which many local communities conserve resources by limiting hunting and fishing to certain times of the year, limiting the cutting of trees, replanting areas, and making full use of what they do take from nature. Often, local populations are doing what they can to help preserve resources for the next generation. Once tourists have a better concept of what life is like for humans in places like the Amazon, they will often have a much better appreciation of the local populations. Another challenge for the anthropologist is to remind tourists that humans do live in most places on the planet and that tourism can be of benefit to the local population and does not need to compete directly for local resources.

BENEFITS TO LOCAL POPULATIONS AND TOUR OPERATORS WHEN ANTHROPOLOGISTS WORK WITH TOURISM

I found that most of the people in the villages I worked with were very receptive to the idea that tour guides should include someone who works in the Amazon and has an understanding of their way of life. As I conducted my ethnographic research, villagers would often use me as a sounding board for ways to improve host–guest interactions. I worked with one village in Peru that was situated near a tourist lodge. When the lodge was built, the villagers dressed up for the visiting tourists and performed traditional dances. However, due to the frequency of the performances, the villagers soon found that the time spent entertaining tourists was taking away from the time they normally spent fishing, hunting, or growing crops. Ten years before my research began with the community, the villagers decided that they would stop performing for tourists and would only sell handicrafts when the tourists visited. The selling of handicrafts could be handled by the women and children while the men participated in other daily activities. When I was conducting my research, a few of the elders in the village approached me for help with negotiations with the lodge owner. They wanted to perform for tourists once again but on a more limited basis than before and for higher pay per performance. They seemed hesitant to approach the proprietor on their own. I was able to suggest ways to negotiate with the owner of the lodge to reach an agreement that would benefit both sides.

When I returned to the city where the lodge had its main office, I met with the owner of the lodge, presented the proposal from the elders, and discussed the villagers' major concerns regarding performances to be staged for the tourists. We discussed ways in which the villagers could work with tourism while continuing their other livelihood activities. The owner was very receptive to the ideas of the elders, and the next time he visited the lodge he negotiated a new contract with the community that would include dance performances on a limited basis. As a result, and with partial funding from the owner of the lodge, a new tribal roundhouse was built where performances would be held for tourists. In subsequent discussions with the villagers and the lodge owner, both sides were satisfied with the new arrangement.

As anthropologists, many of us have conducted research in small communities, often in foreign countries. As a consequence of understanding some of the injustices that communities without influence or money endure from their own governments or from other outsiders who compete for resources, it is often easy to empathize with local populations. In dealing with rural and ethnic tourism, anthropologists may be called upon to be the voices in support of local populations. In the case of tourism to the Amazon, I find that I may be more aware than other guides or tour company leaders of tourist activities that could potentially disrupt the culture or threaten livelihoods or resources used by local populations. Naturalist guides, who work less often with local populations, may not consider the impacts of the host–guest interaction. They may see somewhere like the Amazon as a wild, uninhabited area to be enjoyed and used by all who have money to travel there.

On a particular ship tour in Brazil, we anchored one afternoon just before sunset at the mouth of a tributary located miles from any sizeable town or community. Quickly we disembarked eight Zodiac boats from the hull of the ship and proceeded to board the 90 tourists and guides into the boats for an evening of bird watching and sightseeing up the small tributary. As the first Zodiac approached the tributary, it was met by men in four dugout canoes who were blocking the waterway. The men in the dugouts explained that this tributary was a main area for fishing and that they had strung up their nets across the tributary for the night. When the ship had been there a few weeks earlier, the motors of the Zodiacs had torn up some of their fishing nets, and therefore they did not want the Zodiacs traveling up the tributary again. The tour leader, who spoke fluent Portuguese, was actively involved in a tense conversation with the local men when I arrived in the second Zodiac. Her opinion was that no one owned the tributaries and that she and her 90 tourists had every right to tour this one. She suggested that the men should remove their nets and permit us to proceed.

Since I had worked with fishermen in the Amazon before, I knew the amount of time and energy that it took four men using dugout canoes to position the nets where they wanted them. Once positioned, the nets were usually in place for several hours or overnight. Simply removing the nets to accommodate a group of tourists from outside the area was not a preferred option. I quickly suggested to the tour leader that we visit another nearby tributary that did not have fishing nets in place. She tried to explain to me that it was the principle of the issue: no one owned the tributaries, and therefore no one should be allowed to block the way with nets. I pointed out the amount of time it took to put the nets in place and that, for the fishermen in this region of few houses, the tributary might rightfully be considered as belonging to them. By this time, several tourists had taken note of the conversation and the conflict that had arisen. Many of them were quick to agree with me and suggested that we go somewhere else. As a result, the tour leader grudgingly backed down, and we found an equally suitable tributary for touring not far from where the men were fishing. The point here is that in trying to make the best experience for tourists, tour leaders or tour planners may cross a precarious line with local populations, or they may fail to understand the hardships they can cause as they take tourists into areas that local populations depend upon.

As a researcher in villages where I was also known as a guide, I was often consulted by the villagers on ways to improve the visits for tourists. Villagers expressed their interest in offering more to the tourists, such as in-home visits or staged demonstrations of handicraft production. Since I worked with tourists and knew some of what the tourists wanted from their experiences, I could offer ideas on new ways to work constructively with tourism that would produce more income for locals.

As I continue to work as a guide on trips in the Peruvian Amazon, I work closely with the owner of the boat company and with the villages where I conducted my dissertation research. The owner rarely visits the villages where tourists visit, so I have become an important liaison between him and the villages. On occasions when I visit indigenous villages I studied, I am approached by the chiefs, who seem to feel more comfortable expressing their ideas and concerns about the tourism interaction with me rather than with other representatives of the boat company. As an anthropologist who has studied these groups, I believe I am seen as a supporter of the local villagers. At the same time, the owner of the boat company freely discusses new ideas with me and seeks my input into ways to improve the host–guest relationship.

CONCLUSIONS

The opportunities for anthropologists to work with tourism are numerous. As the fastest-growing industry in the world, tourism has the potential to have a major impact on many rural communities in developing countries. As tourists tread more frequently on land that is used by locals for subsistence agriculture, fishing, hunting, and other economic activities, the potential conflict between tour operators, tourists, and locals increases. Anthropologists are in a prime position to work within the tourism arena, educating tour operators and tourists regarding the communities they encounter, and to help the tourists gain a better appreciation of the cultures they visit. Anthropologists can enlighten tourists and travel companies by explaining how local populations fit into the environment being toured. There is also a need for anthropologists to work as consultants and analysts for the tourism industry and as researchers who can aid in the development of policy regarding tourism in a given area.

Until recently, most studies of tourism have been undertaken by economists, marketing specialists, recreation planners, and, less frequently, by anthropologists. As the tourism industry continues to grow, it is important to understand the impacts tourism has on the natural environment as well as on local human populations. As a field of study, it is important to do more research directly with local communities to find out what impact tourism is having on their culture, their economy, their way of life, and their livelihood strategies. Tourism has now become a legitimate and important field of study for anthropologists, since without humans there would be no tourism. Anthropologists have much to learn from the study of tourism and much to offer as researchers, consultants, guides, and interpreters of other cultures.

REFERENCES CITED

Beavers, John
    1995 Community-based Ecotourism in the Maya Forest: Six Case Studies from Communities in Mexico, Guatemala, and Belize. USAID/MAYAFOR Project. The Nature Conservancy, October.
Brandon, Katrina, Kent Redford, and Steve Sanderson, eds.
    1998 Parks in Peril: People, Politics, and Protected Areas. Washington, DC: Island Press.
Ceballos-Lascurain, Héctor
    1996 Tourism, Ecotourism and Protected Areas. IUCN (World Conservation Union). Switzerland: Gland.
Chambers, Erve
    2000 Native Tours: the Anthropology of Travel and Tourism. Prospect Heights, IL: Waveland Press.
Cohen, Erik
    1988 Authenticity and Commoditization in Tourism. Annals of Tourism Research 15:371–386.
Desmond, Jane
    1999 Staging Tourism. Chicago: The University of Chicago Press.
Graburn, Nelson
    1982 The Dynamics of Change in Tourist Arts. Cultural Survival 6(4):7–11.
Harrison, David, and Martin Price
    1996 Fragile Environments, Fragile Communities? In People and Tourism in Fragile Environments. F. Price, ed. Pp. 1–18. Chichester, UK: John Wiley and Sons.
Healy, Robert
    1994 Tourist Merchandise as a Means of Generating Local Benefits from Ecotourism. Journal of Sustainable Tourism 2(3):137–151.
Ingles, Palma
    2001 Performing Traditional Dances for Modern Tourists in the Amazon. In Tourism in South America. Gui Santana, ed. Pp. 143–159. Binghamton, NY: Haworth Hospitality Press.
Kemf, Elizabeth
    1993 The Law of the Mother: Protecting Indigenous Peoples in Protected Areas. San Francisco: Sierra Club Books.

MacCannell, Dean

 1973 Staged Authenticity: Arrangements of Social Space in Tourism Settings. American Journal of Sociology 79:589–603.

Mansperger, Mark

 1995 Tourism and Cultural Change in Small-Scale Societies. Human Organization 54(1):87–94.

McLaren, Deborah

 1999 The History of Indigenous Peoples and Tourism. Cultural Survival 23(2):27–30.

 2003 Rethinking Tourism and Ecotourism. West Hartford, CT: Kumarian Press.

Smith, Valene

 1989 Introduction. *In* Hosts and Guests: The Anthropology of Tourism. Valene Smith, ed. Pp. 1–17. Philadelphia: University of Pennsylvania Press.

Wells, Michael, Katrina Brandon, and Lee Hannah

 1992 People and Parks: Linking Protected Area Management with Local Communities. Washington, DC: World Bank.

Whelan, Tensie

 1991 Ecotourism and its Role in Sustainable Development. *In* Nature Tourism: Managing for the Environment. Tensie Whelan, ed. Pp. 5–23. Washington, DC: Island Press.

Zeppel, Heather

 1997 Ecotourism and Indigenous Peoples. Issues Paper for Ecotourism Information Centre. Electronic document, http://lorenz.mur.csu.edu.au/ecotour/ecowwwhz.html, accessed January 2001.

THE TRAVELING SEMINAR: AN EXPERIMENT IN CROSS-CULTURAL TOURISM AND EDUCATION IN TAIWAN

DAVID BLUNDELL

National Chengchi University

This article explores the anthropologist's role in facilitating and guiding international educational traveling seminars through interaction with local people, based on my experiences with such seminars in Taiwan. Since the late 1980s, the Taiwanese authorities have reviewed restricted space, converting it into scenic areas and national parks. Martial law was lifted, allowing for changes in the society and introducing a "green" consciousness concerned with examining local roots. In 1992, a method of tourism was developed in which the participants of traveling seminars visited places in Taiwan or other world locations expecting to (1) explore, *(2)* learn, *(3)* interact, *(4)* respect, *(5)* share qualitative feedback with one another, *and (6)* enjoy the process. *When addressing a topic for discussion, such as cultural heritage or the environment, each member of such traveling seminars speaks in his or her own language to share with the group. That is to say, participants explore through travel as a learning process, interacting with others with concern and respect for differences, sharing experiences, and conversing in their mother tongues with translation assistance.* Key Words: traveling seminar, Taiwan, ecotourism, hosts and guests, international education

AN INTRODUCTION TO THE TRAVELING SEMINAR

My objective in this paper is to show how participation in an eco-cultural tourism project is a significant means by which anthropologists can influence the way tourists and hosts perceive themselves, the environment, and one another. The Taiwan traveling seminar project, a unique tour that was developed in 1992 for a visit by the humanist psychologist Jean Houston,[1] works because

NAPA Bulletin 23, pp. 234–251, ISBN 1-931303-22-3. © 2005 by the American Anthropological Association. All rights reserved. Please direct all requests for permissions to photocopy or reproduce article content through the University of California Press's Rights and Permissions website, www.ucpress.edu/journals/rights.htm.

the participants are both hosts and guests and meet one another on the neutral ground of the tour. My current opinion of the value of the seminar resulted from looking at the participation of "seminar members," both en route and at destinations, from the *etic* (expert) and *emic* (local) points of view.

These traveling seminars are organized for the participants to share knowledge on an egalitarian basis in order to (1) explore, (2) learn, (3) interact, (4) respect, (5) share qualitative feedback with one another, and (6) enjoy the process. They learn while traveling, interacting among themselves and with local people, thereby developing concern and respect for differences through cross-cultural and interpersonal sharing. What is unique about this process of conducting a traveling seminar is the dialogue between the tourists, which takes place in each participant's own language. The resulting process of education occurs over several days, as people in the tour learn about the culture, nature, and heritage they witness through interaction with local people and expert guides within the natural environment. Members of the traveling seminar are encouraged to speak in their own languages and to share their thoughts on the topic of discussion with the group. In this way, both visitors and those visited interact among themselves and with one another in order to learn. The outcome is a touring, open classroom without walls.

THE FIELD OF VISITING FOR EDUCATION

The first step in developing a multilingual traveling seminar is researching possible itineraries through consultation with potential participants. For our initial seminars, the Institute of Cultural Affairs, Taiwan,[2] held meetings for people who were interested in visiting a place with a team of like-minded people, academics, and local experts. These individuals told us they expected the traveling seminar to let them experience and learn from something different from their daily lives. In general, participants want to be taken out of their usual routines and into a different physical place, preferably a rural or mountainous environment that is considered relatively inaccessible. Once people visit such places, however, they often wonder why they could not have gone there on their own. When tourists ask this question, our usual response is that it's an effort to take off and explore and that people need a logistical network before taking that first step.

The participants' desire to experience "natural" and "ethnic" aspects of the environment led us to produce the phrase "eco-cultural traveling seminar or tour." We then asked bio-naturalists, geologists, ethnologists, anthropologists—including linguists—and professional recreational specialists to join the tour as specialists who could explain what was "natural" and "ethnic." In the resulting tours, about two-thirds of the participants have been those with a similar interest in "getting away and seeing the world, led by academics and outdoor professionals," and a third have been bio-naturalists, geologists, ethnologists, and local historians. Each traveling seminar has focused on a topic to explore. This topic might be the mountain regions of southern Taiwan, where the Rukai people have almost abandoned their stacked, slate houses on high ridges, or the coastal environs of the Amis people, where elders at Malan Village, Taitung, produced the vocal theme for the 1996 Atlanta Olympic Games (see Anderson 2000).

Cultural tourism is about sharing and learning the local heritage of a people while traveling among them and staying in their homes. Cultural tourism's educational goals are based on an appreciation of cultures and on cultural conservation (Walle 1998). Ecotourism offers similar expectations in the context of a pristine natural environment. Travelers to such places, and their inhabitants, are uniquely aware of an ecosystem's need for equilibrium (see Whelan 1991). This tandem understanding implies an orientation toward visiting that concerns the ethics of getting to know the inhabitants of an ecosystem in places where environmental and cultural conservation are working and open to be observed.

INITIAL CALL FOR A TRAVELING SEMINAR

> The human organism . . . is . . . motivated to keep the influx of novelty, complexity, and information within an optimal range and thus escape the extremes of confusion (This is Tuesday, so it must be Belgium) and boredom (We never go anywhere!). [Berlyne 1962:166]

I call our tour a "traveling seminar" or an "eco-cultural tour." It is imbued with symbols and meanings affecting human life as a meaningful pilgrimage (Graburn 1977). The traveling format for cross-cultural and interpersonal understanding was first developed under the auspices of the Institute of Cultural Affairs, Taiwan, for the 1992 visit of Jean Houston, a psychologist who conducts journeys into the origins of human consciousness through pathways of mythology. Over the years since, I have arranged traveling seminars with a volunteer team and led tours, primarily for people to explore Taiwan, but also to places such as Siberia and Sri Lanka. A special feature of the eco-cultural, traveling tour is that we provide a structure so that all the participants and local hosts can, in their own native languages, communicate and reflect on their tour experience. We have taken care to support an information network among all the different language speakers as part of the sharing process throughout the tour. I believe this tour characteristic is unique in the practice of tourism, yet common in spiritual studies, witnessing, and group psychological therapy.

Traveling seminars begin with acquaintance-building and informational gatherings held in Taipei, the capital and an urban basin in northern Taiwan, by the Institute of Cultural Affairs. Each potential participant is asked to introduce himself or herself and to discuss expectations for a possible traveling seminar, including the route and content. A group of volunteers is selected from the gathering to take responsibility for researching sites and routes. As people sign up, more orientation meetings are held to conduct further research into people's expectations. The scouts, usually myself and others, will then conduct a pre-tour to arrange an infrastructure that is uniquely applicable to the tour's concept. We meet with local people to discuss a route, stops, and places to stay.

The first announcement for a traveling seminar was conveyed by word of mouth. Once several people had agreed to call for a meeting, we gathered at the home of a mutual friend to discuss the theme of our tour. The Institute of Cultural Affairs then sent interested people a notice by e-mail, fax, and post. I then made a two-day, pre-tour experimental run, meeting local people along the route to ask them about the possibility of returning several weeks or months later with 15–20 or 30–42 people. This required the first round of communication to explain what a traveling seminar was about, and to locals at contact points who expressed curiosity about such a plan and interest in its educational outcome. Once back in Taipei, I again called a gathering of the eco-cultural participants to further discuss the route and to share pictures. Eventually, a date was set for the three-day tour to begin and the participants began to prepare themselves for it.

The multilingual, multiethnic aspects of the traveling seminar enhanced the educational process of the initial tour. The delivery of comments in the participants' languages of choice required translation and interpretation. Our winding path into the mountains led us to see how a temple is built and how a garden is planted, and communing with other people through different languages provided a sense of intimacy despite the participants' separate perspectives. We as travelers were also very concerned about the tour's impact on our hosts, the environment, and ourselves. We were careful not just to take only pictures and leave only footprints, but to reach out and embrace the encounter with local people based on friendship.

CULTURAL ANTHROPOLOGICAL ORIENTATION FOR THE TRAVELING SEMINAR

In anthropology, it is known that the past is a scarce resource (Appadurai 1981), making the notion of heritage a rich item or complex system in the present—important as a marker *of*, *by*, and *for* the local people. This heritage is often based on a fragile and eroding environment that has succumbed to industrialization. Once heritage has been recognized and established as a matter of record for the world to observe, the next step is to open the doors for the public to take notice and visit sites they have previously only read about.

For an anthropologist cum guide, the traveling course is about partaking in the experience of taking mental notes or writing notes from the participants' conversations en route, and managing the tour in order to bring people together. Our experiment in an eco-cultural traveling seminar has now taken place regularly over the past ten years. The groups have been composed of Taiwanese, North Americans, Europeans, and nationalities throughout Asia.

For the most part, the people in these tour groups, as well as the others encountered along the way, have been strangers to one another. During encounters that include natural terrain, flora and fauna, food, cultural and personal social norms, and memories, the participants reflect and share with one another. Each person is considered responsible for contributing and sharing thoughts about the encounter. The people who make the journey have made the choice to attend preparatory meetings, to read on the topic, and to participate with interest.

Participants in the initial traveling seminar thought it was best to have diversity among the attendees in terms of age and socio-economic background. Students, the elderly, and children were encouraged to participate to enhance the experience for all participants. When people called the Institute of Cultural Affairs or came to meetings and expressed interest in participating in a tour but stated that they could not afford the set fees, the tour group reduced registration fees for them.

FIGURE 1. At Tzushr Temple (founded in 1769) at Sanshia (Three Gorges of Taipei County), Dr. Blundell points out wood and stone carvings in the architecture.

HOW THE FIRST ANTHROPOLOGICAL TRAVELING SEMINAR TOOK PLACE IN TAIWAN

No relationship significantly entered can ever end—the trouble is with significant entry. [Cooper 1974:113]

As Jean Houston was planning her visit to Taiwan, a coordinator at the Institute of Cultural Affairs, Jo Tai, asked me to arrange a traveling seminar attended by local and international participants to explore the layers of the island's cultures. After careful consideration, I designed a three-day tour.

To make the arrangements, I had to convince local people that Dr. Houston would be interested in sharing indigenous knowledge from Taiwan's prehistory and early history with the other participants. At the time, most local people in Taipei thought that Dr. Houston would only want to reflect on Buddhist and Taoist heritage. I explained that Taiwan was unique because of its indigenous origins and resulting traditions, and that Dr. Houston would be interested in unfolding this heritage to the participants. The Institute of Cultural Affairs was supportive of my idea, but other co-organizers were sure I was wrong. I explained that, having read Houston's books, I knew indigenous knowledge to be an important component of her teachings. I invited an ethnologist,

Professor Bien Chiang, to explain the worth and value of indigenous knowledge, as the Taiwanese seemed to be expressing their roots in terms of the religious origins based on Han Chinese culture. I designed a route that would include both the prehistoric origins of culture and the Han Chinese roots transplanted from the mainland four hundred years ago as a living matrix of the contemporary life in Taiwan.

In preparation, I drove to the east coast of Taiwan to visit the newly established office of National East Coast Scenic Area administrators. Since I had worked for the establishment of the National Museum of Prehistory along the east coast, I was able to select archaeological sites as stops for the seminar. One of these sites was the Paleolithic "Caves of the Eight Immortals" (Pahsientung) dating back long before the Neolithic cultures. It is now thought that the sites could date back 30,000 years. The highway had been widened farther south along the coast, where Neolithic sites were exposed. I decided the road cut would be another stop to observe the strata of pottery and worked slate and Taiwan jade (nephrite). The road continued to Taitung, a county where six Austronesian-speaking indigenous groups reside. I made arrangements to stay at a site near natural thermal springs.

The next day I went to Santimen in the southern central range, where the indigenous Formosan Austronesian-speaking Rukai and Paiwan share ground. The people were receptive to a home stay arrangement and dinner party to celebrate their cultures with the participants. I also made arrangements to meet with Han Chinese Hakka heritage leadership on the hillsides of the plains in Jo Tai's home region of Meinung in Pingtung County. This community of Hakka speakers was important to both indigenous people and Min-nan Han Chinese immigrants from Fujian in terms of its association with cultural and trading interactions.

Then I decided that further exploration was required to understand the descendants of Chinese immigrants. Thus I included the old ruling town of Tainan, the seat of power under Dutch Formosa (1624–1662) and the Ch'ing (Qing) dynasty until the 1880s—when the first governor was appointed to the newly formed province and the capital was moved to Taipei—and Tachia, an ancient harbor dedicated to the sea deity Matsu (Empress of Heaven) at the estuary of the Ta-an River, where early Han Chinese settlers built a town facing the Taiwan Strait.

Eventually, the itinerary was outlined and I headed back to Taipei to present my findings to the institute. The itinerary was accepted, and I then began to plan the logistics of the trip. Below is a map of the tour route, followed by a list

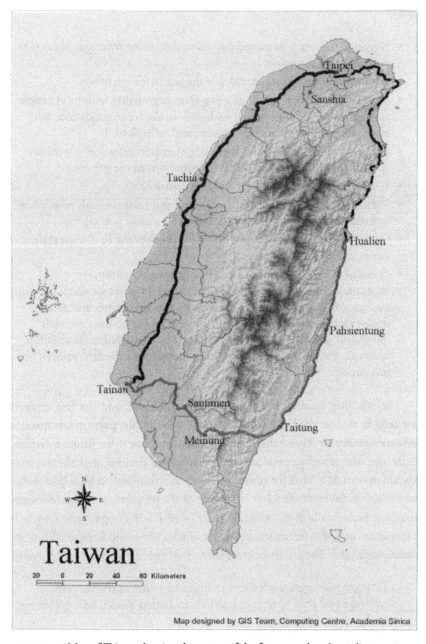

FIGURE 2. Map of Taiwan showing the course of the first eco-cultural traveling seminar.

of the steps I took to make the first eco-cultural tour or traveling seminar a reality.

- Negotiated among interested parties to determine what was important to include on the route.
- Envisioned a route that would suit the seminar's intention.
- Scouted the way by vehicle as a pre-tour, negotiating with local people along the way for a route that included meals, accommodation, rest stops, and sites or venues for lectures and reflections.
- Figured the cost of the tour, including transportation fees of vehicles and other expenses, based on the negotiations of the pre-tour.
- Invited co-speakers and local people to participate.
- Announced the traveling seminar's route and costs through newsletters or broadcasts from the host institution to possible participants.
- Gathered the prospective candidates for the seminar to discuss the route, costs, and conditions.
- Oversaw the tour logistics—accounting, transportation, accommodation, food and drink, honoraria for guest speakers, pre-tour expenses, venue costs, administration by the institution, and other minor expenses—and determined the cost of the seminar for each individual. Discounts applied for those who registered early, children, students, the elderly, and others whose needs were deemed valid by the institution.

The traveling seminar is a not-for-profit enterprise, and the fees assessed are only to recover the basic costs. If a surplus arises, the participants meet to discuss whether to refund the excess money or to save it for future activities. After the first traveling seminar, the participants decided that the seminar should operate as a "club for education" since it is founded on local knowledge and professional research. Later in the life of the program, participants began to gather periodically at the residence of Jo Tai and T. B. Sung to reflect on their experiences and plan future seminars. Eventually, the group became a bit more institutionalized. The group includes the following basic member components:

1. Institute managers work from an office or home to receive calls, circulate and post notices in journals and other media, host gatherings, and account for expenses.
2. A designated person coordinates the tour by planning the traveling seminar theme and route and actively engaging the group prior to and during the seminar.

3. The key coordinator selects lecturers for the traveling seminar based on their expertise with regard to the theme of the tour. Some lecturers travel with the group; others are on location to receive the group at a destination.

4. Participants include all those who attend the seminar to share and learn—both those who travel to each destination and those who are posted at each destination to interact with others.

Gradually a group of volunteers was formed to take responsibility for researching sites in Taiwan and to conduct and document traveling seminars. As they began, a plan emerged to continue tour development and hosting through an association with the Institute of Cultural Affairs. This was established as the Eco-Cultural Tour Association (ECTA) as an initial organization.

AN OUTLINE OF THE FIRST THREE-DAY TRAVELING SEMINAR WITH DR. JEAN HOUSTON

In my role as an anthropologist, I worked as an organizer and shared lecturing with Dr. Houston, who gave a philosophical grand view of humanity. In my lectures, I applied contextual, firsthand knowledge of the archaeology of the sites from Paleolithic and Neolithic cultures in prehistory, the ethnology of indigenous cultures, and the current state of Taoist–Buddhist religions in the ethnographic present for Taiwan (see Blundell 2000, 1992, 1995; Chambers 2000; Hsieh 1994; Tai and Blundell 1994). What follows is an outline of the first three-day, eco-cultural traveling seminar, which has served as the model for subsequent seminars.

Day One

We began the tour by train on a journey to the east coast, where the group visited the hospital and medical training facility of Ven. Cheng Yen, a Buddhist nun who founded the Tzu Chi (Ciji) Foundation in Hualien. People were deeply moved by the caring staff and the hospital's volunteer network, which includes several million supporters across the island. Based on the experience, one person remarked that it was impossible to think of Taiwanese as selfish or greedy. From this point, we proceeded by bus to the sacred shrines of Kuan Yin. Next we visited the ancient Caves of the Eight Immortals (Pahsientung) on the Pacific coast, once inhabited by Paleolithic ancestors. Dr. Houston led the

FIGURE 3. Caves of the Eight Immortals (Pahsientung) with Dr. Jean Houston and participants.

imagining of what it must have been like to live in Taiwan when the ancestors who first called this place home inhabited the caves. Heading farther south, the group visited archaeological sites representing Neolithic cultures. The evening was spent at a thermal spring resort at Chih-pen Valley, Taitung.

Day Two

The second day continued the journey into the southern region, traveling west up and across the south central mountains into Pingtung County and its distinctive Hakka villages and farms in Meinung. The local people treated the group to their culture, cuisine, and history, including a tour of a memorial library dedicated to Jong Li-ho, one of the most influential Hakka writers of the 20th century. From there, the group traveled to the indigenous mountain communities of Santimen, where members of the Paiwan and Rukai welcomed participants for an amazing evening of eating, dancing, and listening to legends. The group members stayed in local homes as overnight guests.

Day Three

The third day of the seminar was a journey to the southwestern region—a visit to the "supermarket of the underworld." The Tung Yueh-dien (a Taoist temple) in Tainan gave everyone a chance to experience firsthand the diversity of local

FIGURE 4. Rukai village leader explains the community's heritage.

beliefs and practices relating to the netherworld. The group was privileged to be present at powerful scenes in which local priests guided trances, presided over the posthumous wedding of a young woman, and facilitated a conversation between a dead son and his mother.

After a downpour of flooding rain, the group moved north along the western coast to visit the old harbor at Ta-an. As the sun set into the Taiwan Strait, the participants sat in a circle and Dr. Houston led a reflection on the last three days' diversity of experiences. Each person in the circle in turn reflected back to the group. Afterwards, the group visited the Tachia Temple of Matsu (Sea Goddess and Empress of Heaven). The group members were empowered by their real, evident ability to travel and to tour the island as a collective.

CONCLUSIONS

Each traveling experience employs both experts in specific fields, who present information, and seminar specialists, who facilitate the educational process,

FIGURE 5. Rukai host prepares breakfast for the traveling seminar group at the mountain stone village of Kochapogan in the vicinity of Santimen.

allowing participants to travel together and explore the ecology and local environment with experienced guides. The local hosts en route share their way of life through an afternoon visit or an overnight stay. And the translators that accompany the tours are able to convey what each person has said, giving participants and leaders the opportunity to lead the discussion and effectively communicate their points of view. Thus, the learning process is active, not passive.

The first eco-cultural traveling seminar happened to occur a few years after the lifting of martial law in Taiwan, and matched the growth of a "green" consciousness that promoted indigenous and ethnic revival at the grass roots. City folk gathered for our tour to encounter the "simple life." Local people joined the group en route. The Taiwan Institute of Cultural Affairs modeled a program in which the urban participants (who were roving off their beaten track) demonstrated an attitude of respect for those they met in rural areas. The route also included possibilities for the establishment of local world heritage sites, from a mountain ridge with an almost abandoned Rukai stone village in Pingtung County to a primeval grove of giant cypress in a perpetually misty valley. Experts from the university on geomorphology, timber, fauna, and ethnology accompanied the tour to enter the conversations at hand.

The basic structure of the traveling seminar can serve as a replicable model, but tour specifics will vary according to the countries in which they occur and the places to be visited. Each traveling seminar depends on a loose yet cohesive gathering of people committed to working together for a mutually beneficial learning experience composed of changing landscapes and conversations with strangers who are knowledge-sharers and potential friends. Frequent meetings for interpersonal exchange and discussion of the tour content are required for the sustainability of the process. This model, with its localized sustainability, could be employed in any community where people embrace the concept that reflective education through travel-based sharing is a valuable, eye-opening resource and experience.

For an individual or a tour group, the empowerment of travel lies in its opportunities for connecting with a global trend of affluence. In Valene Smith's pioneering work, *Hosts and Guests: The Anthropology of Tourism* (1977), she introduces tourism as a major factor in economic growth worldwide. Of course, our informal traveling group is an aspect of globalization in a world of contending perspectives on what life means (see Langness 1977; Morrow 1989; Wu 1995; Barber 1996; Bauman 1998; Held et al. 1999; Friedman 2000, 2002; Webster 2000, 2002). Both hosts and guests consider their roles to be part of an international trend in growing awareness. In the introduction to her book, Smith states that tourism can be classified as exotic tourism, cultural tourism, heritage tourism, environmental tourism, and recreational tourism (Smith 1977:1–14). Again, our traveling seminar, as an eco-cultural tour, includes environmental elements as well as exotic, cultural, and heritage elements, depending on the theme of the tour. Some participants have mentioned that regardless of the theme, the outing is also recreational, or simply a way to get some fresh air and a break from the daily routine. When I studied pilgrimage in Sri Lanka (see Blundell 1994:140–143), I found that the Sinhalese villagers connected with one another through the stream of people visiting the sacred shrines, and in turn connected with the respect felt for their deity. People with the ability to travel seek to connect with something greater than what they usually do.

The ethos for this type of travel rests in a "charter" of mutualization through interaction that inspires participatory commitment. Through immersion in the local people's way of life, tourists come to have an ecological sense of place and people. Interactive events in daily life encourage participants to share their own experiences and interests while learning from one another and the experts on the tour. This combination of activities tends to build a sense of respect for diverse lifestyles. The tours also involve many accepted experts on local societies and cultures as well as geography, linguistics, ecology and other arenas of academic exploration. The past tours have involved many organizations, both public and private. Volunteers gave of their own expertise and time to bring a new reality of understanding of the locations to the group participants.

Sustainability of our tour encounters is our mutual goal for a common future (See Wahab and Pigram 1997; Hall and Lew 1998; Butler 1999; Aronsson 2000; Cheung 2003). In three days, we cannot expect fully to grasp other realities, yet accepting sustainability of the life cycle (Cooper 1997:78) as a guiding resource for global interaction and the managing principle for continuance of relationships has become the ethos of the program. It is indeed our view that first encounters should be the beginnings of relationships in other places. Therefore, our tacit understanding has been that we address our hosts in friendship, who in turn treat us as personal guests. The hosts may then be invited by the guests to be personal guests at their own homes in the future. Thus the seminar becomes the impetus for the reciprocation of hosting or a reunion of hosts and guests on an individual basis.

Eco-cultural tours have taken off in Taiwan, although my colleagues in the forestry department at the university where I have taught would say that it isn't eco-tourism, since that's about visiting pristine nature. Once you add cultural to eco-, then you have another species. Yet both types of tourism rely on a faithful and respectful coming together with the "other": a caring tourism. This caring aspect is the tour's draw, especially since the participants can rely on using their native languages to share and express heartfelt reflections on their experiences. I believe that the eco-cultural seminars work for cross-cultural and ecological understanding. Even though the tour participants who come as guests have the affluence and leisure time to partake in this kind of education, the Institute of Cultural Affairs is interested in having economically disadvantaged people share in the experience as well by conducting the not-for-profit tours. The hosts also learn from the experience of this cultural cross-fertilization and "green" education. The most important keys of success for these activities are to have aware, responsible, and interested people who will share and articulate their personal and cultural observations as traveling seminar participants, hosts, and guests, in an ethos of living, interrelated friendship. The centerpiece of eco-cultural travel is this vital dialogue, which builds lasting, cross-cultural friendships.[3]

Dedicated to Jo Tai

NOTES

1. Jean Houston, a student of Joseph Campbell and the "adopted daughter" of Margaret Mead, is a leader of the human potential movement in the United States. More than twenty years ago, Dr. Houston founded the Mystery School, which is dedicated to the process of self-discovery through cross-cultural studies. Jean Houston conducts transformational workshops and seminars drawing on the strength of legendary and indigenous knowledge. See her works *A Mythic Life*, 1996; *The Possible Human*, 1998; and *Evolution*, 1998.

2. The Institute of Cultural Affairs is a consultant to the United Nations registered as a self-sustaining office providing services that envision heritage as a resource for the future. The institute is a unique, global organization of people who care for the human factor in world development. This international yet locally based institute facilitates a process of constructive change in which individuals dedicated to practical problem-solving use their knowledge of policy and development methods to improve the lives of local participants based on their aspirations and vision of life.

3. A note of appreciation: I offer my heartfelt thanks to Tim Wallace for prompting this article on a traveling seminar as an example of practicing anthropology for public education. I would like to thank Renée Wolcott for her copyediting talents, Hsuing-ming Liao for creating the map of Taiwan, and the staff at the University of California Press. Hui-ji Wang, Betty Rothenberger, and Christian A. Anderson also assisted by making suggestions for the final draft.

REFERENCES CITED

Anderson, Christian A.
    2000 The New Austronesian Voyaging: Cultivating Amis Folk Songs for the International Stage. *In* Austronesian Taiwan: Linguistics, History, Ethnology, Prehistory. David Blundell, ed. Berkeley: Phoebe A. Hearst Museum of Anthropology. pp. 282–319.
Appadurai, Arjun
    1981 The Past as a Scarce Resource. Man 16(2):201–219.
Aronsson, Lars
    2000 The Development of Sustainable Tourism. London: Continuum.
Barber, Benjamin R.
    1996 Jihad versus McWorld. New York: Ballantine.
Bauman, Zygmunt
    1998 Globalization: The Human Consequences. Cambridge: Polity.
Berlyne, D. E.
    1962 New Directions in Motivation Theory: Anthropology and Human Behavior. T. Gladwin and W. C. Sturtevant, eds. Pp. 150–173. Washington, DC: Anthropological Society of Washington.
Blundell, David
    1992 Tourism Resources and Cultural Preservation: Comparison of Traditional Contemporary and Prehistoric Heritage of Taiwan. Paper presented at the International Symposium of Tourism and Leisure Management (Pacific Cultural Foundation, Chinese Culture University, and Tourism Society), Taipei, May 21–24.
    1994 Masks: Anthropology on the Sinhalese Belief System. American University Studies, Series VII: Theology and Religion, 88. New York: Peter Lang Publishing, Inc.

1995 Eco-Cultural Tourism: Taiwan's Living Pride. Travel in Taiwan, 1(2):34–36.

2000 Languages Connecting the World. *In* Austronesian Taiwan: Linguistics, History, Ethnology, Prehistory. David Blundell, ed. Berkeley: Phoebe A. Hearst Museum of Anthropology. pp. 401–457.

Bowlin, John, and Peter Stromberg

1997 Representation and Reality in the Study of Culture. American Anthropologist 99(1): 123–134.

Butler, Richard W.

1999 Sustainable Tourism: A State of the Art Review. Tourism Geographies 1(1):7–21.

Chambers, Erve

2000 Native Tours: The Anthropology of Travel and Tourism. Prospect Heights, IL: Waveland Press.

Cheung, Sidney

2003 Remembering through Space: The Politics of Heritage in Hong Kong. International Journal of Heritage Studies 9(1):7–26.

Cooper, Chris

1997 The Contribution of Life Cycle Analysis and Strategic Planning to Sustainable Tourism. *In* Tourism, Development and Growth: The Challenge of Sustainability. S. Wahaband and J. J. Pigram, eds. Pp. 78–94. London: Routledge.

Cooper, David

1974 The Grammar of Living. New York: Pantheon Books.

Friedman, Thomas L.

2000 The Lexus and the Olive Tree: Understanding Globalization. New York: Anchor Books.

2002 Longitudes and Attitudes: Exploring the World After September 11. New York: Farrar, Straus and Giroux.

Graburn, Nelson H. H., ed.

1983 The Anthropology of Tourism. New York: Pergamon Press.

Hall, C. Michael, and Alan A. Lew, eds.

1998 Sustainable Tourism: A Geographical Perspective. Harlow, Essex: Addison Wesley Longman.

Held, David, A. McGrew, D. Goldblatt, and J. Perraton

1999 Global Transformations: Politics, Economics and Culture. Cambridge: Polity.

Houston, Jean

1996 A Mythic Life: Learning to Live Our Greater Story. New York: Harper Collins.

1998 Evolution: Awakening the Power of Our Social Potential. Novato, CA: New World Library.

1998 The Possible Human: A Course in Enhancing Your Physical, Mental, and Creative Abilities. Collingdale, PA: Diane Publishing Co.

Hsieh, Shih-chung

1994 Tourism, Formulation of Cultural Tradition, and Ethnicity: A Study of the Daiyan Identity of the Wulai Atayal. *In* Cultural Change in Postwar Taiwan. Stevan Harrell and Chun-chieh Huang, eds. Pp. 184–201. Prospect Heights, IL: Westview Press.

Langness, L. L., ed.

1977 Other Fields, Other Grasshoppers: Readings in Cultural Anthropology. Philadelphia: J. B. Lippincott.

Morrow, Lance

    1989 Welcome to the Global Village. Time Magazine, May 29:41.

Smith, Valene L., ed.

    1977 Hosts and Guests: The Anthropology of Tourism. Philadelphia: University of Pennsylvania Press.

Tai, Jo, and David Blundell

    1994 Eco-Cultural Tourism Takes Root in Taiwan. Initiatives, ICA in Western USA, 10(3).

Webster, Frank

    2000 Information, Capitalism and Uncertainty. Information, Communication and Society 3(1):69–90.

    2002 Information Society Theory in the Age of Globalization. Paper presented at the 3rd Wen Shan Conference, Cultural Diversity, National Chengchi University, Taipei, October 26–27.

Wahab, Salah, and John J. Pigram

    1997 Tourism, Development and Growth: The Challenge of Sustainability. London: Routledge.

Walle, Alf H.

    1998 Cultural Tourism: A Strategic Focus. Boulder, CO: Westview Press.

Whelan, Tensie, ed.

    1991 Nature Tourism: Managing for the Environment. Washington, DC: Island Press.

Wu, David Y. H.

    1995 McDonald's in Taipei: Hamburgers, Betel Nuts, and National Identity. *In* Golden Arches East: McDonald's in East Asia. J. L. Watson, ed. Pp. 110–135. Stanford: Stanford University Press.

ANTHROPOLOGISTS IN THE TOURISM WORKPLACE

VALENE L. SMITH
California State University, Chico

Anthropology and tourism melded at a symposium at the 1974 American Anthropological Association meeting in Mexico City, believed to be the first social science discussion of tourism in the Western Hemisphere. Tourism has increased dramatically to become one of the world's largest industries, and anthropology has also extended its interests in theory and methodology. Few articles have linked career options for anthropologists to the tourism workplace. Our disciplinary strengths in heritage conservation, economic development—especially among indigenous cultures—and conflict resolution, as well as our cross-cultural orientation, lead to employment with governments, NGOs, visitor and convention bureaus, and management. Regrettably, many industry employers are unfamiliar with our professional skills; a job search in the tourism workplace may become a personal quest, often bolstered by a sales pitch and with bilingualism as a major asset. Key Words: cross-cultural communication, travel industry, convention and visitor bureaus, business anthropology, environmental sustainability

The doors that lead from the anthropology classroom to the travel industry are many and varied—some are part-time, but many are career paths. Nolan (2002) offers sound general counsel for anthropology students who seek careers "outside the academy." This article attempts to provide an overview of occupations and opportunities for anthropologists in the highly diverse field of travel and tourism. The travel industry develops and sells many fundamental anthropological specialties including culture, ethnicity, and heritage. By encouraging travel, the industry helps to maintain and market the anthropological cross-cultural perspective. In many ways, the travel industry might be viewed as "real world" anthropology, and it offers increasing opportunities for significant anthropological involvement.

NAPA Bulletin 23, pp. 252–269, ISBN 1-931303-22-3. © 2005 by the American Anthropological Association. All rights reserved. Please direct all requests for permissions to photocopy or reproduce article content through the University of California Press's Rights and Permissions website, www.ucpress.edu/journals/rights.htm.

Unfortunately, the empirical data to validate this observation do not exist. Neither the American Anthropological Association (AAA) nor the Society for Applied Anthropology (SFAA) maintain employment information about their members. Similarly, the American Society of Travel Agents (ASTA) and the Institute for Certified Travel Agents (ICTA) do not show any interest in the academic majors or training of their members. Thus the content of this article derives from my role as participant observer, from information requests circulated on Internet bulletin boards, and from years of personal experience. My personal ties to the industry are almost lifelong, as my family owned a small-town travel agency for twenty years. I earned the Certified Travel Counselor (CTC) designation in 1982, and subscribe to and read several weekly trade journals.

CONTRIBUTIONS OF ANTHROPOLOGY
TO THE TRAVEL INDUSTRY

In the post-World War II era, and thanks largely to articulate spokespersons such as Margaret Mead and Ashley Montague, writers Loren Eiseley and Brian Fagan, and novelists such as Farley Mowat, Tony Hillermann, Jane Auel, and others, anthropology has gained increasing public awareness. In the 1960s, only a few hundred people attended AAA meetings; now the attendees are in the thousands. Some two decades ago, it was said that every U.S. agency "has an anthropologist on their staff but they do not always know what to do with them."

This article is patently directed towards alerting anthropologists to the diversity of opportunities within the travel industry. If anthropologists enter the field in numbers, the anthropological perspective of cultural relativism is certain to dominate. Globalization is irrevocably altering the human perspective. Many individuals no longer have a "nationality" because their "place of origin" can be literally whatever they choose to describe. From refugees to tourists, humans move around the globe in great numbers. According to the 2002 Global Refugee Survey, "uprooted people" number between 37 and 40 million. Many refugees will become expatriates and will eventually travel to visit family, friends, and a former homeland. In 2002, air terminals are already global melting pots and virtual Babylons of multiple languages, distinctive dress, and differing lifestyles. The December 2004 tsunami that devastated major tourist destinations and killed thousands of both hosts and guests reinforces the need for skilled crisis management. The anthropologist has a central role as facilitator wherever people live, move, and travel.

The principal contribution of anthropologists to the travel industry is the theoretical bulwark for the tasks that many in the industry already realize and perform. Tourism scholars principally attend academic conferences but rarely venture even to the quasi-academic Travel and Tourism Research Association (TTRA), let alone to the annual meeting of the American Society of Travel Agents (ASTA) or the largest global marketplace, International Tourism Berlin (ITB). Thus, many professors are unfamiliar with the research on issues such as ecotourism, best practices, and sustainability that is undertaken by industry and reported at their seminars. Anthropologists in industry link theory and practice. Every long-term tour operator and carrier realizes that a blighted environment is no longer a viable destination, and they exert every reasonable (and sometimes unprofitable) measure to ensure environmental protections. All too often it is the tourist who is the culprit and lacks a sense of environmental stewardship. If litter is a problem, trash cans are an obvious solution—but if the tourist fails to use them, who is to blame? College campuses, like national parks, provide designated and paved paths to protect the environment and aesthetics, but students, like tourists, create shortcuts.

Tourism faces enormous challenges in the decades ahead due to increased demographics, with the global population expected to swell from 6.1 billion in 2000 to 9.4 billion in 2050. Urbanization will similarly increase in this time frame from 47 percent of the global population in 2000 to 69 percent in 2050 (Smith and Brent 2001:336). The demand for water and for energy, which is especially heavy in tourism, will strain existing resources (Perkins 2002:42–43). Empty space will dwindle with further degradation of the physical landscape. The real need is to work and plan locally, at the chamber of commerce and visitor and convention bureau level, for the wisest use of the landscape and hinterland resources. Geographic planners can do this, but tourism anthropologists have a broader perspective:

If the bus that arrives today or the conference that begins tomorrow hosts visitors from China, India, or Brazil, what special needs must we provide? And what special instructions should the guide give the group to protect our destination assets?

EMPLOYMENT WITH A B.A. IN ANTHROPOLOGY

Finding employment in travel with a B.A. in anthropology is analogous to finding a first job in almost any other social science. My criteria for success include a willingness to work and to learn, to show respect and courtesy for the public and co-workers, and to maintain personal accountability in ethics and behavior. However, because travel involves diverse sites and locations as well as an increasingly cosmopolitan population, two additional assets are often important in the job search.

The first of these assets is a knowledge of geography. Our travel office offers two examples—which could be replicated in many travel industry situations—that illustrate this need. One client asked about travel to Venezuela, and after some delay, the puzzled employee was still poring over literature on Venice. Another client asked to reserve a hotel in Washington to attend some congressional hearings. After a prolonged search, an employee informed the client that "there are no hotels in Washington." (This employee thereafter never forgot that the capital city of the United States is located in the District of Columbia and that, like a telephone directory, tourism resources are alphabetically arranged.)

A second and increasing need in the U.S. travel industry is for bilingual specialists. Unfortunately, current recruitment is drawn largely from immigrant populations whose knowledge of the United States and American culture is sometimes limited. The U.S. National Park Service (USNPS) has been at the forefront in the preparation of descriptive literature and displays to better serve the 41 million foreigners who now visit the United States annually. Most national and state parks do not record the precise number of foreign visitors, but many staff will acknowledge that at least one-third of their attendance is foreign. To meet the demand, the USNPS recruits bilingual staff, and most bookshelves are well stocked with reference works in five or six languages.

The global economic decline that began in late 1998 initiated a reorganization of the travel industry. As sales slowed, the airlines and other carriers sought ways to cut their costs. A cap on the commissions paid to travel agents hurt their retail sales, and, in 2002, the airlines terminated all commissions. Almost simultaneously, travelers with access to the Internet discovered they could often find cheaper fares through online consolidators. Literally the hand-held mouse was destroying the local travel agency and changing employment patterns. The terrorist attack on the World Trade Center on September 11, 2001, further impacted the travel industry, with reduced revenues to hotels, restaurants, and car-rental agencies. The combined effect destroyed some of the presumed "perks" of the industry—in the form of free or greatly reduced travel—which originally attracted potential new employees (Henricks 2004).

These current trends do not sound the death knell to the travel agency facet of the industry, which was created by Thomas Cook more than 150 years ago. The knowledge and experience attained by travel agents over a period of years remain highly marketable skills. Many seasoned travelers prefer and will continue to solicit their expertise, and will pay service fees to obtain personalized travel arrangements, often with savings in time, money, and hassle. This remains a viable job market, offering careers with the carriers (airlines, cruise lines, car-rental agencies) and major tour and motor coach operators. The domestic resort industry is thriving and also offers many seasonal jobs and summer internships, including those with properties operating in Arizona winters and Alaskan summers.

Chambers of Commerce and Convention and Visitor Bureaus

Within the framework of anthropology and tourism, chambers of commerce and visitor and convention bureaus are two important venues in which to work. The two entities have different constituencies, but their goals and expertise often overlap. Chambers of commerce were originally established to coordinate and benefit local businesses. Some metropolitan chambers now are seeking anthropologists for their staffs, to assist with tourism-related ethnic and heritage projects and to ensure that local natural preserves, including parks, are managed with an awareness of sustainability. For many cities, domestic tourism remains the bread-and-butter mainstay for restaurants and hotels, built around farmers' markets, concerts in the park, parades, and other specialized events. One example is Waynesville, North Carolina, whose tourism revitalization is built around a downtown renovation along a rustic, mountain theme. The town also hosts several festivals in the autumn, attracting groups of tourists to see the changing colors of the leaves.

Convention and visitor bureaus (often identified with the acronym CVB) are commonly funded from local general tax revenues, and are expected to reach out for new inbound tourism. Equipped now with elaborate web sites and toll-free phone lines, their agenda is to establish *name* or *place markers* for the host community. Each bureau's very survival depends on generating new money in the area with its well-known multiplier effect. The actual cash outlays may be spent in marketing or communication, but the important decision-maker roles are essentially the natural landscape, ethnicity, and heritage—three major areas of anthropological interest. If the CVB is successful in attracting one or more major conventions per year, the bureau may create or hire a special team to finalize the arrangements because of large staff requirements.

Networking and Event Management

A new class of tourist has developed in recent years—generally referred to as alternative tourists (Smith and Eadington 1992) or post-Fordist travelers (Mowforth and Munt 1998:142–143). Their new travel patterns have the potential to open up expanded opportunities for entry-level employment for students with degrees in anthropology. The concept of networking as a source of information and socialization for an increasingly mobile population has heightened an already flourishing convention and conference business. Event management involves far more than providing accommodations and meals, and includes theme development, promotion, attractions, and entertainment (Getz 1997). Conventions are a lucrative source of domestic tourism revenue, and competition among potential host communities is often keen. The special "foreign" ambience of a place like New Orleans, the western motif of a city like Denver, or the antebellum charm of Atlanta enables these cities to showcase their destination attraction with exhibits, field trips, folklore, and heritage. Other cities have successfully created identities through special events. For example, Gilroy, California, attained national fame and fortune as the "garlic capital of the world" with its annual festival of food (including garlic candy) and crafts.

A successful venue must be able to offer a diversity of activities, with fine dining, interesting entertainment options, and shopping. In the United States, the two most frequently cited reasons for tourism are to visit family and relatives (Jafari 2000:621) and to shop. Las Vegas, the premier convention city, maintained an unprecedented 85 percent annual occupancy in its 126,000 hotel rooms until September 11, 2001, by offering outstanding entertainment, inexpensive meals, competitive hotel rates, themed hotels—some with masterpiece art galleries—*and* seven major shopping malls ranging in price from outlet to upscale (Berns 2001:1). In addition, Las Vegas developed several one- or two-day excursions to nearby attractions, including visits to Boulder Dam, an aerial excursion to the Grand Canyon, and trips to see restored historic Western memorabilia (Metro Guide Network 2004). Every extra day a convention-goer remains in the city boosts the per capita revenue appreciably.

Event Management

Event management is an important travel industry adjunct and offers a foundation on which to build community support for heritage. The American Museum Association notes that in 2001, more people visited museums than attended sporting events. Globalization contributes to a widening interest in ethnic diversity, together with a greater need for meeting planners to be aware of and to provide for the social and cultural needs of their guests—whether in terms of dietary restrictions, nonsmoking areas, religious holidays, or culturally offensive language or attire. Anthropologists, with their cross-cultural perspective, are ideally positioned to move into this field. Several U.S. universities now have event management majors (e.g., Indiana University at Indianapolis and George Mason University), and a scholarly journal, *Tourism and Event Management*, serves the academic community.

Tour Guides and Travel Escorts

The United States is notoriously lacking in professional, trained guides, but exceptional opportunities exist for bilingual individuals to create their own jobs, and in so doing, to create a new labor pool. Local or so-called "step on" guides usually register with their local chamber of commerce or with local motor coach companies to offer services either in English or their second language. In major cities such as New York, many work almost full time, and some firms such as GrayLine provide training. The role of tour manager (also termed "escort" or "courier") involves traveling with a group on a pre-booked program, with responsibility for handling luggage, maintaining the time schedule on the itinerary, facilitating compatible socialization among tour members, and managing illness, accidents, and other crises en route. The hours are often long and the pay barely minimum wage, but the tips for a successful tour manager are often substantial. A former student worked almost full time for nine years, escorting Americans to Mexico and vice versa. With living expenses paid, she enjoyed an upscale lifestyle, and her earnings paid in full for a condo and a nice car. Tour manager training is offered principally in large metropolitan proprietary schools.

Consulting and Context Research

The remarkable growth of tourism in the past two decades has created greater product diversity—trekking in the Himalayas (including tourist ascents on Mt. Everest), flights to the South Pole, icebreaker cruises in the High Arctic and Antarctic, submersibles to view the *Titanic* and other sunken vessels— as well as increased tourism on African safaris, visits to coastal resorts, and ecotourism into Costa Rica and the Amazon jungles. Commensurate with this destination proliferation, the travel industry needs marketing information. What clientele by age, education, occupation, and income are potential sales prospects for these (and more mundane) travel offerings? Where do they live? How does a tour operator or a carrier best commit the advertising budget to reach the targeted audience?

Market surveys are a standard industry tool, and in the scholarly tourist literature they are best known from the psychographic study initially published by Stanley Plog (1974). His bell-shaped curve was the first to identify the psychological preferences of travelers—as adventurers or stay-at-homes—and to associate them with specific destination choices. Plog Research Inc. and other consulting firms continue to develop and administer market survey instruments at industry request (http://www.plogresearch.com). Students are sometimes employed in this process.

Travel Industry of America (TIA) is a trade organization based in Washington, D.C. Their publications address broader issues of tourism research, and TIA hosts an annual travel forum that forecasts potential tourism activity for the upcoming year. Among their recent publications, *The Minority Traveler* (2000) assesses the travel behavior of three American ethnic groups: Hispanics, African Americans, and Asians. *The Profile of Travelers Who Participate in Gambling* was published in 2001, and publications covering other topics have included *Senior Travelers and Youth Travelers*.

The importance of market surveys and their value in support of the travel industry is the genesis for a new academic consortium based in Baltimore: Context-Based Research Group (www.contextresearch.com). Founded in 1998, its focus extends beyond the travel industry, as its members have undertaken a wide variety of tourism-related research, including (1) in-depth ethnographic analyses of Asian tourists, (2) studies of Gore-Tex fabrics—important to adventure tourism—(3) visitor satisfaction, and (4) conflict resolution involving ethnic employer–employee differences. In its first three years, the group has employed more than two hundred anthropologists in ethnographic projects and paid them more than $250,000.

In summary, there are very few official job listings in tourism that start with the word "anthropologist." The traditional advice holds true here: job applicants need to assess the needs of the employer and adjust their application and interviews accordingly. Many students have created their employment through internships (paid or unpaid) by contributing new ideas and skills on the job.

Institutional Employment

Government agencies offer many career opportunities for anthropologists with graduate degrees. The U.S. National Park Service may be regarded as a primary agency to protect national heritage, but it also hosts millions of visitors each year in a variety of settings. Park historians research the continuum of human land use. Other staff mount exhibits and fill important interpretive roles as curators, naturalists, lecturers, and guides. Park planners must address the complex issues of tourist use and tourist overload, possibly even to the level of de-marketing their attraction. The Grand Canyon, Yosemite, and Yellowstone are prime examples of small but fragile physical environments that face ongoing problems of balancing site carrying capacity with an ever-increasing number of tourists. Other federal agencies—including the Forestry Service, Bureau of Land Management, and Bureau of Indian Affairs, as well as their state-level counterparts—employ anthropologists in cultural resource management, as curators, and as public liaisons.

Inbound tourism by foreign visitors is now a leading U.S. business. A DRI-WEFA report (2003) noted that tourism in 2000 was a $283 billion industry and provided 3.9 million jobs in the leading 100 metropolitan areas. The magnitude of tourism has created new employment in federal agencies such as the Department of the Interior and the Department of Commerce. Immigration and refugees have increased cultural diversity in the United States, which in turn demands deeper awareness of ethnic variation. This, combined with the war on terrorism, has prompted the FBI to solicit cultural anthropologists with ethnographic and linguistic skills. The CIA faces a similar need for personnel with culturally specific interpretive skills for areas outside the United States.

Within the travel industry, the international hotels, airlines and cruise operators recognize the increasingly multiple levels of cultural diversity whose specific criteria must be met. The airlines accept individual orders for, and prepare, a dozen different culinary entrees to meet religious and medical needs. Most international hotels seek middle-management employees who have a business background but are also bilingual and have a double major such as anthropology. Such candidates are prized for their ethnic insights as well as their skills in conflict resolution involving hotel staff or guests.

Innovative Careers

Anthropologists with graduate degrees have pioneered a variety of career paths in tourism, but the supportive data is scarce. Some, like Trevor Sofield, work extensively in political administration and economic development involving tourism in Third World environments, then decide to return to the university for a terminal degree and teaching career. University alumni tours, the U.S. National Museum (the Smithsonian), and adventure-tour operators often feature en route lectures by professors with special expertise on the culture of the indigenous people or the archaeology of the destination area. These lecturers usually receive a small stipend and a free trip that becomes a cost-free return to the field, an opportunity to revisit an area of former research. The lecturers' professional presence is an additional marketing incentive.

A number of individuals, like David Blanton and myself, opt to venture into ownership and day-to-day management of a tour operation or retail travel agency. Both of us felt that our academic training and experience facilitated offering a better travel product to the public, and that our hands-on knowledge of the industry was an asset to our academic careers, especially in teaching and counseling students. Between these two named alternatives lie myriad other personal choices, best demonstrated through three diverse case studies.

The Arts and Crafts Entrepreneur Gordon Bronitsky, who had earned his Ph.D. in anthropology, accepted an academic appointment, but teaching was not his forte. He worked for several years as a tour organizer and guide in Mexico and the Yucatan, then served as a senior Fulbright professor at Goethe University in Frankfurt, Germany. His experience at the Institute of American Indian Art in Santa Fe then led to his 1994 founding of Bronitsky and Associates, a firm headquartered in Denver, Colorado, with an office in Bergamo, Italy.

Initially the company worked with Native American tribal groups to market their jewelry and other crafts overseas. Bronitsky knew firsthand the traditional German fascination with North American Indians—dating to the time of Maximilian—and with the paintings by artists Kurt Bodmer and George Catlin. For several summer seasons, the firm maintained a small Native American theme park in Austria. Subsequently the firm has expanded into international marketing of traditional and contemporary art, music, dance, fashion, film and video, photography, theater, speakers and writers in both native languages and English, food products, and American Indian-owned tourism. The first Spirit of a Planet Festival, held in Italy in May 2000, was representative of their ethnic booking services and included participants from Kazakhstan, Australian Aboriginals, Apache Indians, Wodaabe from Niger, and Indians from Mexico, as well as an Irish band. In 2002, the company expanded its geographical coverage to include the Xavante tribe in Brazil.

In 2001, the firm arranged for performances of the Fernando Cellicion Traditional Zuni Dancers in Taiwan, the Gummilami Yanni Yulidji Dancers (Australian Aboriginals) in Mexico, the Dukwakada Dancers (Yukon Territory) in Mexico, the Pa'a Taotao Tano Dancers (Guam) in the Netherlands, and the Yellow Bird Dancers (Apache) in Ireland. Traveling theatrical performances in 2002 included the Fernando Cellicion Traditional Zuni Dancers in Australia and Lithuania, the Chinle Valley Singers (Navajo) in the Netherlands, the Naa Luudisk Gwaii Yatx'i Dancers (Alaska) in Mexico, the Pa'a Taotao Tano Dancers (Guam) in Mexico, and the Yellow Bird Dancers (Apache) in Italy.

Archaeoastronomy and the Ute Mountain Tribal Park Virginia Wolf, an anthropology instructor at Butte Community College in Chico, California, had a long and deep-seated interest in the Anasazi (ancestral Puebloan) culture of the American Southwest. When the Mountain Ute Indians announced the first tour of representative sites on their reservation in 1978, Wolf signed on and was impressed with the ruins, the artifacts, and the absence of other tourists.

The reservation includes Mancos Canyon, a steep-walled, 1,000-foot-deep canyon of multilayered sandstone carved by the river of the same name, which defines much of the southern boundary of Mesa Verde National Park. The valley bottom, filled with rich sandy loam, apparently supported a substantial population, from the early Basketmakers (A.D. 400) to late Puebloan Farmers (A.D. 1300). In the nearly thousand years of occupancy, these settlers left immense quantities of pottery sherds, tools, and village sites. The Mountain Ute tribe currently live in a relatively barren land with little outside revenue. They have long eyed the tourism money that pours into nearby Mesa Verde, Monument Valley, and Canyon de Chelly, hoping to augment earnings from their own Mountain Ute Casino in Towoac.

Wolf began to visit the area regularly and to photograph the many petroglyphs, and eventually identified a sun calendar similar to the one at nearby Chaco Canyon (Wolf and Wheeler 1994). Several Ute became interested in their heritage and inspired in Wolf a strong sense of commitment to create a profitable, sustainable tourist enterprise that would benefit the Ute and also preserve their heritage. Working with faculty colleague Ed Wheeler, Wolf's first step was to consolidate the data into a commercially produced video, *Sun*

Calendars of the Ancient Puebloans (1999), updated in 2004 to DVD. It is sold at the Anasazi Heritage Center, on the Ute Reservation, and at various businesses in southern Colorado. A group of teachers at nearby Monticello, Utah, came forward to organize the Four Corners School of Outdoor Education, which uses tribal facilities to host field trips and Elderhostel groups. The tribal council asked both Wolf and Wheeler to serve as advisors, to qualify the Tribal Park and the Four Corners School for nonprofit status.

In summer 2001, Wolf initiated the first archaeological and rock art record-ing tours, and thus became the only "Anglo" on the tribal park payroll. By December 2004, more than 6,000 of what are estimated to be some 20,000 identifiable sites had been recorded, and on December 22, the first public tour documented the solstice on a Mancos Canyon sun calendar (Wolf and Wheeler 2004). In the future, tribal leaders hope to expand the sustainable tourism pro-gram using native guides and also to construct accommodations for visitors. Wolf summarizes her now 25-year commitment, saying it is "exciting to be part of this regional research effort and to pass on some of this information through the tours to visitors who genuinely want to learn more about the ancient farms of the Four Corners."

MAPATO and African Tourism Education   David C. Blanton completed his B.A. with a burning desire to see the world and joined the Peace Corps to work in Uganda. With his strong background in communication skills, Blanton became involved in several international development projects, the best known of which was the creation of MAPATO, a program whose acronym stands for "Media Analysis of Problems in African Tourism."

MAPATO was introduced in 1979 to Kenya's primary hospitality training school, Utalii College in Nairobi. Tourism to Africa was then in its infancy, although the European (dominantly German) charter tourism that would ul-timately fill the beaches of Mombasa with sunbathers was incipient. Kenya and neighboring Uganda and Tanzania wanted and needed the tourist rev-enues, but there were few natives trained to meet labor demands. In its initial form, MAPATO had three primary goals: (1) to bring potential employees from their tribal homelands into Nairobi and introduce them to the amenities of tourist hotels, including service requirements such as toilets and show-ers; (2) to provide training in basic skills for maids, drivers, barmen, and ultimately for tour guides and front-desk managers; and (3) to heighten na-tive self-esteem and provide them with an awareness of client interests and needs.

Funded with Swiss support, MAPATO developed into a multimedia project using available technology to illustrate the issues. Of particular interest to me were the case studies which profiled four types of tourists. As anthropology and tourism students know, most residents in Third World countries regard their foreign guests as "rich," which is largely true by local standards. However, MAPATO students are made aware of the fact that for many of their guests this visit is a once-in-a-lifetime experience for which they have saved and planned for many years. The profiles also highlight ethnic differences. In each profile, the portrayal begins with a visit to the tourists' homeland (the United States, Germany, Britain, or Switzerland), their residence, their occupation, and the planning for their trip. Each profile then continues with the visitors' experiences in Kenya: sightseeing, hotels, shopping, et cetera. Students who have never traveled begin to understand the effects of jet lag, client irritability, food preferences, and travel style differences.

MAPATO has been greatly expanded and modified. On a May 2002 visit to Utalii College as fieldwork for this article, I viewed a new, Kenya-made video that traces the history of human origins in Olduvai Gorge, the role of melanin in hair and skin color, the history of the slave trade, and modern tourism. The 30-week MAPATO curriculum is mandatory for every student, whether enrolled in the culinary, hotel management, or tour guide program, and includes four themes:

1. Who Am I?—includes the traditions of African hospitality
2. Professional Attitudes—considers the image of Africa, prejudice, and use of time
3. Who are They?—history of tourism, motivations, and tourist profiles that include the tour-bus traveler and the backpacker
4. Problem-Solving—traveler behavior, the rights of hosts, and the rights of guests

The significance of MAPATO is its universal application. With minimal modification, the curriculum is applicable to other developing countries, and graduates are easily identified by their professionalism and self-confidence. In its original format, MAPATO was a grassroots opportunity that, in the words of one graduate, "provided an education and a job. Otherwise I would still be living on the land and my children would have no school and no future."

In Kenya, MAPATO training has proven so effective that Utalii College is now designated by the World Tourism Organization (WTO) as a TEDQUAL (Tourism Education and Quality) institution, both in business management and for tour operator training. Utalii is the only sub-Saharan TEDQUAL school except for South Africa. TEDQUAL also emphasizes upper-level management training and presupposes the student has completed secondary school and is relatively sophisticated and metropolitan.

Blanton returned to the United States and his hometown of Ithaca, New York, in search of a new career. From what he had seen and learned about tourism in Africa, he was convinced that he could offer better services to travelers, and founded his own company as a wholesale tour operator.

The combined experience of the Peace Corps and active industry involvement demonstrated to Blanton (and others) the importance of tourism training. Some countries have excellent training and recruitment, and returning travelers uniformly praise the services accorded them, while other nations provide virtually no learning opportunities. As a consequence, Blanton is developing a guide-training program for Tanzanians in cooperation with staff at the University of Southern Michigan. He also plans further use of his communication skills in new films for the touring public and for staff training.

THE FUTURE

Globalization is having a major effect on the world, and tourism is one of the main agents of this process. The transfer of jobs from the West to countries such as China and India also means that the availability of disposable income for outbound tourism is greater. The relocation of formerly rural peoples to urban areas increases the flow of information about places of interest in other countries. Already, the enhanced income is generating more outbound tourism from both China and India. These trends highlight two new areas of importance to anthropology and tourism.

Guide Training

This article has already addressed some aspects of the need for and value of trained guides, but a major concern lies within the United States. This country always ranks among the leading destinations for inbound tourism. Yet the United States is the only major nation that has no policy or program to train, certify, and license guides. This lack blights the United States and its economy in three ways:

1. Our educated population is denied the opportunity to earn an income from guiding because we have no requirement—as is the case almost everywhere else in the world—that a tour group must have a *licensed* local guide.

2. Many foreign tour groups arrive in the United States with their own national escorts, who also assume the role of local guides. Many of these guides are not expert in American culture and provide incorrect or misleading information. The United States as a nation is losing an important opportunity to explain American values and lifestyles to the people who voluntarily spend their leisure time and discretionary money to visit us.

3. Our foreign guests are deprived of the privilege of meeting and learning about the United States from its own citizens. Many travelers note that "it is the people we meet whom we most remember." Because of language deficiencies, some foreign guests travel across the land and never meet or hear an American speak to them. They visited the place but do not know the people.

Americans could enhance stewardship of our nation and our heritage with a concerted letter campaign to members of Congress and the president. These are "new jobs" at minimal cost per employee and per taxpayer. U.S. high schools already teach the basics; it is not necessary to draft elaborate new curricula, only to develop the requisite tests, administer them, and license the guides accordingly.

ETHNIC PSYCHOGRAPHS

Psychographics are the summary description of tourists who share values, attitudes, motives, and travel preferences (Pearce 2000:471). These characteristics are often identified within a nationality by age, gender, education, and even occupation. American tourists traveling overseas in the 1960s were often labeled "ugly" Americans for their unseemly displays of wealth, braggadocio manner, and Hawaiian shirts (among many other distinguishing traits). In the 21st century, the impact of global television and extensive travel has minimized that nomenclature and the behavior that caused it. Now the important shared factors among western tourists tend to be age, gender, and language rather than nationality.

Through its consultancies, the U.S. travel industry has become quite expert at defining the travel behaviors of five age groups of Americans: Depression

Kids, Swing Generation, baby Boomers, Generation X, and Generation Y (Smith and Brent 2001:118). Each of the five generations has special tastes in tourism, preferential styles, and represent particular marketing niches. Through globalization and cultural reterritorialization, members of many European nations are scarcely distinguishable from their American counterparts. Hoever, these generational categories are entirely different for Asian tourists, and each Asian nationality—whether Chinese, Indian, Korean, or Malaysian—is also believed to be unique, because of linguistic and heritage differences.

Reisinger and Turner (2002) were pathfinders in the study of cross-cultural behavior in tourism and provide models for cross-cultural analysis. The travel industry needs broad-based studies of Asian visitors as ethnographic samples to plan for better visitor satisfaction, and it needs them now, given the impending arrival of increased Asian tourism. Further, Moeran (1998) illustrates with reference to Japanese tourism that overseas visitor attitudes and expectations change through time and experience. Anthropologists ought to be one of the key travel industry resources in the psychographic identification of inbound Asian visitors.

In summary, as a tourism anthropologist, I have often felt that our discipline made us "jacks of all trades and masters of none"—except synthesis. However, this is indeed our forte. Our awareness of cross-cultural variation and our expertise in cultural relativism provide a wealth of skills that are directly applicable to the world's growing travel industry. As anthropologists, we help ourselves to gainful employment and extended social networking—and potentially build a more peaceful world—when we directly contribute to a better travel experience for both hosts and guests of all social classes, cultures, and backgrounds. The world of tourism and travel experiences is out there: step out and try it!

NOTE

1. Further information is available from Utalii College, P.O. Box 31052, Nairobi, Kenya, and online at www.utalii.co.ke.

REFERENCES CITED

Allyn and Bacon
    2004 Public Speaking. Electronic document, http://wps.ablongman.com/ab_public_ speaking_2/0,9651,1593257-,00.html, accessed November 30, 2004.

Berns, Dave
    2001 Local Economy: Hotel Occupancy Rates Rise Again. Las Vegas Review-Journal, October
        8. Electronic document, http://www.reviewjournal.com/lvrj_home/2001/Oct-08-Mon-
        2001/business/17172450.html, accessed November 30, 2004.
DRI-WEFA
    2002 Report to the U.S. Mayor's Conference, Lexington, MA, August 17.
Getz, Donald
    1997 Event Management and Event Tourism. Elmsford, NY: Cognizant Communication
        Corp.
U.S. Committee on Refugees
    2002 Global Refugee Crisis Report. Washington, DC: U.S. Committee on Refugees.
Henricks, Mark
    2004 A Business for People Who Love to Travel. Startup Journal: The Wall Street Jour-
        nal Center for Entrepreneurs. Electronic document, http://www.startupjournal.com/
        columnists/startuplifestyle/20040513-lifestyle.html, accessed November 30, 2004.
Jafari, Jafar, ed.
    2000 Encyclopedia of Tourism. New York: Routledge.
Mayaka, Melrphon, and Brian King
    2002 A Quality Assessment of Education and Training for Kenya's Tour-Operating Sector.
        Current Issues in Tourism 5(2):112–133.
Metro Guide Network
    2004 Las Vegas Attraction Guide. Electronic document, http://attractionguide.com/las_
        vegas/, accessed November 30, 2004.
Moeran, Brian
    1998 Rereading the Language of Japanese Tourism. In Tourists and Tourism: A Reader. Sharon
        B. Gmelch, ed. Pp. 111-126. Prospect Heights, IL: Waveland Press.
Mowforth, Martin, and Ian Munt
    1998 Tourism and Sustainability: New Tourism in the Third World. London: Routledge.
Nolan, Riall
    2002 Anthropology in Practice: Building a Career Outside the Academy. Boulder, CO: Lynne
        Rienner Publishers.
Perkins, Sid
    2002 Crisis on Tap? Pollution and burgeoning population stress Earth's water resources.
        Science News, July 12:42–43.
Plog, Stanley
    1974 Why destinations rise and fall in popularity. Cornell Hotel and Restaurant Administra-
        tion Quarterly:11–13.
Reisinger, Yvette, and Linda Turner
    2002 Cross-Cultural Behavior in Tourism: Concepts and Analysis. London: Butterworth-
        Heineman.
Smith, Valene, and William R. Eadington, eds.
    1992 Tourism Alternatives: Potentials and Problems in the Development of Tourism. Philadel-
        phia: University of Pennsylvania Press.
Smith, Valene, and Maryann Brent
    2001 Hosts and Guests Revisited: Tourism Issues of the 21st Century. Elmsford, NY: Cog-
        nizant Communication Corp.

Travel Industry of America (TIA)
  2000 The Minority Traveler. Washington, DC: Travel Industry of America.
Wolf, Virginia, and Michael Roebuck
  1993 Anasazi Pueblo I–Basket Maker III: Multi-Component Solstice Observatory in the Lower Mancos River Canyon. Southwestern Lore 59(2):34–39.
Wolf, Virginia, and Edward Wheeler, dirs.
  1999 Sun Calendars of the Ancient Puebloans. 47 min. Wheelwolf Productions. Chico, CA.
Wolf, Virginia, and Edward Wheeler
  2004 Two Archaeoastronomical Solstice Techniques Utilized in Mancos Canyon. Southwestern Lore 70(2):33–48.

Biosketches of the Authors

Kathleen M. Adams is an associate professor of anthropology at Loyola University Chicago and an adjunct curator at the Field Museum of Natural History. She has published articles on tourism in insular Southeast Asia in a variety of journals, including *American Ethnologist, Ethnology, Annals of Tourism Research,* and the *Southeast Asian Journal of Social Science*. Her current research interests include identity politics, danger zone travel, and cultural displays. She is currently completing a book on the politics of tourism, ethnicity, and the arts in Tana Toraja.

David Blundell (Ph.D., Department of Anthropology, University of California, Los Angeles) is a visiting scholar in the International and Area Studies Program of the University of California, Berkeley. He has contributed articles on the anthropology of tourism since 1992. About that time, he began to organize and lead traveling seminars for the Institute of Cultural Affairs, Taipei, based on the experience he gained from the Experiment in International Living at the School of International Training, Brattleboro, Vermont, South Asia Program. Since the 1980s, Dr. Blundell has been teaching at National Taiwan University and National Chengchi University in Taipei. His works include *Masks: Anthropology on the Sinhalese Belief System* (New York: Peter Lang, 1994) and *Austronesian Taiwan: Linguistics, History, Ethnology, Prehistory* (Berkeley: Phoebe A. Hearst Museum of Anthropology, University of California, 2000).

Erve Chambers is a professor of anthropology at the University of Maryland. He has served as a Special Fulbright Scholar in appropriate tourism development at Kasetsart University in Bangkok, Thailand, and is an affiliate professor with the International Graduate Course in Tourism Management with the Associazione Instituzione Libera Universita Nuorese in Sardinia, Italy. Dr. Chambers maintains strong interests in community-based tourism and heritage resource management. He is currently completing work on a monograph devoted to heritage concepts and tourism as they are applied to the Chesapeake Bay region of Maryland and Virginia. Dr. Chambers' publications include *Places in Mind: Archaeology as Applied Anthropology* (with Paul Shackel), 2004; *Native Tours: The Anthropology of Tourism*, 2000; *Tourism and Culture: An Applied Perspective*, 1997; *Housing, Culture, and Design: A Comparative Perspective* (with Setha M. Low), 1989; and *Applied Anthropology: A Practical Guide*, 1985.

Quetzil Castañeda is a cultural anthropologist and ethnographer. He has taught at the University of Houston, Lake Forest College, the University of Hawaii, and Princeton. Since 1985, he has been doing ethnographic research in Yucatán, Mexico, on tourism and its intersections with anthropological institutions, practitioners, and practices. In 2003, Dr. Castañeda founded OSEA—The Open School of Ethnography and Anthropology, a non-degree training program and field school—where he continues to teach and develop ethnographic methods for use in academic and applied settings. He is currently writing on the theory and practice of experimental fieldwork. In recent years, Dr. Castañeda has collaborated with archaeologists on questions of ethics, the study of heritage, and ways to develop ethnographic methods within the discipline and practices of archaeological research.

Daniela N. Diamente is currently a master's student in applied anthropology at the University of Arizona, Tucson. Previously, she served as the assistant director of the NCSU Ethnographic Field School in Costa Rica for one year and around Lake Atitlán, Guatemala, for two years. While in Guatemala, she also worked for the Universidad del Valle de Guatemala on a project by The Nature Conservancy and conducted research with small coffee farmers on the impacts of market and climatic vulnerability. Presently she works with the Bureau for Applied Research in Anthropology (BARA) on community-level environmental research and outreach in Nogales, Arizona, and Sonora, Mexico.

William A. Douglass is professor emeritus with The Center for Basque Studies at the University of Nevada, Reno. He has published extensively on ethnicity, migration, and nationalism. His recent work includes articles on Las Vegas and Basque tourism.

Palma Ingles received her master's and doctoral degrees in anthropology from the University of Florida. For her doctorate, she studied the impacts of tourism on four indigenous tribes in the Amazon region of Peru. During the same time, she worked as a tour guide with tourists who were visiting the Amazon, including the villages she was studying. Dr. Ingles is currently a cultural anthropologist for NOAA Fisheries in the Southeast region of the United States, where she does research on the impacts of fishing regulations on fishermen and their communities.

Julie Lacy received her doctorate in anthropology in 2002 at University of California, Davis. She remains engaged by anthropology's theoretical debates, particularly regarding tourism issues. She recently coauthored "Beyond Authenticity: The Meanings and Uses of Cultural Tourism," *Tourist Studies*, 2002.

Mary B. LaLone is a professor of anthropology in the Department of Sociology and Anthropology at Radford University in Virginia. Her specialties are in applied, economic, and historical anthropology and experiential teaching. She received her Ph.D. in anthropology from UCLA in 1985. Her research began in Latin America and then shifted to the Appalachian region, where she focused on Appalachian coal mining and farming cultures. Since the early 1990s, she has organized and directed numerous oral history and applied heritage tourism projects in Appalachia. For descriptions of her projects, see http://www.radford.edu/~mlalone.

Amanda Mason is an applied anthropologist with specific interests in tourism, participatory planning, and resource management. She has worked in New York State for tourism projects involving historic preservation, economic development, and natural resource preservation at heritage sites in the Adirondack mountains and along western portions of the Erie Canal. During the three years of applied research that formed the basis for this paper, she was greatly assisted by several other ethnographers working as interns and consultants. For their solid research, suggestions, and assistance, she would like to thank Rosemary Riel, Aaron Tobler, Pellegrino Luciano, Judy Tso, Kathyrn Shaffer, Amanda Bundrun, Barbara Waldern, and Casey Schneider. For its attention to the concept of heritage and developing innovative approaches to combining anthropological theory and methods with tourism, she also thanks the Center for Heritage Resource Studies at the University of Maryland, College Park, especially Dr. Erve Chambers.

Valene L. Smith, research professor of anthropology at California State University, Chico, organized the first American Anthropological Association symposium on tourism in 1974, resulting in the book entitled *Hosts and Guests: The Anthropology of Tourism* (1977). She is the co-editor of the first comprehensive textbook on social–cultural tourism, *Hosts and Guests Revisited: Tourism Issues of the 21st Century* (2001, Cognizant Communications Corp., Elmford, New York).
vsmith@csuchico.edu

Susan C. Stonich is professor of environmental studies, anthropology, geography, and marine science at the University of California, Santa Barbara, and serves as chair of the environmental studies program. She is the author of *I Am Destroying the Land: The Political Ecology of Poverty and Environmental Destruction in Honduras* and *The Other Side of Paradise: Tourism, Conservation, and Development in the Bay Islands* and the editor of *Endangered Peoples of Latin America: Struggles to Survive and Thrive.* She is a member of the National Academy of Sciences, the National Research Council, the Committee on the Human Dimensions of Global Change, and the Panel on New Research on Population and the Environment.

Amanda Stronza is an assistant professor in recreation, park, and tourism sciences at Texas A&M University. She has a Ph.D. in anthropology from the University of Florida and has been studying linkages between local participation and conservation in Madre de Dios, Peru, since 1993. Funding for her research on Posada Amazonas was provided by the National Science Foundation, the Wildlife Conservation Society, the Inter-American Foundation, and the Tropical Conservation and Development Program at the University of Florida. In 2003, Dr. Stronza directed the "Trueque Amazónico," an initiative funded by the Critical Ecosystem Partnership Fund to compare and exchange lessons learned between three community-based ecotourism projects in Ecuador, Peru, and Bolivia.

Cameron Walker is an archaeologist with a special interest in how archaeology and archaeological sites are presented to the public. After almost ten years of fieldwork in

Bronze Age Crete, she now works in Mexico's Yucatán Peninsula and has found that the issues of archaeological tourism necessitate ethnographic and applied anthropological methodology. Dr. Walker currently teaches in the Department of Anthropology at California State University, Fullerton, holds the position of vice president for the Archaeological Institute of America, and serves on the Public Education Committee of the Society for American Anthropology.

Tim Wallace is an associate professor and applied anthropologist in the Department of Sociology and Anthropology at North Carolina State University, Raleigh, North Carolina. His applied research work in tourism has taken him to Madagascar to do an impact assessment for a Duke University–NCSU ecotourism project; to Hungary to study the economic effects of tourism in the post-Soviet transition; to Costa Rica, where he led six summers of ethnographic field schools on tourism topics; and now to Guatemala. In 2002, he was a Senior Fulbright Scholar at the Universidad del Valle de Guatemala and returned in 2003 as a senior specialist in anthropology. In 2004, he completed his third summer ethnographic field school around Lake Atitlán, Guatemala. He is a member of the Executive Board of the Society for Applied Anthropology, and is co-editor of the *NAPA Bulletin*.
http://www4.ncsu.edu/~twallace
tim_wallace@ncsu.edu

American Anthropological Association

AAA Membership Benefits

You'll Receive:

❖ *Anthropology News*, published nine times a year, with news and commentaries on trends, issues and activities across the discipline.

❖ The most comprehensive listings of anthropological job and grant opportunities available.

❖ Listings of new anthropology publications from all major university and trade presses.

❖ Information on hundreds of conferences and academic meetings.

❖ Access to the *Anthropology News* online.

❖ Opportunities to participate in the AAA Annual Meeting, the world's largest, most prestigious meeting of anthropologists.

❖ Reduced prices for the Association's many publications.

❖ Listing in Annual *AAA Guide* Membership Section a widely consulted anthropological publication, a comprehensive directory of anthropologists and anthropological institutions.

❖ Access to the *E-Guide*, the online searchable database containing all the listings from the *AAA Guide*.

❖ Listing in the AAA's online searchable database of anthropologists.

❖ Access to the members only area of the AAA Web site where you can access information and resources not available to the public.

❖ Access to AAA's on-line Career Center, where you can use our interactive job-search, post your resume, and manage your career strategy.

❖ Access to AAA member insurance, options for health/life insurance, short-term/long-term disability, hospital income plan, Medicare supplement and professional liability (US members).

❖ Access to over 30 Sections representing the broad field of anthropology (archaeology, biology, linguistics, ethnology, medical, visual and practice).

❖ Extensive networking opportunities among researchers, teachers and practitioners.

Visit Our On-Line Career Center at
http://www.aaanet.org/careers.htm
AAA
2200 Wilson Blvd Ste 600
Arlington VA 22201-3357
ph 703-528-1902 x 3030
fx 703-528-3546
rthomas@aaanet.org

AMERICAN
ANTHROPOLOGICAL ASSOCIATION
JOURNALS
AVAILABLE IN JSTOR!

For over two years, the American Anthropological Association has
worked with JSTOR, a not-for-profit online digital archive,
to provide access to the complete back runs of several AAA journals
and preserve them in a long-term archive. Users may search,
browse, view, and print full-text PDF versions of articles in five AAA
journals, from their first year published through 1996:

American Anthropologist (1879)
American Ethnologist (1974)
Cultural Anthropology (1986)
Ethos (1973)
Medical Anthropology Quarterly (1968)

Members of the AAA who are at institutions that participate in
JSTOR's Arts & Sciences II Collection can search and browse these
journals directly at www.jstor.org. AAA is currently working
on plans to offer individual access as part of their membership in 2005.
For more information, please visit www.aaanet.org.

The American Anthropological Association is proud to
collaborate with JSTOR to preserve and make widely available the
historic literature of our field.

JSTOR is an independent not-for-profit organization with
a mission to create a trusted archive of scholarly journals and to
increase access to those journals as widely as possible.
Information regarding JSTOR is available at www.jstor.org.

Printed and bound by CPI Group (UK) Ltd, Croydon, CR0 4YY

09/06/2025

14686137-0003